GREAT FOOD

GREAT FOOD

Over 175 Recipes from Six
of the World's Greatest Chefs

WEST 175 PUBLISHING

Credits

GREAT FOOD PRODUCTION TEAM

Editor – Chris Rylko   Culinary Director – Jenny Steinle
Publisher – Greg Sharp   Executive Assistant – Kate Terhaar
Book Design – Connie Lunde   Photographer – Christopher Conrad
Cover Design – Kathy Kikkert   Food Stylist – Cindy Alice
Production Assistant – Susan Albers   Stylist's Assistant – Carol Phillips

Grateful Acknowledgments

Chief Executive Officer, West 175 Enterprises, Inc. – John McEwen
Director, International Sales & Marketing, BBC Worldwide Publishing – Charles Hyde
Regional Head, Americas – International Sales & Marketing, BBC Worldwide Publishing – Rachael Williams

WEST 175 PUBLISHING
POST OFFICE BOX 84848
SEATTLE, WASHINGTON 98124
www.greatfoodtv.com

Excerpts from *Antonio Carluccio's Italian Feast*, ©Antonio Carluccio 1996, First Published by BBC Books 1996
Excerpts from *Ken Hom's Hot Wok*, ©Taurom Incorporated 1996, First Published by BBC Books 1996
Excerpts from *Madhur Jaffrey's Flavours of India*, ©Madhur Jaffrey 1995, First Published by BBC Books 1995
Excerpts from *Wild Harvest 2, Nick Nairn,* ©Nick Nairn 1997, First Published by BBC Books 1997
Excerpts from *More Rhodes Around Britain, Gary Rhodes,* ©Gary Rhodes 1995, First Published by BBC Books 1995
Excerpts from *Delia Smith's Winter Collection,* ©Delia Smith 1995, First Published by BBC Books 1995
Excerpts from *Delia Smith's Winter Collection* by Random House, Inc., New York, ©Delia Smith 1995

Introduction by Molly O'Neill

Library of Congress Cataloging-in-Publication Data
Great food : over 175 recipes from six of the world's greatest chefs. –– 1st U.S. ed.
p. cm.
Includes index.
ISBN 1-884656-05-6
1. Cookery, International. 2. Cooks. I. Great food (Television program)
TX725.A1G722 1998   98-17732
641.59––dc21   CIP

Printed in Hong Kong
1 2 3 4 5 6 7 8 9 10
First U. S. Edition

DISTRIBUTED BY PUBLISHERS GROUP WEST

TABLE *of* CONTENTS

INTRODUCTION
BY MOLLY O'NEILL

FROM TIME TO TIME,
THOSE OF US WHO LIVE TO
TRAVEL AND EAT FORGET
WHY WE'RE OBSESSED
WITH THE FLAVORS OF
THE WORLD. The adventures,
whether discovering the glory
of Scotland's wild harvest, or the rustic soulful-
ness of a Sunday dinner in Tuscany, or the
beguiling mystery of lunch in West Bengal –
are, in the end, ways of knowing the world.

To recreate these meals at home
is to remember that the borders
between continents and cultures are
permeable. Every time we cross those
borders, we shrug off the constrictions
of our own setting, as well as the harried
time-deprivation of modern life.

Great food from another part of the world
can free you ... at least for the duration of dinner.

Of course, recipes devoid of the sights and
sounds and smells of the culture from which
they arise are far less potent in this regard.
Which is why the Great Food television series –
and this cookbook – are so compelling. Finally,
the arm-chair traveler can truly enter disparate
and far-flung worlds of food with all their senses
primed.

Having logged, by now, hundreds of thousands of miles in the pursuit of flavor, I'm
impressed – if not a little
jealous. With Great Food, you
watch, you read, you cook,
and you've (almost) been
there. The only thing lacking
is frequent flyer points.

The people whose recipes
follow aren't merely cooks, they are more like
culinary anthropologists. They know the geogra-
phy and climate, the social leanings, habits,
history and underlying mythology of the cultures
that spawned the recipes they present.

Antonio Carluccio may in fact, own a restaurant and an Italian specialty food shop in
London's Convent Garden, but the loamy
earth from Italy's forests is under his
nails. He is an incurable amateur
mycologist, who has deveined
subterranean white truffles in Italy's
Piedmont and uncovered Tuscany's
prized Porcini mushroom with the
diligence and cunning of Scotland Yard.

Carluccio's recipe for wild mushroom salad,
therefore is not merely a blueprint for a dish.
It is also haiku for the land that sprouts the
mushrooms, and the people whose instinct
for cooking with them is bred in the bone.

Knowing the context of a cuisine, a cook
instinctively recreates the ambiance of a time
and place in his recipes. Carluccio, for instance,

delivers the sort of joyful anachronism of the Italian kitchen. Closer to home, when for instance, Gary Rhodes celebrates Great Britain, the challenge is to become an observer of his native culture.

As the minting of the "New American Cuisine" has shown over the past several decades in the United States, the dance between the familiar (prosaic) and exuberant discovery (infusing the mundane with the vitality that may have been lost over the centuries) is a delicate one. The natural tendency is toward the precious, the archaic – dishes whose pleasure can be eclipsed by the fussiness of their preparation.

Mr. Rhodes, chef of the Michelin-starred, Greenhouse Restaurant in London, has, nevertheless, managed to breathe new life – and streamlined technique – into Britain's traditional country cooking.

A bite of his battered fried cod, for instance, delivers a sense of simplicity and purity that the dish boasted before the invention of fast-food: the dish would seem to justify modern nostalgia and rose-colored glasses.

Likewise, Delia Smith, Britain's best-selling cookbook author, makes traditional dishes like *Traditional Yorkshire Pudding* or *Classic Roast Pork with Cracklings* new again by distilling away modern *frou frou* in recipes that epitomize the sturdy heart of England.

In a Tuscan farm house, where I often retreat to write cookbooks, my closest neighbors in the summer are British. They come to Italy, they say, "to eat, don't you know; it's impossible to eat well in England." Ms. Smith has played no small part in dispelling such notions. And she's had help.

Nick Nairn, for instance, the self-taught chef whose restaurant, Braeval, in Glasgow, Scotland garnered a Michelin star, is such an ebullient life force that his ways with the country's wild harvests are irresistible.

A dedicated outdoorsman, Mr. Nairn creates dishes that celebrate Scotland's landscape and waterways. The sense of wonder and adventure that he himself feels, at the top of a craggy mountain, or navigating snappy waves when windsurfing the country's coast, for instance, takes the form of surprising seasonings and exotic techniques in his recipes.

Only a Scot who has experienced transcendence in his native landscape could imagine a dish like *Warm Smoked Eel and Apple Tartlets with Cider Dressing* or *Pan-Fried Mallard with Stir-Fried Greens and a Whiskey, Soy, Honey and Lemon Sauce.*

From mountain tops and the open sea you can experience a world without national boundaries. Mr. Nairn is irrepressible: he captures these moments in recipes.

Personally, my first experience with culinary transcendence was having a decent meal. The American Midwest of the 1950's, 60's and even 70's wasn't exactly known for its cuisine.

In fact, Columbus, Ohio, where I grew up, was the test market capital of the country at that time. If fast food chains could make it in Columbus, they could make it anywhere. A full-fledged member of the "Generic White Bread Generation," you can imagine my shock when, as a college student in Paris, I ate a croissant.

For the next fifteen years, first as a chef and later, as a food writer, I was obsessed: first with French, then Italian, then Mediterranean, then Mexican cooking. I traveled, ate, cooked and learned a lot. Only recently did I realize that, however thorough my study, my specialties remained Western, the food of French knives and sauté pans, the wheat-based cuisine that pre-dated, but ultimately lead to sliced bread and pizza.

Intellectually, I under-stood the significance of the rice-based cuisines of the Orient. And I was smitten with the fresh, fiery flavors that Indian, Chinese, Indonesian and Southeast Asian cooking delivered. But it wasn't until I dove into Asia that I fell in love with my subject again.

I began a five year plan to become fluent in Asian cuisine in Singapore, Asia Light. And found, much to my chagrin, that after two weeks of Singaporean cooking, I was chaffing for a big arugula salad with balsamic vinaigrette, a plain grilled hunk of pacific salmon, roasted potatoes and seasoned only with pepper and salt.

It took a number of trips, countless interludes with home cooks and restaurant chefs, and hours of wander-ing through food markets, sampling street food, as well as fruits and vegetables and herbs and spices of another hemisphere before I found comfort and then delight in some of the world's more exotic cuisines.

Great guides smoothed the way. Ken Hom's Chinese cookbooks and Madhur Jaffrey's books about Indian cuisine were indispensable to me.

Mr. Hom, a Chinese American, is an astute cultural translator who demystifies while simulta-neously connecting the cuisine of his parents to the Western context in which he was reared.

He understands the time-pinched modern Western world with all its odd dietary fears and long held cooking habits. And selects the recipes he provides to appeal to Western concerns without diminishing the integrity of their classic Chinese soul.

Hom's characteristic ebullience makes it easy to pass from the familiar to the unknown, without culture shock. His books were, for me, a source of direction far more important than maps or guide books in my Asian adventures.

And I can say the same of Madhur Jaffrey's books. I couldn't have navigated the deeply nuanced flavor of Indian cooking without her careful dissection of its ingredients. Confusion, like that I experienced initially in Singapore, would have made the seam between Western and Eastern cooking impassable.

Instead, I was gently delivered to a more expansive world view, a wider breadth in cooking, an ever opening heart.

To me, the whole point is to cook through cultural bias toward an ever widening world view. For whatever reason – and bear in mind that no religion lacks food protocol, food prohibition and food ritual – this exercise seems to translate into an open heart, or soul, depending on your vernacular.

I know for sure that when my heart closes, my cooking constricts and *violà!* I've lost an essential capacity for wonder and joy.

My mother, an elegant Midwestern lady, accompanied me on a recent tour for one of my own cookbooks. She was amazed by the lines of people waiting for a signature and one evening asked an equally elegant woman of her own age, "Do you really cook this stuff?"

Waiting for her book, the other woman laughed. "Of course not," she said. "I don't have time to cook anymore. But I love to dream about the day that I will have time and the dishes that I will cook when that time arrives."

I'd long suspected that my own painstaking efforts to recreate recipes that sang of their place and time was as much about providing a fantasy for readers as it was about delivering a workable formula.

My mother's conversation made me think that writing about food is like writing fairy tales for grown ups. Recipes display that the extraordinary can triumph over the mundane, that magic is possible, that a well-lived life is – at least in part – the sum of its meals.

Unfortunately, I couldn't tell this reader to turn onto Great Food. The series, and this book, was more a fantasy than a reality at that time. But I know there are thousands like her, who are hungry for the sort of life that that sheer pace of modern living endangers. Two week vacations, after all, are often only a tantalizing introduction to unfamiliar frontiers.

Great Food takes you where years of traveling to eat can leave you soul-fed and satiated. Enjoy your trip.

Antonio Carluccio

INSPIRED BY THE FINEST INGREDIENTS AND FLAVORS OF NORTHERN ITALY, Antonio Carluccio presents the classic dishes of Italian cookery in his television series for Great Food, *Italian Feast.*

Although often simple, this is never fast food. A great enthusiast for the pleasure of eating, Antonio's recipes are to be enjoyed at your own pace.

"During recent visits to the northern regions of Italy, I have been excited to find that the cuisine has not been compromised or watered down by the temptation to cut corners. It is true that, like everywhere else, the hectic pace of life in the big cities has dictated a faster way of eating without necessarily improving the quality of life.

"And it was with great relief that, on one of my journeys, I encountered the *Slow Food Society* which was started by Carlo Pertini in 1986 and has its combined central office and restaurant in the small charming Piemontese town of Bra. This society simply encourages its members to enjoy thoughtfully and masterfully produced food, in peaceful and tranquil surroundings, in the company of other like-minded people. This society invites you to take it easy – that's what I call civilization!"

Antonio Carluccio is the proprietor of the popular *Neal Street Restaurant* in London's Covent Garden and *Carluccio's,* a specialty Italian food shop next door, which he owns with his wife Priscilla.

A wild mushroom enthusiast and great gastronome, Antonio's cuisine is at the forefront of the new wave of Italian cookery in Britain and the United States. He appears regularly on British television and has previous best-selling books which include *An Invitation to Italian Cookery, A Passion for Mushrooms* and *Passion for Pasta.*

CREST HERB SOUP

Zuppa Di Erbe Del Crest - Serves 4

When my friend Nina, who lives in the Aosta Valley in Italy, wants a soup made with fresh greens, she just pops out to the fields in front of her house with a basket and returns with a collection of dandelion, wild sorrel, nettles and pimpernel. Nina's herbs are especially wonderful because they grow organically high in the mountains. But dandelions and nettles grow every-where, so you can try this soup with whatever wild herbs you can find in non-polluted places.

Chop the onion, potato and carrot into chunks. Heat the oil in a large stockpot set on medium-high heat. Add the vegetables and cook for 1-2 minutes. Add the stock, bring the mixture to a boil, and add all the herbs. Turn the heat to low and cook for 15 minutes. Add the butter, then pour the mixture into a blender or food processor. Blend just until smooth, then pour into warm bowls and top with croutons.

1 small onion

1 small potato

1 carrot

2 tablespoons olive oil

1 ounce (25 g) stinging nettle

1 ounce (25 g) sorrel

1 ounce (25 g) white dead nettle

¾ ounce (20 g) yarrow (if this is not collected in spring, strip the leaves)

2 ounces (50 g) dandelion greens (pre-boil for 5-10 minutes to remove the bitterness)

1 ounce (25 g) watercress

1 ounce (25 g) fresh spinach leaves

3½ cups chicken stock, or vegetable stock

2 tablespoons butter

NETTLES, YARROW, SORREL, WATERCRESS AND DANDELION grow wild throughout the United States. Still, for those of us who live in cities, identifying and gathering them can be a daunting task. You can make this soup with an assortment of various greens – just make sure you have a total of ½ pound (225 g) of greens. Try using beet greens, collard greens, Swiss chard, arugula, amaranth, turnip greens, mustard greens or kale. All can be found at large grocery stores.

Opposite: Rosalba's Ravioli (page 22).

Melon *and* Parma Ham Soup

Zuppa di Melone e Prosciutto - Serves 4

1 very ripe (2¼-3 pound)
    (1-1.5 kg) cantaloupe

Juice of 1 orange

Juice of ¼ lemon

½ teaspoon sea salt

½ teaspoon coarsely ground
    pink peppercorns
    (see note)

Sugar to taste

4 large slices Parma ham,
    cut into thin slices

This is a wonderful way to enjoy Parma ham and melon. It adds another dimension to summer eating. The combination of a little orange and lemon juice gives it a special spiciness. In summer, this is one of the bestsellers in my restaurant.

Peel the melon and place it in a food processor or blender. Add the orange and lemon juices, salt, pepper and sugar, and blend until smooth. If you find a melon that is ripe and flavorful, you won't need to add much sugar. Stir in one quarter of the Parma ham. Pour the soup into 4 bowls and top with the remaining ham and a twist of freshly ground pepper.

PINK PEPPERCORNS are available in gourmet food stores. They are worth seeking out, as they are much sweeter and impart a more delicate flavor than black peppercorns. If you can't find them, substitute half the amount of black or white peppercorns. The soup will still taste good.

SAN GIOVANNI FISH SOUP

Zuppa di Pesce di San Giovanni · Serves 6

*T*he San Giovanni restaurant in Casarza is where I came across this Ligurian specialty. The fairy queen of that kitchen, Pinuccia, is an ex-fishmonger and knows the importance of freshness to a good fish soup. This soup is known locally as cacciucco.

To make the fish stock, take the fish heads and bones and place in a large pan with the fennel and the water. Bring to a boil, then turn the heat down to low and simmer for half an hour.

Heat the oil in a large frying pan, add the onion and chili and fry for 2-3 minutes. Stir in the crushed tomatoes. Add the chunks of monkfish, John Dory, red mullet, octopus, squid and cuttlefish to the pan and 3½ cups of the fish stock and leave to simmer for 10 minutes. Then add the clams, mussels, prawns and scallops and cook for a further 5-6 minutes. Add the parsley and season with the salt and pepper.

When dividing the soup, make sure that it is done equally and fairly so that everyone gets a bit of everything. Please note that if you prefer a thicker consistency, add a very thinly sliced potato during cooking.

THE MONKFISH, JOHN DORY AND RED MULLET FISH mentioned above may be difficult to find outside of Italy. You can substitute several kinds of firm-fleshed white fish, such as flounder, sole, halibut, cod, red snapper etc. If you can't find the cuttlefish or octopus, just use squid. It will taste just as good.

2 pounds (900 g) fish heads and bones (you can purchase these at a fish market)

2 green fennel tops

9 cups water

6 tablespoons olive oil

1 small onion, finely chopped

1 small fresh red chili

4 tablespoons canned crushed tomatoes

12 ounces (350 g) monkfish, cleaned, filleted and cut into 1 inch (2.5 cm) chunks

12 ounces (350 g) John Dory, cleaned, filleted and cut into 1 inch (2.5 cm) chunks

11 ounces (300 g) red mullet, cleaned, filleted and cut into 1 inch (2.5 cm) chunks

4 ounces (100 g) octopus, cut into 1 inch (2.5 cm) slices, tentacles removed

4 ounces (100 g) squid, cut into 1 inch (2.5 cm) rings

4 ounces (100 g) cuttlefish, cut into 1 inch (2.5 cm) strips

12 clams

12 mussels

4 ounces (100 g) large prawns, peeled and deveined

6 scallops, shelled

2 tablespoons coarsely chopped fresh parsley

Sea salt to taste

Freshly ground black pepper to taste

RISOTTO SOPHIESTICATED

Risotto all'Acetosa · Serves 4 as an appetizer.

5 cups chicken stock or
   5 bouillon cubes dissolved
   in 5 cups boiling water

3 tablespoons olive oil

6 tablespoons butter

1 small onion, chopped

2 cups raw risotto rice
   (carnaroli, vialone nano
   or arborio)

5 ounces (125 g) wild or
   cultivated sorrel, stems
   removed

½ cup freshly grated
   Parmesan cheese

Sorrel leaves, to garnish
   (optional) (see note)

I created this risotto in Italy on the day my niece, Sophie, was getting married in England. I thought it was so delicious that I decided to dedicate it to her. I sent her a fax with the recipe and good wishes for the occasion. That is why it is called Risotto Sophiesticated.

You may find wild sorrel during your early summer outings in the country, but cultivated sorrel is available from good grocery stores and gourmet markets.

Bring the chicken stock to a boil in a saucepan set on medium heat. Reduce the heat to a low simmer. In a separate saucepan set on medium heat, heat the oil and 2 tablespoons of the butter. Add the onions and fry until soft. Turn the heat up to medium high and add the rice, stirring continually. After 1 minute, pour some stock into the rice and stir until it is absorbed. Add the sorrel and continue stirring.

Keep adding stock a little at a time, stirring constantly, until all the stock is absorbed and the rice is cooked. After 18 minutes, remove the rice from the heat. The rice should be cooked al dente and not be too dry. Add the rest of the butter and the Parmesan cheese and beat until creamy. Serve immediately on warm plates and garnish, if you wish, with a small sorrel leaf.

If you have any leftover rice, you can mix it with a beaten egg and a little more Parmesan. With wet hands, form balls a little larger than a walnut and deep fry until crispy. These delicious rice balls are called arancini (little oranges).

SORREL IS A PERENNIAL HERB which grows wild in Asia, Europe and North America. Its tart, lemony flavor is a good accent in salads and with other cooked greens. Look for it in the produce section of your grocery store.

BUCKWHEAT PASTA

Pizzoccheri - Serves 10

≈

Valtellina is a valley in the Italian Alps not far from Milan. It is famous for bresaola, the thinly sliced air-dried beef which is served as an antipasto, pizzoccheri, the only buckwheat pasta made in Italy and Bitto, a delicious local cheese. Taleggio is a neighboring valley, where the famous cheese of the same name comes from. I had great fun cooking this dish for students of a fashion school in Milan who were preparing for their end-of-year exams. In exchange I received a series of outrageous and impractical aprons specially made for me that only a school with lots of imagination could invent.

Boil the pasta, beans, potatoes and cabbage together and cook for about 18 minutes or until tender. Drain and set aside. Put the butter and olive oil in a pan and gently fry the garlic slices until they are golden brown. Then add the nutmeg. Remove from the heat and set aside.

Preheat a large casserole dish. Layer the pasta, vegetables, Bitto and taleggio cheese cubes and Parmesan cheese. Repeat the layers until the ingredients are all gone. Pour the garlic butter mixture on top – it should be warm enough to slightly melt the cheese. Mix well, season with the salt and pepper and serve immediately. This is a sensational dish for vegetarians.

1¼ pounds (550 g) buckwheat or wheat pasta

11 ounces (300 g) French beans, ends trimmed

14 ounces (400 g) potatoes, peeled and cut into cubes

1¼ pounds (550 g) Savoy cabbage, cut into strips

14 tablespoons butter

4 tablespoons olive oil

2 garlic cloves, sliced

Pinch of freshly grated nutmeg

11 ounces (300 g) Bitto or Fontina, provolone or mozzarella cheese, cut into small cubes

11 ounces (300 g) taleggio or Fontina, provolone or mozzarella cheese, cut into small cubes

4 ounces (100 g) freshly grated Parmesan cheese

Sea salt to taste

Freshly ground black pepper to taste

FRESH PASTA

Pasta all'Uovo ~ Makes about 1 pound (450g) pasta.

2½ cups flour (use 1¾ cups
  all-purpose flour and
  ¾ cup pastry flour, or
  2 cups all-purpose flour
  and ½ cup cake flour)

2 eggs

Pinch of salt

This recipe is the basis for all types of home-made pasta. The best flour to use is a mixture of all-purpose flour and pastry flour or cake flour made from very finely milled tender wheat. You may also need to add a little durum wheat semolina if you want to make special shapes like trofie. Standard tagliatelle are made with about 6 whole eggs per 2¼ pounds (1 kilo) of flour, plus a little water if required. Sometimes, for example, if you are making ravioli, pansotti or other filled pasta, you will want a softer, more workable pasta dough, and this can be achieved by using about 3 eggs and the necessary water to 2¼ pounds (1 kg) flour.

The important thing to remember when making pasta is to work the dough well with a lot of elbow grease and then to rest it for an hour before using it. Then, once you have rolled and cut the dough to the required shape, leave it to dry for half an hour or so on a clean cloth. Home-made pasta cannot be kept for long because of its egg content. You should not refrigerate it – the best thing is to freeze it, although this will of course have an adverse effect on the quality of the finished dish. Bought dried pasta is dried industrially for 12 hours in commercial machines.

Never add oil to the water when cooking pasta except for large squares of pasta like open ravioli. Never rinse pasta in cold water – if you want to cool it down and interrupt the cooking process, add a couple of glasses of cold water to the pot when you take it off the stove.

Sift the flour onto a clean work surface (marble is ideal), forming it into a volcano-shaped mound with a well in the center. Break the eggs into the well and add the salt. Incorporate the eggs into the flour until it forms a coarse paste. Add a little more flour if the mixture is too soft or sticky, and scrape up any pieces of dough.

Before kneading the dough clean your hands and the work surface. Lightly flour the work surface, and start to knead with the heel of one hand. Work the dough for 10-15 minutes until the consistency is smooth and elastic. Wrap the dough in plastic wrap or foil and let it rest for half an hour.

Lightly flour your work surface and rolling pin. Gently roll the dough out, rotating it in quarter turns. Roll the dough to a sheet ⅛ inch (3 mm) thick.

If you are making filled pasta, go ahead and add the filling as directed in the recipe. If you are making flat pasta or shapes, leave the pasta on a clean dish towel to dry for about half an hour.

PASTA *with* PESTO

Trofie al Pesto - Serves 4

Try taking this dish to your next picnic. The combination of a beautiful day outside and this delicious dish is a great pleasure for the eye, the palate and the soul. Trofie is a particular pasta shape from Liguria. It is usually homemade, but you can find it in good Italian shops. Strozzapreti or fusilli pasta would work well too.

To make the pesto by hand, place the garlic, basil, sea salt and pine nuts in a mortar. Use a pestle to grind the mixture to a smooth paste. Add a splash or two of the olive oil and continue to grind. Add the Parmesan and continue adding olive oil and grinding until the sauce is smooth and well-incorporated.

To make the pesto in a food processor, add the basil, garlic, sea salt, pine nuts and a little olive oil to a food processor and pulse until the mixture forms a smooth paste. Add the Parmesan cheese and pulse until well incorporated. With the machine running, slowly drizzle additional olive oil into the bowl and continue to process until the mixture is smooth.

Boil the pasta according to the directions on the bag. Drain, transfer to a bowl, and mix thoroughly with the pesto sauce. Garnish with the fresh basil leaves and serve.

4 garlic cloves

40-50 fresh basil leaves

1 teaspoon sea salt

½ cup pine nuts

⅓ cup extra virgin olive oil

½ cup freshly grated
  Parmesan cheese

1¼ pounds (550 g) dried
  trofie, strozzapreti
  or fusilli pasta

Basil leaves, for garnish

Rosalba's Ravioli

Ravioli di Rosalba - Serves 4

3 cups water

½ teaspoon salt

1 tablespoon olive oil

2 cups chopped cabbage

½ pound (225 g) ground
   pork, veal or beef

1 egg

½ cup freshly grated
   Parmesan cheese

1 recipe Fresh Pasta
   (see page 20)

4 tablespoons unsalted
   butter

12 fresh sage leaves

One of the best traditions of Italian cooking is making handmade ravioli. My sister-in-law, Rosalba, makes some of the best. Everyone has their own favorite formula for the filling, which varies enormously from fish to meat to vegetables to cheese. This filling includes braised cabbage, but feel free to try any combination of ingredients. To make life easier, buy a raviolatrice, an aluminum tray which has square molds with a jagged border. These can be bought at specialty cooking shops. (Illustrated on page 14.)

Bring the water, half of the salt and the olive oil to a boil. Add the chopped cabbage, cover, turn the heat down to low and simmer for 5-10 minutes or until al dente. Drain and mix with the ground meat, the egg and half the Parmesan.

Roll out the pasta dough into a thin rectangular sheet to cover the raviolatrice. Gently press the dough into the raviolatrice. Top each individual mold with a teaspoon of the filling, then cover with another sheet of pasta. Gently roll with a rolling pin over the top and remove each ravioli onto a floured surface. Cook in boiling water with the remaining salt for 3-4 minutes.

Meanwhile, melt the butter in a pan, add the sage leaves and pour over the ravioli on individual plates. Serve with the remaining Parmesan cheese.

BRAISED BEEF *in* NEBBIOLO WINE

Brasato al Nebbiolo - Serves 4

The Nebbiolo grape is the father and mother of Barolo wine and is also used for making many other Piemontese wines, like Carema. Piemontese beef is particularly tasty. The union with Nebbiolo wine brings out the best in it and after two hours of cooking, it is tender and juicy. The alcohol evaporates during the cooking, so you won't get tipsy when eating this robust but very tasty dish!

Chop the onions, carrots and celery into small pieces and set aside.

Set the rosemary on the chuck roast, roll the roast around it and tie with string. Season with the sea salt and pepper.

Heat the butter and oil in a large frying pan set on medium high heat. Add the meat and fry until browned on all sides. Add the chopped vegetables, sage leaves and chopped garlic and cook until the onions are golden brown. Pour in the wine and the beef stock, turn the heat down to low, cover the pan with a lid and simmer for 1¾ hours. To serve, place the beef on a serving dish with the vegetables and spoon the sauce on top.

2 onions

2 carrots

3 celery stalks

2 sprigs fresh rosemary

1 (2¼ pound) (1 kg) chuck roast

½ cup butter

⅓ cup olive oil

5 fresh sage leaves

2 garlic cloves, chopped

3½ cups Nebbiolo, Barolo or other dry red wine

2 cups beef stock

Sea salt to taste

Freshly ground black pepper to taste

CASTELLUCCIO LENTILS *with* SAUSAGE

Lenticchie di Castelluccio con Salsicce - Serves 4

8 sausages, approximately
   1½ pounds (750 g), either
   pure pork or wild boar

2 cups (400 g) Castelluccio,
   Puy or green lentils

Leaves from 2 stalks of celery,
   chopped

2 garlic cloves

4 tablespoons virgin olive oil

1 fresh chili, finely chopped

10 sun-dried tomatoes,
   halved

Salt to taste

Stock, as required (a bouillon
   cube is fine)

Umbrian food is, in my opinion, one of the most authentic Italian cuisines and the least contaminated by modern catering methods. This recipe uses Castelluccio lentils which are full of iron and have a thin skin so they cook in a short time. You could, of course, use Puy lentils or green lentils instead.

Norcia pork sausages are made with locally raised animals and are the best I have ever tasted. Some people mix the pork with wild boar meat when in season and this adds a certain extra something.

Boil the sausages in water for 30 minutes, then peel off the skins. Cover the lentils with water and then bring to the boil. Add the celery leaves and one whole clove of the garlic and continue to cook until soft.

In another pan, heat the olive oil and fry the chili, the other garlic clove, finely chopped, and the sun-dried tomatoes for one minute.

After removing and discarding the whole garlic clove, mix the lentil mixture with the tomatoes and chili, and add the sausages. Allow to cook on a moderate heat for 10 minutes. The consistency must not be too soupy but neither must it be too thick so add stock if necessary. Add salt to taste and serve with bread.

VERDI-STYLE DUCK

Anitra alla Verdi - Serves 4

I prepared this dish for the first time in Busseto, Italy, birthplace of the great maestro Giuseppe Verdi, for finalists in the vocal competition dedicated to him. The delicious simplicity of this dish would certainly meet the approval of one of the greatest composers of all time – at least I hope it would! It perfectly combines the local ingredients, duck and Parma ham.

Preheat the oven to 425°F (220°C). Wash and peel the carrots, then chop the carrots and onion into small pieces and scatter in a roasting pan. Wash and dry the duck, then place on top of the carrots and onion. Rub the duck with the olive oil and sprinkle with the minced Parma ham. Top with the sprig of rosemary, cover with foil and place into the oven. After 1 hour, remove the foil and roast for 15 more minutes or until crisp and golden-brown. Remove the vegetables from the fat at the bottom of the pan, and serve them with the roasted duck.

This is delicious with Peppers in Balsamic Vinegar (see page 34).

2 carrots

1 onion

1 (3 pound) (1.5 kg) duck, cleaned

2 tablespoons olive oil

⅓ pound (150 g) well marbled Parma ham, finely diced

Sprig of fresh rosemary

Antonio Carluccio 25
Entrées

FRIED MEAT PIEMONTESE-STYLE

Fritto Misto Piemontese - Serves 6

Olive oil for frying

5 eggs, beaten

Sea salt to taste

Dried bread crumbs

6 (2½ inch) (6 cm) square,
    flat pieces of each of
    the following meats:
    beef, lamb, pork,
    chicken, turkey, veal

6 small pork sausages

6 (2½ inch) (6 cm) square
    pieces of pork liver,
    calves' liver, kidney,
    brain or sweetbread

6 slices apple, peeled and
    cored

6 Amaretti biscuits

6 zucchini blossoms

6 eggplant slices

6 zucchini slices

Lemon halves

The work involved in making this dish is completely justified by the result for those who like food fried in bread crumbs. A respectable fritto misto has to have at least thirteen different types of meat which are carefully prepared and shallow-fried at the last minute to arrive crispy and succulent on your plate. It is impossible to make this for many people; at the most it is for four or six. This is without doubt the Piemontese specialty "par excellence" and only enjoyable either in private or at a very good restaurant. You can choose any combination of ingredients, but take care to check the quantities of each.

Gather all the ingredients and arrange near the stove. Pour a little oil into a large frying pan on medium heat.

Add salt to taste to the beaten eggs. Dip the pieces of meat, vegetables, apple, etc., into the egg, then coat on both sides with bread crumbs. Shake off any extra coating, then fry the pieces until golden on each side. You may have to do this in batches. Continue until all the pieces are cooked. Then serve with the lemon halves and a salad.

GUINEA FOWL *with* PEVERADA SAUCE

Farona con Peverada - Serves 4

*T*his dish is the specialty of Treviso, a charming Italian town not far from Venice. Treviso is also famous for its radicchio, which the local restaurants serve cooked in hundreds of different ways, and sopressa, a local type of salami. Guinea fowl is an elegant bird, which somehow tastes more like pork than chicken. This is an easy to prepare Sunday lunch which I make using smoked ham rather than sopressa.

Preheat the oven to 400°F (200°C). Rub the guinea fowl or chicken with 1 tablespoon of the oil and sprinkle it with the salt. Place in a roasting pan and cook for about 1 hour, or until golden brown.

Meanwhile, heat the remaining olive oil in a large frying pan set on low heat. Add the onions and cook until transparent. Add the carrots, chicken livers and ham and cook for 10 minutes. Pour in the chicken stock, wine and vinegar and cook for 8 minutes. Remove from the heat, add the parsley and check the seasoning, adding salt and pepper to taste. Serve the cooked guinea fowl with the sauce.

1 (3 pound) (1.3 kg) guinea fowl or chicken, cleaned

6 tablespoons olive oil

Sea salt to taste

1 onion, finely chopped

1 carrot, finely chopped

1 pound (450 g) chicken livers, finely chopped

4 ounces (100 g) Parma, Black Forest or other smoked ham

5 tablespoons chicken stock

4 tablespoons white wine

1 tablespoon white wine vinegar

Coarsely chopped fresh parsley to taste

Freshly ground black pepper to taste

Mixed Fried Fish Burano-Style

Fritto Misto di Burano - Serves 4

Olive oil for frying

14 ounces (400 g) fresh eel,
  cut into chunks

8 giant prawns, peeled and
  deveined

⅓ pound (150 g) squid

Sea salt to taste

Flour for dusting the fish

2 lemons, cut into halves

On the small and very pretty island of Burano near Venice, once Italy's center of handmade embroidery, the gondola regatta is quite a prestigious event. The entire village (about 800 people) takes part. While the youngsters row in the race, the others prepare the most delicious Fritto Misto di Pesce which is sold to the thousands of people who travel from all over the area. Every coastal region in Italy has its own Fritto Misto di Pesce, but only a few have a lake from which they can catch such delicious fish.

Pour the olive oil into a deep fryer and heat to 375°F (190°C). Sprinkle all the seafood with the salt and coat each piece with the flour. Shake off any excess flour, then place the seafood pieces in the hot oil and fry for 2-3 minutes, or until golden brown. You may have to do this in batches. Drain on paper towels and serve with the lemon halves on warm plates.

Ragout *of* Lamb Offal

Coratella di Agnello - Serves 6

*B*ecause the Padrone (or boss) always used to get the better parts of an animal when it was slaughtered, the offal was usually discarded and given to the poor. Not today, however. Lamb's heart, liver and lungs are now a delicacy commanding very high prices. This specialty is also cooked, though slightly differently, in southern Italy, but this is the Umbrian method. The original also includes the spleen and intestines, but for obvious reasons I suggest you use only the liver, heart and lungs.

Be brave, believe me, this is a very delicate and tasty dish.

Clean the offal of any fat and unwanted pieces. Cut into very small pieces. Heat some oil in a pan and cook the onion with the chili and whichever herb you are using. When golden, add the offal and stir from time to time. When the meat starts to brown, add some of the wine and tomato if desired. Cook, adding more wine as necessary, until soft and tender, about 30 minutes.

Serve with bread, rice, polenta or as a sauce for pasta.

1 (2¼ pound) (1 kg) lamb's heart, liver and lungs

Virgin olive oil, for frying

2 onions, finely chopped

1 fresh chili pepper, very finely chopped

1 sprig rosemary, bay leaves or sage (not together)

1 bottle dry white wine

Salt to taste

1 ripe tomato, seeded and cut into cubes (optional)

SAN DOMENICO RABBIT

Coniglio San Domenico - Serves 4

1 (2¼ pound) (1 kg) rabbit,
   cleaned

3 artichokes

Juice of 1 lemon

6 tablespoons olive oil

1 large onion

25 black Taggiasca olives
   (see note)

6 fresh sage leaves

1 sprig fresh marjoram

Sea salt to taste

Freshly ground black pepper
   to taste

1 cup white wine

1½ cups chicken stock

1 teaspoon tomato paste

2 teaspoons chopped
   fresh parsley

This recipe is dedicated to Padri Francesco Gusberti, Mario Raffaelo Icardi, Francesco Merlino and Attilio Pichino. These four Dominican monks I met at the fifteenth-century monastery of Taggia seem to have escaped the pressures of twentieth-century life. They grow everything they use in their back garden just as they did centuries ago and the artichokes, onions, salads, fruit and even their rabbits looked so tempting that I had to cook this recipe for them. They enjoyed the feast very much and they invited me to return and spend some time with them.

Joint the cleaned rabbit and cut into medium-sized chunks. This can be done by your butcher.

Trim the artichokes up to the tender heart and cut into quarters. Put them in a bowl of water with the lemon juice to prevent discoloration.

In a large frying pan set on medium-high heat, fry the chopped onions until they soften. Add the rabbit pieces, olives, sage, marjoram, salt and pepper to taste, wine and the chicken stock. Turn the heat down to low, stir well, cover the pan with a lid and leave to simmer for 30 minutes. Add additional stock if necessary, then add the artichokes, tomato paste and parsley and simmer for a further 10-15 minutes.

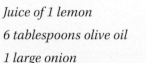

IF YOU CANNOT FIND BLACK TAGGIASCA OLIVES, try substituting another black Italian olive such as San Remo or Gaeta olives. You could also simply use ordinary black olives.

TROUT *in a* BAG

Trota in Cartoccio - Serves 4

*W*rapping a fish in a leaf, clay or salt is a clever cooking method used by the ancient Romans. This form of cooking retains the juices in the envelope and fills food with flavor. You can try this with aluminum foil or waxed paper. Be careful not to wrap the fish too tightly, or the skin will come off when you open the package. The best way is to open the package at the table, and let your guests inhale the wonderful aroma.

Preheat the oven to 400°F (200°C). Clean, gut and scale the trout or ask your fishmonger to do it. Chop the fennel into small pieces. Cut each lemon in half lengthwise. Then cut each half into 6 slices. Scatter the chopped fennel and a couple lemon slices over 4 sheets of aluminum foil or waxed paper. Season the fish with the salt and pepper and place on top of the fennel and lemon. Tuck a couple of lemon slices and a sprig of parsley inside each fish, then top each fish with a lemon slice and a dot of the butter. Fold the foil or paper around the fish, place on a baking sheet and cook for 20 minutes.

Serve on a long plate, opening the parcel in front of your guests.

4 trout

1 fennel bulb

2 lemons

Sea salt to taste

Freshly ground black pepper to taste

4 sprigs parsley

5 tablespoons butter

Braised Chicory

Cicoria in Umido - Serves 4

1¾ pounds (750 g) Belgian
    endive or radicchio

4 tablespoons extra virgin
    olive oil

2 garlic cloves, coarsely sliced

1 tablespoon small capers,
    drained

2 small tomatoes, sliced

Sea salt to taste

1 cup chicken stock or
    a bouillon cube dissolved
    in 1 cup boiling water

When in Italy, I make this dish with an Italian chicory called puntarelle. Belgian chicory, also known as Belgian endive, is available in America, and is also ideal for this recipe as it offers a certain interesting bitterness. Radicchio is another possibility.

Cut the chicory in half lengthwise and remove and discard the tough central core, which may be bitter. Cook in boiling water for 2 minutes. Drain well and place in a saucepan. Sprinkle with the olive oil, garlic, capers, tomatoes and salt. Pour the chicken stock on top, cover with a lid and cook on low heat for about 30 minutes, or until tender.

NINA'S POLENTA

Polenta di Nina - Serves 6

*O*n a recent trip to Italy I saw my friend Nina, from Champoluc, a small town in the Aosta Valley. Her polenta is famous all over the area. This is not only because the ingredients like the butter and Fontina cheese come from her own cows and taste sublime, but also because of her traditional way of making it. She recently modernized the kitchen in her hotel, but the old wood-fired heavy-duty cooker remains, probably just to make polenta, which needs a traditional slow stove. It is served to everyone eating in her charming hotel in a simple way, with the tastiest chicken, salsiccia (pork sausage) or coniglio (rabbit) in tomato sauce.

Bring the water to a boil, then add the salt and let it dissolve. Pour the polenta a little at a time into the boiling water and stir the mixture constantly. Take care to cover your hands with an oven glove as the polenta tends to splatter as it boils. Continue to stir and cook the polenta for 40 minutes; then add the Fontina, Parmesan and butter. Stir until all the ingredients are incorporated and the polenta comes off the walls of the pan. Serve with meat, fish or mushroom ragù.

If you have any leftover polenta, spread it onto a flat surface, let it cool and solidify and cut it into slices. Grill or fry the pieces and enjoy. Even without any accompaniments, polenta is a substantial and delicious dish.

7 cups water

1 tablespoon sea salt

2½ cups cornmeal or polenta flour

5 ounces (150 g) Fontina cheese, cut into small cubes

1 cup freshly grated Parmesan cheese

½ cup plus 2 tablespoons butter

Peppers *in* Balsamic Vinegar

Peperoni al Balsamico - Serves 4

3 red bell peppers

3 yellow bell peppers

6 tablespoons olive oil

2 garlic cloves

Sea salt to taste

2 tablespoons balsamic
vinegar

One of the most famous producers of traditional balsamic vinegar is Signora Giacobazzi of Modena, who loves her wooden barrels so much that she treats them as if they were her best friends. A wooden barrel that holds cooked-down unfermented wine for up to 50 years and turns it into one of the most sublime and precious condiments on earth has to be your friend! It is not necessary to use a 50-year-old balsamic vinegar in this dish – a good quality younger one is fine.

Cut the peppers in half. Scrape out the seeds and the pith and cut into strips. Heat the olive oil in a frying pan set on high heat. When it begins to sizzle, add the peppers and cook until lightly browned. Add the garlic and cook for 1-2 minutes, then add the salt and balsamic vinegar. Continue cooking until the vinegar has evaporated.

This dish goes well with Verdi-Style Duck (see page 25) or it can be eaten by itself.

STUFFED ZUCCHINI FLOWERS

Fiori di Zucchini Ripieni - Serves 4

I can still remember the face of Padre Emiliano, a very nice orthodox Catholic father from Grotta Ferrata near Rome, when I invited him to come and eat some stuffed zucchini flowers with me. I don't think he had ever eaten anything like them before. The expression on his face after tasting one or two was of complete beatitude.

After zucchini flowers, we went on to eat gnocchi with Gorgonzola cheese and my tiramisù, and later on he had a huge steak as well! When I mentioned that he might perhaps have overdone it, he said with a smiling face that his work had been very hard that morning and that was his caloric reward!

4½ ounces (120 g) chopped fresh spinach leaves

½ cup fresh ricotta cheese

4 tablespoons chopped fresh basil

3 tablespoons freshly grated Parmesan cheese

2 eggs

Large pinch freshly grated nutmeg

1 garlic clove, crushed

Sea salt to taste

Freshly ground black pepper

8 zucchini flowers (see note)

Oil for shallow or deep-frying

Wash the spinach well, and cook in boiling salted water for about 3-4 minutes. Drain and allow to cool. Mix the cooled spinach with the ricotta cheese, basil, Parmesan, 1 of the eggs, nutmeg, garlic, salt and pepper. Spoon the filling into a piping bag, then pipe into each zucchini flower until they are about three-quarters full. Beat the remaining egg and brush each flower with it. Shallow or deep-fry the flowers until golden. Serve at once.

THERE ARE TWO TYPES OF ZUCCHINI FLOWERS; the one sold with the little zucchini attached to it is the female. However, if you know a farmer or a gardener who grows zucchini, go and see if he or she will give you male flowers, which are the ones attached to a stem without the zucchini.

Doges' Delight Ice Cream

Makes 6 servings of each flavor.

I invented this recipe during a New Year's holiday in Venice in honor of the Doges, who are known for returning from their Mediterranean expeditions with all sorts of spices previously unknown in Italy. It uses saffron, the most precious of all spices, plus cardamom and cinnamon to make three ice creams whose flavors blend marvelously well together. The method is similar for each ice cream flavor.

For the Cinnamon Ice Cream

2 cups whole milk

2 tablespoons ground cinnamon

2 cloves

6 egg yolks

2 tablespoons honey (optional)

⅔ cup sugar

½ cup heavy whipping cream

For the Cardamom Ice Cream

2 cups whole milk

1 tablespoon cardamom seeds, crushed

6 egg yolks

2 tablespoons honey (optional)

⅔ cup sugar

1 cup pistachio nuts

Green food coloring

½ cup heavy whipping cream

For the Cinnamon Ice Cream

Heat a saucepan on medium high heat. Bring the milk, cinnamon and cloves to a boil. Turn the heat down to low and simmer for 5-10 minutes. Allow to cool, then strain through a mesh strainer.

In a separate bowl, mix the eggs, honey (optional) and sugar. Add the flavored milk, a little at a time, and whisk until it is all used up. Set the bowl over a pan of simmering hot water, and cook, stirring constantly, for 15 minutes or until the mixture coats the back of a spoon. Remove from the heat, allow to cool and refrigerate overnight. Then place in an ice cream machine and churn for about 30 minutes.

While the ice cream is churning, whip the heavy cream with a whisk for about 1 minute. Fold into the ice cream in the last 5 minutes, continuing to churn and freeze. To serve, scoop onto a chilled saucer with the other 2 ice creams.

For the Cardamom Ice Cream

Heat a saucepan on medium high heat. Bring the milk and cardamom seeds to a boil. Turn the heat down to low and simmer for 5-10 minutes. Allow to cool, then strain through a mesh strainer.

In a separate bowl, mix the eggs, honey (optional) and sugar. Add the flavored milk a little at a time and whisk until it is all used up. Set the bowl over a pan of simmering hot water, and cook, stirring constantly, for 15 minutes or until the mixture coats the back of a spoon. Remove from the heat, allow to cool and refrigerate overnight. Then place in an ice cream machine and churn for about 30 minutes.

While the ice cream is churning, whip the heavy cream with a whisk for about 1 minute. Add the pistachios, 2-3 drops of the green food coloring and heavy cream to the ice cream in the last 5 minutes, continuing to churn and freeze. To serve, scoop onto a chilled saucer with the other 2 ice creams.

FOR THE SAFFRON ICE CREAM

    Heat a saucepan on medium high heat. Bring the milk and saffron to a boil. Turn the heat on down to low and simmer for 5-10 minutes. Allow to cool, then strain through a mesh strainer.

    In a separate bowl, mix the eggs, honey (optional) and sugar. Add the flavored milk a little at a time and whisk until it is all used up. Set the bowl over a pan of simmering hot water, and cook, stirring constantly, for 15 minutes or until the mixture coats the back of a spoon. Remove from the heat, allow to cool and refrigerate overnight. Then place in an ice cream machine and churn for about 30 minutes.

    While the ice cream is churning, whip the heavy cream with a whisk for about 1 minute. Fold into the ice cream in the last 5 minutes, continuing to churn and freeze. To serve, scoop onto a chilled saucer with the other 2 ice creams.

FOR THE SAFFRON ICE CREAM

2 cups whole milk

Pinch of saffron

6 egg yolks

2 tablespoons honey (optional)

½ cup sugar

½ cup heavy whipping cream

KEN HOM

KEN HOM, BORN IN AMERICA OF CHINESE EXTRACTION, SHOT TO FAME IN BRITAIN with the debut of his 1984 BBC television series Ken Hom's *Chinese Cookery*. He is now widely regarded as one of the world's greatest authorities on Chinese cooking and delights viewers of Great Food with his dishes whipped up easily and quickly in his beloved wok. Indeed, Ken Hom's *Hot Wok* tells you absolutely everything you need to know about successful and foolproof wok cookery – what Ken believes to be the fast food of the future.

"The wok has been central to my life as a professional chef and food writer. But it was central to my childhood and youth as well.

"To grow up Chinese means enjoying wonderful foods prepared in the wok. My mother put together three or four course meals every night in a tiny kitchen, ill-equipped by modern Western standards. In my eyes, she did this quickly and smoothly. I never heard her complain of any technical problems. Our dinner was on the table within an hour of her coming home from work.

"With today's hectic lifestyle, in which time is limited and yet people are so mindful of health and nutrition, the wok is something of a wonder. The richly blackened, perfectly seasoned family wok, expertly manipulated by a cook can become the indispensable tool for making wonderful meals."

Ken Hom travels extensively as a food and restaurant consultant, dividing his time among America, Europe, Asia and Australia. His book *Chinese Cookery*, published by BBC Books in 1984, has sold over half a million copies and its successors, *Ken Hom's Quick and Easy Chinese Cookery*, *Ken Hom's Illustrated Chinese Cookery* and *Ken Hom's Vegetarian Cookery*, have ensured Ken an ever-growing band of culinary admirers around the world.

THAI CRISPY PRAWN-COCONUT TREATS

Serves 4

On my frequent visits to Bangkok, I often cook at the famous Oriental Hotel kitchen. Whenever I get the chance, I observe the excellent chefs in the Thai food section of the kitchen. I have discovered that there are many similarities between Chinese and Thai cuisine, but the addition of certain Thai ingredients adds another depth or dimension to Chinese food.

Here is a simple Thai appetizer which would be quite Chinese but for the added twist of coconut and curry paste. These touches turn the dish into a wonderful party treat or a splendid opener for any dinner.

The filling can be made in advance, but the actual stuffing should be done at the last moment, otherwise the pasta will become soggy. These treats should not be frozen. (Illustrated on the opposite page.)

FOR THE FILLING

12 ounces (350 g) raw prawns, peeled and coarsely ground

4 ounces (100 g) ground pork

1 teaspoon salt

½ teaspoon freshly ground black pepper

4 tablespoons finely chopped green onions

3 tablespoons dried coconut

2 teaspoons light soy sauce

2 tablespoons oyster sauce

1½ tablespoons finely chopped orange zest

1 teaspoon Madras curry paste

1 teaspoon sugar

9 ounces (250 g) wonton skins

2 cups peanut oil or vegetable oil for deep-frying

Put the prawns and pork in a large bowl, add the salt and pepper and mix well, either by kneading with your hand or by stirring with a wooden spoon. Then add the rest of the filling ingredients and stir them well into the prawn and pork mixture. Wrap the bowl with plastic wrap and chill it for at least 20 minutes.

When you are ready to stuff the parcels, put 1 tablespoon of the filling in the center of the first wonton skin. Dampen the edges with a little water and bring up the sides of the skin around the filling. Pinch the edges together at the top so that the wonton is sealed; it should look like a small, filled bag.

Heat a wok or large frying pan over high heat until it is hot. Add the oil, and when it is very hot and slightly smoking, add a handful of wontons and deep-fry for 3 minutes until golden and crispy. If the oil gets too hot, turn down the heat slightly. Drain the wontons well on kitchen paper. Continue to fry the wontons until they are all cooked.

Opposite: Cantonese-Style Chicken Wings with Oyster Sauce (page 52). Thai Crispy Prawn-Coconut Treats (page 45), Crispy Beggar's Purses (pages 46-47).

DOUBLE-STEAMED CHINESE CABBAGE SOUP

Serves 4

1 pound (450 g) Chinese or Napa cabbage

1 ounce (25 g) dried shiitake mushrooms

2 ounces (50 g) Parma ham or lean smoked bacon

4 slices fresh ginger root

4 cups chicken stock

4 whole green onions

2 tablespoons Shaoxing rice wine or dry sherry

½ teaspoon salt

¼ teaspoon freshly ground white pepper

2 teaspoons sesame oil (see note)

Yet another wok-friendly soup, the unusual technique for making this soup is not difficult to master. Double-steaming is a process in which rich ingredients are steamed for hours in a covered casserole filled with soup. This diffuses and marries all the flavors of the different ingredients. It is a technique often used for making the classic Shark's Fin and Bird's Nest soups.

The result is a distinctive consommé, clear and rich but also light. Here the delicate sweet flavor of the cabbage plays gently with the subtle taste of the ham. This elegant soup is a refreshing starter for any dinner party. It can be made in advance and frozen, as it reheats well.

Using a sharp, heavy knife or cleaver, cut the cabbage leaves in half lengthwise, then into 2 inch (5 cm) segments. Soak the mushrooms in warm water for 20 minutes. Drain them and squeeze out the excess liquid. Remove and discard the stems and finely shred the caps into thin strips. Cut the Parma ham or bacon into very fine shreds and cut the ginger into 2 x ¼ inch (5 cm x 5 mm) slices.

Next set up a steamer or put a rack into a wok or deep pan and fill it with 2 inches (5 cm) of water. Bring the water to the boil.

Meanwhile, bring the stock to the boil in another large pan and then pour it into an ovenproof glass or china casserole. Add the cabbage leaves, ham, ginger, green onions, Shaoxing rice wine or dry sherry, salt, pepper and sesame oil to the casserole and cover it with a lid or foil. Put the casserole on the rack and cover the wok or deep pan tightly with a lid or foil. You now have a casserole within a steamer, hence the term "double-steaming." Turn the heat down and steam gently for 1½ hours. Replenish the hot water from time to time. An alternative method is simply to simmer the soup very slowly in a conventional pan, but the resulting taste will be quite different.

When the soup is cooked, place the contents into a large soup tureen. The soup can be served immediately or cooled and stored in the refrigerator or freezer to be reheated when required.

SESAME OIL has a distinctive, nutty flavor and aroma. It is widely used as a seasoning but not normally as a cooking oil, because it heats rapidly and burns easily. It is often added at the last minute to finish a dish.

AROMATIC FIVE-SPICE TROUT

Serves 4

*F*resh trout makes an elegant centerpiece for lunch or dinner. With its clean and delicate taste and texture, it is a foundation course in any meal, a light and wholesome treat.

All that it needs is a touch of seasoning to complement its own unique flavor. Here I have dusted it with aromatic five-spice powder, the subtle flavors of which enhance the special qualities of trout.

This is an easy dish to put together; it browns quickly and perfectly in the wok.

Blot the trout dry inside and out with paper towel. Combine the cornstarch with the salt and five-spice powder. Dust the trout on the outside thoroughly with this mixture.

Heat a wok or large frying pan over a high heat until it is hot. Add 2 tablespoons of the oil and, when it is very hot and slightly smoking, turn the heat down to medium and cook the trout. You may have to do this in 2 batches, depending on the size of your wok or pan. When the fish is brown and crispy, turn it over and cook the other side for about 4 minutes. When the fish is cooked, transfer it to a warm platter.

Reheat the wok with the remaining oil. When it is hot, add the garlic, ginger and green onions and stir-fry for 2 minutes. Pour this mixture on top of the trout, arrange the lemon wedges on the platter and garnish with the cilantro. Serve at once.

4 small trout, cleaned

2 tablespoons cornstarch

1 teaspoon salt

1 teaspoon five-spice powder (see note)

3 tablespoons peanut oil

1 tablespoon finely chopped garlic

2 teaspoons finely chopped fresh ginger root

3 tablespoons finely chopped green onions

1 lemon, quartered

Fresh cilantro leaves, for garnish

FIVE-SPICE POWDER, five-flavored powder or five-fragrance spice powder is a mixture of star anise, Szechwan peppercorns, fennel, cloves and cinnamon. A good blend is pungent, fragrant, spicy and slightly sweet at the same time. It keeps indefinitely in a well sealed jar.

Braised Garlic Chicken

Serves 4

≈

2 pounds (900 g) chicken thighs with bone-in

2 teaspoons salt

1 teaspoon freshly ground black pepper

2 tablespoons all-purpose flour

3 tablespoons peanut oil (see note)

15 whole garlic cloves, unpeeled

2 tablespoons Shaoxing rice wine or dry sherry

1 tablespoon light soy sauce

3 tablespoons chicken stock or water

2 tablespoons finely snipped fresh chives, for garnish

The wok is a perfect cooking utensil for any type of cookery, not just Chinese or Asian. Its versatility is what makes it so universally popular. This recipe was inspired by a friend's mother from the south of France. Madam Taurines often braised veal with whole garlic. I have substituted chicken and added my own Chinese touches, which work just as well. Braised in this way, the whole garlic becomes mild and sweet. Most of the resulting sauce cooks off, leaving a tender, aromatic chicken dish, and the bonus is that it is quick to make. Serve this dish with potatoes or plain rice and another vegetable dish.

Blot the chicken thighs dry with a paper towel. Sprinkle them evenly with the salt and pepper, then sprinkle with the flour, shaking off any excess.

Heat a wok or large frying pan over a high heat until it is hot. Add the oil and, when it is very hot and slightly smoking, turn the heat to low. Add the chicken skin-side-down and slowly brown on both sides for about 10 minutes. Drain off all the excess fat, add the garlic and stir-fry for 2 minutes. Then add the Shaoxing rice wine or dry sherry, soy sauce and stock or water. Turn the heat to as low as possible, cover and braise for 20 minutes until the chicken is tender.

When the chicken and garlic are cooked remove them from the wok with a slotted spoon and place them on a warm platter. Sprinkle with the chives and serve at once.

PEANUT OIL is the most commonly used oil in Chinese cookery. It has a pleasant, unobtrusive taste and its ability to be heated to a high temperature without burning makes it perfect for stir-frying and deep-frying. Corn oil can be used instead if peanut is not available. I prefer peanut over corn oil because I find the corn oil taste rather bland and feel it has a slightly disagreeable smell. Other vegetable oils, like soy and sunflower, can be used in Chinese cooking, but they smoke and burn at lower temperatures than peanut oil, and care must be taken when cooking with them.

BURMESE-STYLE CHICKEN

Serves 4

Although I have never been to Burma, I have visited a number of Burmese restaurants that have opened in California. The food seems to be a cross between Chinese-Vietnamese and Thai. It is an aromatic and fragrant style of cooking that uses spices to coax flavors from foods.

Here I have adapted a favorite Burmese chicken dish I have enjoyed. It is a dry-braised dish that is slowly cooked in spices and its own juices. Again, it is easy to make and delicious to eat. Serve it with plain rice and another vegetable dish for a wholesome meal.

Blot the chicken dry with paper towel and sprinkle evenly with the salt and pepper.

Peel the lemon grass to reveal the tender, whitish center, crush the stalk and cut into 3 inch (7.5 cm) pieces.

Heat a wok or large frying pan over a high heat until it is hot. Add the oil and, when it is very hot and slightly smoking, turn the heat to low. Add the chicken, skin-side-down, and slowly brown on both sides. Remove the chicken and drain on paper towel.

Drain off all but 1 tablespoon of the oil and fat. Add the onion, garlic, ginger and lemon grass and stir-fry for 3 minutes. Add the turmeric, chili powder, soy sauce and water. Return the chicken to the wok and stir-fry to coat with this mixture. Turn the heat to as low as possible, cover and braise for 20 minutes until the chicken is cooked. Transfer to a warm platter and serve at once.

2 pounds (900 g) chicken thighs with bone in

2 teaspoons salt

1 teaspoon freshly ground black pepper

2 stalks fresh lemon grass

3 tablespoons peanut oil

1 small onion, thinly sliced

6 garlic cloves, crushed

1 tablespoon finely chopped fresh ginger root

1 teaspoon ground turmeric

1 teaspoon chili powder

1 tablespoon light soy sauce

3 tablespoons water

CANTONESE-STYLE CHICKEN WINGS
with OYSTER SAUCE

Serves 4

1½ pounds (675 g)
   chicken wings

3 cups peanut oil

FOR THE MARINADE

1 tablespoon light soy sauce

1 tablespoon Shaoxing rice
   wine or dry sherry

2 teaspoons sesame oil

½ teaspoon salt

¼ teaspoon freshly ground
   black pepper

2 teaspoons cornstarch

FOR THE SAUCE

1 tablespoon peanut oil

3 garlic cloves, crushed

1 (1 inch) (2.5 cm) thick piece
   fresh ginger root, unpeeled
   and crushed (see note)

3 tablespoons oyster sauce

1 tablespoon light soy sauce

2 tablespoons Shaoxing rice
   wine or dry sherry

2 cups chicken or
   vegetable stock

A thrifty, economical dish my mother used to make which I still love today is this one of chicken wings simmered in a rich oyster sauce. It is extremely easy to make and reheats quite well. In fact, the chicken wings are also tasty served cold and terrific for picnics. (Illustrated on page 44.)

In a large bowl, combine the wings with the Marinade ingredients and mix well. Let sit in the refrigerator for 30 minutes.

Heat a wok or large frying pan over a high heat until it is hot. Add the oil, and, when it is very hot and slightly smoking, add the chicken wings and fry them for 5 minutes or until they are golden brown. Remove them from the wok with a slotted spoon and drain on paper towel. You may have to do this in batches.

Drain off the oil and fat from the wok and wipe it clean. For the Sauce, reheat the wok until it is very hot. Add the oil, garlic and ginger and stir-fry for 30 seconds. Add the oyster sauce, soy sauce, rice wine or dry sherry and stock and bring to a simmer.

Return the chicken to the wok. Reduce the heat to very low, cover and simmer for 30 to 35 minutes or until the chicken is very tender. Remove the wings with a slotted spoon to a warm platter. Turn up the heat and boil to reduce the sauce until it is slightly thick. Pour this over the chicken and serve at once.

FRESH GINGER ROOT is pungent, spicy and fresh tasting, adding a subtle but distinctive flavor to soups, meats and vegetables. It is also an important seasoning for fish and seafood, since it neutralizes fishy smells. Ginger root can be found in many sizes. Its pale brown, dry skin is usually peeled away before use. Select ginger which is firm with no signs of shriveling. It will keep in the refrigerator wrapped in plastic for up to two weeks. Dried powdered ginger has quite a different flavor and should not be substituted for fresh ginger root.

FRAGRANT STIR-FRIED BEEF *with* PEPPERS

Serves 4

My many trips to Thailand have led me to elevate the virtues of lemon grass almost to the status enjoyed by garlic and ginger. It has a subtle but quite distinctive flavor that adds a certain something to the most prosaic recipes.

Fortunately, lemon grass has become generally available in most metropolitan areas in Western countries and it is well worth searching for.

Here I have adapted the Thai version by pairing the lemon grass with sweet red bell peppers, which add color as well as contrasting tastes and texture.

Cut the beef into thin slices 2 inches (5 cm) long, cutting against the grain. Put the beef into a bowl together with the Marinade ingredients, mix well and then let the mixture marinate for about 20 minutes.

Peel the lemon grass stalks to reveal the tender, whitish center and cut into 2 inch (5 cm) pieces, then crush them with the flat of a cleaver or knife.

Heat a wok or large frying pan over high heat until it is very hot. Add the oil and, when it is very hot and slightly smoking, remove the beef from the marinade with a slotted spoon. Add it to the pan and stir-fry for 2 minutes until it browns. Remove it and leave to drain in a colander or sieve.

Pour off all but 1 tablespoon of the oil. Reheat the wok or pan over a high heat and then add the lemon grass, ginger, shallots and garlic slices and stir-fry for 20 seconds. Then add the peppers, soy sauce, Shaoxing rice wine or dry sherry, salt, pepper and sugar and continue to stir-fry for 3 minutes. Then return the beef to the wok and stir-fry for 4 minutes, mixing well. Drizzle in the sesame oil and give the mixture a few stirs. Transfer to a warm platter and serve at once.

1 pound (450 g) lean beef steak

3 stalks fresh lemon grass (see note)

3 tablespoons peanut oil

2 teaspoons finely chopped fresh ginger root

1 cup thinly sliced shallots

3 garlic cloves, thinly sliced

1½ cups coarsely diced red or green bell pepper

1 tablespoon light soy sauce

1½ tablespoons Shaoxing rice wine or dry sherry

½ teaspoon salt

½ teaspoon freshly ground black pepper

1½ teaspoons sugar

2 teaspoons sesame oil

FOR THE MARINADE

1 tablespoon light soy sauce

1 tablespoon Shaoxing rice wine or dry sherry

2 teaspoons sesame oil

2 teaspoons cornstarch

FRESH LEMON GRASS IS A SOUTH-EAST ASIAN ORIGINAL that has a subtle lemony fragrance and flavor. Fresh lemon grass is sold in stalks that can be 24 inches (60 cm) long. It is fibrous, so lemon grass pieces are always removed after the dish is cooked. Some recipes may call for lemon grass to be finely chopped or pounded into a paste, in which case it becomes an integral aspect of the dish. Avoid dried lemon grass, as it is mostly used for herbal tea purposes. Fresh lemon grass can be kept, loosely wrapped, in the bottom of your refrigerator for up to one week. Neither fresh lemon nor citronella grass should be used as a substitute for the unique flavors of lemon grass.

MALAYSIAN-STYLE RICE NOODLES

Serves 2 to 4

8 ounces (225 g) broad flat
   dried rice noodles

8 ounces (225 g) raw prawns

6 ounces (175 g) Chinese
   sausages or ham

2 eggs, beaten

2 teaspoons sesame oil

Pinch of salt

½ teaspoon freshly ground
   black pepper

3 tablespoons peanut oil

4 green onions, shredded

2 tablespoons coarsely
   chopped garlic

3 fresh red or green chilies,
   seeded and finely
   chopped

2 small onions, thinly sliced

3 tablespoons light soy sauce

3 tablespoons oyster sauce

2 tablespoons Shaoxing
   rice wine or dry sherry
   (see note)

2 teaspoons chili bean sauce

½ cup chicken stock

6 ounces (175 g) fresh bean
   sprouts

½ cup loosely packed fresh
   cilantro leaves

One of the most exciting aspects of visiting Malaysia is eating at all the food hawkers' stalls. Here you can find all manner of food that is skillfully prepared and extremely savory and tasty. The strong aromas of garlic, ginger and chilies permeate: a food lovers' paradise. A favorite of mine is made with rice noodles. The Chinese influence can easily be detected in the use of the Chinese sausages, which are rich and sweet. This recipe is substantial enough for a lunch or makes a delightful side dish to a main course.

Soak the rice noodles in a bowl of warm water for 25 minutes then drain in a colander or sieve. Peel the prawns and discard the shells. Using a small sharp knife, remove the fine digestive cord. Wash the prawns and pat them dry with paper towel. Slice the sausages on a slight diagonal to about 1 inch (2.5 cm) thick, and do the same with the green onions.

Combine the eggs with the sesame oil, salt and half the pepper and set aside.

Heat a wok or large frying pan over a high heat until it is hot. Add 1 tablespoon of the peanut oil and, when it is very hot and slightly smoking, add the egg mixture and stir-fry for 2 minutes or until the egg has set. Remove it and place on a platter.

When it is cool enough to handle, chop it lengthwise and set aside.

Reheat the wok over a high heat and, when it is very hot, add the remaining peanut oil. Add the shredded green onions, garlic, chilies and onions and stir-fry for 2 minutes. Add the prawns and sausages and stir-fry for 1 minute. Then add the rice noodles, soy sauce, the rest of the black pepper, the oyster sauce, Shaoxing rice wine or dry sherry, chili bean sauce and stock and stir-fry for 2 minutes. Finally, add the bean sprouts and cooked egg and cook for 2 minutes. Stir in the fresh coriander leaves for 30 seconds. Transfer to a warm platter and serve at once.

RICE WINE IS USED EXTENSIVELY FOR COOKING AND DRINKING throughout all of China. I believe the finest rice wine to be from Shaoxing in Zhejiang Province in eastern China. It is made from glutinous rice, yeast and spring water. Now readily available in Chinese markets and in some wine shops in the West, it should be kept tightly corked at room temperature. A good quality, dry pale sherry can be substituted but cannot equal its rich, mellow taste. Do not confuse it with sake, which is the Japanese version of rice wine and quite different. Western grape wines are not an adequate substitute either.

QUICK *and* HEALTHY STEAMED CHICKEN

Serves 4

Steaming is not only a healthy way to cook food, it also brings out the subtle flavors. By keeping food moist and cooking it slowly in warm vapors, good chicken comes out even better. Chinese cooks tend to steam the entire chicken, but, when I am in a hurry, I simply steam chicken breasts. The result is a quick but healthy meal that takes little time to prepare. The juices from the steamed chicken taste delicious over rice.

Combine the chicken with the salt, soy sauce, Shaoxing rice wine or dry sherry, pepper, egg white, cornstarch and sesame oil. Leave to marinate for at least 20 minutes.

Next set up a steamer or put a rack into a wok or deep pan and fill it with 2 inches (5 cm) of water. Bring the water to the boil over a high heat. Put the chicken in one layer on an ovenproof plate and scatter the ginger evenly over the top. Put the plate of chicken into the steamer or on to the rack. Cover the pan tightly and gently steam the chicken until it is just white and firm. It will take about 8-10 minutes to cook, depending on the thickness of the chicken.

Remove the plate of cooked chicken and sprinkle on the green onions. Heat the two oils together in a small pan. When they are hot, pour the oil mixture over the top of the chicken. Serve at once.

1 pound (450 g) skinless, boneless chicken breasts

1 teaspoon coarse sea salt or plain salt

1 tablespoon light soy sauce

1 tablespoon Shaoxing rice wine or dry sherry

½ teaspoon freshly ground white pepper

1 egg white

2 teaspoons cornstarch

1 teaspoon sesame oil

1½ tablespoons finely shredded fresh ginger root

3 tablespoons finely shredded green onions, for garnish

1 tablespoon peanut oil, for garnish

2 teaspoons sesame oil, for garnish

RICH EGGPLANT *with* TOMATO *and* BASIL

Serves 4

1 pound (450 g) Chinese eggplant or ordinary eggplant

8 ounces (225 g) fresh or canned tomatoes

⅓ cup extra-virgin olive oil

5 garlic cloves, peeled and crushed

2 teaspoons salt

½ teaspoon freshly ground black pepper

2 teaspoons sugar

3 tablespoons finely chopped basil leaves

1 tablespoon lemon juice

This savory treat combines two of my favorite vegetables, eggplants and tomatoes. The smaller, long, thin Chinese eggplants are preferable to the thicker European variety because of their slightly sweeter and milder taste. However, you may use the European type. Leave the skins of the eggplants on as they enhance the texture of the dish.

Ordinarily, such a dish is oven-baked but because many Chinese homes lack modern cookers, the wok is used instead. It is, in practice, the perfect utensil for preparing this Italian-inspired dish. It can be served hot or at room temperature, and is delicious as a vegetarian plate or as a wonderful accompaniment to grilled meats.

Trim the eggplant and cut them on the diagonal into 2 x ½ inch (5 x 1 cm) slices.

If you are using fresh tomatoes, plunge them into a large pan of boiling water for a few seconds, removing them with a slotted spoon. Then peel, seed and cut them into 1 inch (2.5 cm) chunks. If you are using canned tomatoes, chop them into small chunks.

Heat a wok or large frying pan over a high heat until it is hot. Add the oil and, when it is moderately hot, add the garlic and stir-fry for 30 seconds. Then add the eggplant slices, salt and pepper and continue to stir-fry for 2 minutes.

Add the tomatoes and sugar and continue to cook for 5 minutes. Turn the heat to low, cover and cook slowly for 15 minutes until the eggplant is quite tender. Stir in the basil leaves and lemon juice and give the mixture several good stirs. Transfer to a warm platter and serve at once or allow to cool and serve at room temperature.

SINGAPOREAN-STYLE CURRY CRAB

Serves 4

Singapore is an Asian city rich in many different cultures. One of the joys of visiting such a fascinating city is to sample its diverse foods. The blending of disparate traditions can be seen in the street hawkers' stalls. A dish I often love to eat is Singapore's Curry Crab, which is a mixture of Chinese and Indian influences. Although the authentic recipe has ingredients which may be difficult to obtain outside Singapore, I have adapted the idea and made my own mixture with delicious results. The spices are a wonderful contrast to the sweet crab meat. Serve it with plain rice and another vegetable dish for a complete meal.

Remember, it is important to buy the freshest crab available, preferably live. It is perfectly good manners to eat the crab with your fingers, but I suggest that you have a large bowl of water decorated with lemon slices on the table so that your guests can rinse their fingers.

To cook a live crab, bring a large pot of water to the boil, drop in the crab and boil until there is no movement, about 2 minutes. Remove the crab and drain thoroughly.

Remove the tail-flap, push the body with legs still attached away from the shell (see drawing A) and remove the stomach sac and feathery gills (see drawing B). Using a heavy knife or cleaver, cut the crab, shell included, into large pieces.

Cut the lemon grass into 2 inch (5 cm) segments. With the flat side of a large knife or cleaver, smash the lemon grass pieces to release their aromatic oils.

Heat a wok or large frying pan over high heat until it is hot. Add the oil and, when it is very hot and slightly smoking, add the lemon grass, garlic, ginger and onions or shallots and stir-fry for 1 minute. Add the green onions and crab pieces and stir-fry for 2 minutes. Add the remaining ingredients and continue to stir-fry for 2 minutes. Turn the heat to low, cover and simmer for 10 minutes. Spoon the curry onto a large warm serving platter and serve.

3 pounds (1.4 kg) live or freshly cooked crab on the shell

2 stalks fresh lemon grass

2 tablespoons peanut oil

8 garlic cloves, thinly sliced

2 tablespoons finely shredded fresh ginger root

4 tablespoons thinly sliced small onions or shallots

3 tablespoons finely shredded green onions

3 tablespoons Madras curry paste

1 (15 ounce) (400 ml) can coconut milk

1 teaspoon salt

2 teaspoons sugar

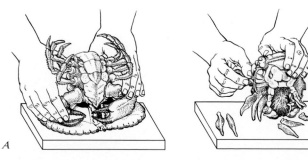

A   B

SPICY CHICKEN *with* MINT

Serves 4

1 pound (450 g) skinless,
    boneless chicken breasts

1¼ cups peanut oil or water

1 tablespoon peanut oil

1½ cups coarsely chopped
    red or green bell peppers

1 tablespoon thinly sliced
    garlic

⅔ cup chicken stock

1½ tablespoons Madras
    curry paste

2 teaspoons chili bean sauce

2 teaspoons sugar

1½ tablespoons Shaoxing
    rice wine or dry sherry

1 tablespoon light soy sauce

1 teaspoon cornstarch
    blended with 1 tablespoon
    water

8 mint leaves

FOR THE MARINADE

1 egg white

1 teaspoon salt

2 teaspoons cornstarch

The wok is ideal for making quick but tasty dishes. Here is a lovely, spicy chicken dish with fresh mint as a counterbalance. If you grow your own mint, it is likely to be even more delicate and subtle than the shop-bought variety. Mint is probably the most widely used of all the aromatic herbs and the one most readily accessible. A touch of curry is used with the chili bean sauce to give this dish a real kick. The chicken is velveted to preserve its juiciness and flavor. You can use the traditional oil method or, for a less fattening version, substitute water instead. The peppers provide the dish with a crunchy texture that makes a wonderful complement to the soft tender chicken. Serve this with plain steamed rice and a salad for a quick delicious meal.

Cut the chicken breasts into 1 inch (2.5 cm) cubes. Combine them with the Marinade ingredients in a small bowl. Put the mixture into the refrigerator for 20 minutes.

Heat a wok or frying pan over a high heat until it is hot, then add the 1¼ cups of oil. When the oil is very hot, remove the wok from the heat and immediately add the chicken pieces, stirring vigorously to keep them from sticking. When the chicken pieces turn white (about 2 minutes), quickly drain the chicken.

If you choose to use 1¼ cups of water instead of oil, bring the water to the boil in a pan. Remove the pan from the heat and immediately add the chicken pieces, stirring vigorously to keep them from sticking.

When the chicken pieces turn white (about 2 minutes), quickly drain the chicken.

Wipe the wok or pan clean and reheat until it is very hot. Add the 1 tablespoon of oil. When it is very hot, add the peppers and garlic and stir-fry for 2 minutes. Add the rest of the ingredients, except the cornstarch mixture and mint leaves, and cook for 2 minutes. Add the cornstarch mixture and cook for 20 seconds, stirring. Add the cooked chicken and stir-fry for 2 minutes, coating the chicken thoroughly with the sauce. Finally, add the mint leaves and stir to mix well for 1 minute. Transfer to a warm platter and serve at once.

SPICY FISH CURRY

Serves 2 to 4

I have eaten this wonderful fish curry many times in Singapore and Malaysia. In those countries, surrounded as they are by water, fresh fish is a standard staple in every home and on every menu. This recipe is a simplified version of the original. Most fish have a delicate taste and texture and one must be careful in applying any seasoning or spice. I have found Madras curry paste a great convenience; it works almost as well as the time-consuming handmade curry paste. Added to a firm white fish fillet, it makes a fragrant, savory, delectable treat that goes perfectly with plain rice.

Cut the fish into 2 inch (5 cm) pieces and then combine them with the egg white, salt, pepper and cornstarch in a medium bowl. Mix well and chill for 20 minutes.

Heat a wok until it is very hot, then add the oil. When the oil is very hot, remove the wok from the heat and immediately add the fish pieces, stirring vigorously to prevent them from sticking. When the fish turns white (about 2 minutes), quickly drain the fish and all of the oil into a stainless steel colander set in a bowl. Reserve 2 tablespoons of the oil and discard the rest.

If you choose to use water instead of oil, bring it to the boil in a pan. Remove the pan from the heat and immediately add the fish pieces, stirring vigorously to keep them from sticking. When the fish pieces turn white (about 2 minutes), quickly drain the fish in a stainless steel colander.

Reheat the wok, add 2 tablespoons of the reserved oil (or, if you used the water method, add 2 tablespoons of fresh oil), and when it is hot, add the onion, ginger and garlic and stir-fry for 3 minutes. Add the curry paste, soy sauce, salt, sugar and coconut milk. Bring the mixture to a simmer and cook for 5 minutes. Add the fish pieces and heat for 3 minutes. Garnish with the green onions and serve at once.

1 pound (450 g) fresh boneless, skinless, firm white fish fillets, such as cod, halibut or sea bass

1 egg white

1 teaspoon salt

½ teaspoon freshly ground black pepper

2 teaspoons cornstarch

2 cups peanut oil or 3½ cups water

1 small onion, coarsely chopped

1½ tablespoons finely chopped fresh ginger root

1 tablespoon finely chopped garlic

3 tablespoons Madras curry paste

1 tablespoon light soy sauce

1 teaspoon salt

1 teaspoon sugar

⅔ cup canned coconut milk

2 tablespoons finely chopped green onions, for garnish

SPICY ORANGE LAMB

≋

1 pound (450 g) lean boneless lamb chops

3 tablespoons peanut oil

1½ teaspoons finely chopped
  fresh ginger root

2 tablespoons thinly sliced
  garlic

1 tablespoon grated orange
  zest

1 teaspoon roasted Szechuan
  peppercorns, finely
  ground (optional)
  (see page 69)

2 tablespoons orange juice

1 tablespoon dark soy sauce
  (see note)

2 teaspoons chili bean sauce

½ teaspoon salt

½ teaspoon freshly ground
  black pepper

1 teaspoon sugar

2 teaspoons sesame oil

FOR THE MARINADE

1 tablespoon light soy sauce
  (see note)

2 teaspoons Shaoxing rice
  wine or dry sherry

1 teaspoon sesame oil

2 teaspoons cornstarch

Although Chinese ordinarily do not like lamb, they have not tasted lamb in the West, where it is delicate and more subtle than the stronger-tasting one from China.

Here I have combined the lamb with orange for a lovely contrast to the rich meat. The tartness of the fresh orange peel works well to balance the robust taste of the lamb. It is an easy dish to make and the spicy flavors add to its appeal. Serve it with plain rice and vegetables for a wholesome meal.

Cut the lamb into thin slices 2 inches (5 cm) long, cutting against the grain. Put the lamb into a bowl together with all the Marinade ingredients. Mix well and then let the mixture marinate for about 20 minutes.

Heat a wok or large frying pan over a high heat until it is very hot. Add the oil and, when it is very hot and slightly smoking, remove the lamb from the marinade with a slotted spoon. Add it to the pan and stir-fry it for 2 minutes until it browns.

Remove it and leave to drain in a colander or sieve. Pour off all but about 2 teaspoons of the oil.

Reheat the wok or pan over a high heat and then add the ginger, garlic, orange zest and peppercorns, if using. Stir-fry for 20 seconds. Then return the lamb to the pan, add the rest of the ingredients and stir-fry for 4 minutes, mixing well. Serve the dish at once.

SOY SAUCE IS MADE FROM SOY BEANS, FLOUR AND WATER which is aged for some months. Light soy sauce is lighter in color and tastes saltier than dark soy sauce. Dark soy sauce, which is aged much longer, also has a thicker consistency and tastes sweeter.

SPICY PORK *with* FRAGRANT BASIL

Serves 4

This is a mouth-watering Thai-inspired dish. The ground pork is quickly stir-fried and tossed with so much fragrant basil that the seasoning almost plays the role of a green vegetable. Thai cookery, it seems, can never use too much basil. And here it is used to such good effect, helping to produce a marvelously aromatic dish that goes extremely well with plain rice. It is easy to make and is therefore ideal for a quick but exotic family meal.

Heat a wok or large frying pan over a high heat until it is hot. Add the oil and when it is very hot and slightly smoking, add the garlic and chilies and stir-fry for 30 seconds. Then add the pork and continue to stir-fry for 3 minutes. Then add the cilantro, fish sauce, oyster sauce, sugar and stock. Continue to stir-fry for 3 minutes. Then add the basil and stir-fry for another minute. Turn on to a warm platter and serve at once.

1½ tablespoons peanut oil

3 tablespoons coarsely chopped garlic

3 tablespoons seeded and finely chopped

Fresh red chilies

1 pound (450 g) ground pork

2 tablespoons finely chopped fresh cilantro

2 tablespoons Thai fish sauce

1 tablespoon oyster sauce

2 teaspoons sugar

⅔ cup chicken stock

A large handful of fresh basil leaves

STEAMED SCALLOPS *with* CHILI *and* GINGER

Serves 4

1 pound (450 g) fresh
    scallops, including the
    corals

2 fresh red chilies, seeded
    and chopped (see note)

2 teaspoons finely chopped
    fresh ginger root

1 tablespoon Shaoxing rice
    wine or dry sherry

1 tablespoon light soy sauce

¼ teaspoon salt

¼ teaspoon freshly ground
    black pepper

3 tablespoons finely chopped
    green onions

Fresh scallops are sweet and rich. Perhaps the best way to preserve their qualities is the Chinese technique of steaming. Using hot, wet vapors, this method brings out the succulent texture of scallops without overcooking them. Their briny seafood taste is emphasized, and the bonus is that they are very simple to prepare and take literally minutes to cook. This dish is ideal for a quick and easy, as well as a healthy, meal and I think it makes an ideal opener for any dinner party.

Place the scallops evenly on an ovenproof platter. Then evenly distribute the chilies, ginger, Shaoxing rice wine or dry sherry, soy sauce, salt, pepper and green onions on top.

Next set up a steamer or put a rack into a wok or deep pan and fill it with 2 inches (5 cm) of water. Bring the water to the boil over a high heat. Carefully lower the platter of scallops into the steamer or on to the rack. Turn the heat to low and cover the wok or pan tightly. Steam gently for 5 minutes. Remove and serve at once.

CHILIES ARE THE SEED PODS of the capsicum plant and can be obtained fresh, dried or ground. Fresh chilies should look bright with no brown patches or black spots. Red chilies are generally milder than green ones. To prepare, rinse them in cold water and slit them lengthwise. Remove and discard the seeds. Rinse under cold running water and then follow recipe instructions. Wash your hands, knife and chopping board before preparing other foods and do not touch your eyes.

STIR-FRIED BEEF CURRY

Serves 2 to 4

Although curry, as such, is not a Chinese seasoning, it has nevertheless made its way into Chinese cuisine in a rather mild form. The hint of exotic spices adds a special, very subtle flavor to any Chinese dish. Curry works extremely well when beef is matched with vegetables.

This is a substantial dish that easily makes a filling meal for two or three. It may also be served as part of a multi-course Chinese-style menu.

The best type of curry paste or powder to use is the Madras variety. It is favored by most Chinese cooks.

Cut the beef into thin slices 2 inches (5 cm) long and ¼ inch (5 mm) thick and put them into a bowl. Add the Marinade ingredients and let stand for 20 minutes.

Heat a wok or large frying pan until it is very hot. Add the oil and, when it is very hot and slightly smoking, add the beef slices and stir-fry for 3 minutes or until they are lightly browned. Remove them and drain well in a colander set inside a bowl.

Wipe the wok or pan clean and reheat it over a high heat until it is hot. Add 1 tablespoon of the drained oil, then add the onions and garlic and stir-fry for 1 minute. Add all the Curry Sauce ingredients and bring the mixture to a simmer and cook for 3 minutes. Return the drained beef slices to the wok or pan and toss them thoroughly with the sauce. Transfer the mixture to a warm serving platter, garnish with the green onions and serve at once.

1 pound (450 g) lean beef steak

3 tablespoons peanut oil

1 onion, sliced

2 tablespoons coarsely chopped garlic

1½ tablespoons finely chopped green onions, for garnish

FOR THE MARINADE
1 tablespoon light soy sauce

2 teaspoons sesame oil

1 tablespoon Shaoxing rice wine or dry sherry

2 teaspoons cornstarch

FOR THE CURRY SAUCE
1 tablespoon Shaoxing rice wine or dry sherry

1 tablespoon Madras curry paste or powder

1 tablespoon dark soy sauce

1 teaspoon light soy sauce

1 teaspoon sugar

2 tablespoons chicken stock or water

STIR-FRIED FISH *with* BLACK BEAN SAUCE

Serves 4

1 pound (450 g) fresh, firm white fish fillets, such as cod, halibut or sea bass

2 teaspoons salt

3 tablespoons peanut oil

1½ tablespoons coarsely chopped salted black beans (see note)

1 tablespoon finely chopped garlic

2 teaspoons finely chopped fresh ginger root

3 tablespoons finely chopped green onions

1 tablespoon light soy sauce

1 teaspoon dark soy sauce

1 tablespoon Shaoxing rice wine or dry sherry

1 teaspoon sugar

1 tablespoon water

2 teaspoons sesame oil

3 tablespoons finely shredded green onions, for garnish

My mother loved making this dish because it was quick, easy and delicious. The pungency of the black beans, garlic and ginger turn an ordinary fish into a gourmet's delight. When served with vegetables and rice, it becomes the type of light, wholesome, satisfying meal that is the hallmark of the best Chinese home cooking.

Cut the fish fillets into strips 1 inch (2.5 cm) wide and sprinkle evenly with the salt. Let them stand for 20 minutes.

Heat a wok or large frying pan over high heat until it is hot. Add the oil and, when it is very hot and slightly smoking, turn the heat down to medium and add the fish strips. Stir-fry these gently for about 2 minutes or until they are brown on both sides, taking care not to break them up. Remove them with a slotted spoon and drain on paper towel. Drain off all but 1½ tablespoons of the oil from the pan.

Reheat the wok. When it is hot, add the black beans, garlic, ginger and chopped green onions and stir-fry for 30 seconds. Add the soy sauces, rice wine or dry sherry, sugar and water and bring to a simmer. Return the fish to the wok and gently finish cooking in the sauce for about 1 minute. Add the sesame oil and give the mixture a good stir. Using a slotted spoon, arrange the fish on a warm serving platter, garnish with the shredded green onions and serve at once.

THESE SMALL BLACK SOYA BEANS, also known as salted black beans, are preserved by being fermented with salt and spices. They have a distinctive, slightly salty taste and a rich pleasant aroma. Thus prepared, they are a tasty seasoning, especially when used in conjunction with garlic or fresh ginger.

Black beans are inexpensive and can be obtained from Chinese grocers, usually in tins labeled 'Black Beans in Salted Sauce,' but you may also see them packed in plastic bags. These should be rinsed before use; I prefer to chop them slightly, too, as it helps to release their pungent flavor. Transfer any unused tinned beans and liquid to a sealed jar and the beans will keep indefinitely if stored in the refrigerator.

STIR-FRIED PASTA *with* ORANGE *and* CURRY

Serves 4

*O*ne of the quickest and easiest ways to prepare Italian pasta is in the wok. I love using whatever leftovers I have in the refrigerator and quickly stir-frying cooked pasta with some curry paste. With a bit of imagination, the wok turns a simple pasta dish into an ambrosial delight.

This recipe makes a fine starter for a multicourse meal or can easily be a main course with salad. In warm weather, serve it at room temperature.

Cook the pasta in a large pan of salted water, according to the instructions on the packet. Drain well and set aside.

Heat a wok or large frying pan over a high heat until it is hot. Add the olive oil and, when it is very hot and slightly smoking, add the garlic, ginger, onion and orange zest and stir-fry for 2 minutes. Then add the bacon and continue to stir-fry for 3-4 minutes or until the bacon is browned. Next add the peppers, sugar, stock, tomatoes, curry paste, tomato paste, salt and pepper. Turn the heat down, cover and simmer for 30 minutes.

Add the drained pasta and mix well in the wok. Turn the mixture out onto a large warm platter, garnish abundantly with plenty of the basil and chives and serve at once.

1 pound (450 g) dried Italian pasta, such as fusilli or farfalle

3 tablespoons olive oil

3 tablespoons coarsely chopped garlic

1 tablespoon finely chopped fresh ginger root

1 small onion, chopped

2 tablespoons finely chopped orange zest

6 bacon slices chopped

1½ cups cut up red bell pepper, cut into ½ inch (1 cm) dice

1½ cups cut up yellow bell pepper, cut into ½ inch (1 cm) dice

2 teaspoons sugar

1¼ cups chicken stock

1 (14 ounce) (400 g) can chopped tomatoes

3 tablespoons Madras curry paste

2 tablespoons tomato paste

1 teaspoon salt

½ teaspoon freshly ground black pepper

Handful of chopped fresh basil, for garnish

Handful of fresh chives, snipped, for garnish

Thai-Style Prawns *with* Lemon Grass

Serves 4

1 pound (450 g) raw prawns

FOR THE SAUCE

2 stalks lemon grass

1 (14 ounce) (400 ml) can
    coconut milk

2 tablespoons seeded and
    chopped fresh red chili

1 tablespoon coarsely
    chopped fresh cilantro

3 tablespoons coarsely
    chopped garlic

2 tablespoons coarsely
    chopped shallots

3 tablespoons water

2 tablespoons Thai fish sauce
    (see note)

1 tablespoon sugar

2 teaspoons shrimp paste
    (see note)

Basil leaves, for garnish

This is a dish inspired by one of my many visits to Bangkok where I frequently conduct food promotions for the Oriental Hotel. Working with their superb Thai chefs, I was able to learn the essentials of their rich and aromatic cuisine. One of my favorites consists of prawns and lemon grass, a very popular standard for their luncheon buffet.

Their version is made in a quite unusual brass wok. Your usual wok will do nicely, however. Note that, rather than being stir-fried, the prawns are simmered, and in coconut milk at that. The delicate taste of the prawns benefits from such tender care. The result is a hearty, satisfying main dish, redolent of chilies and ginger. It goes well with plain rice.

Peel the prawns and discard the shells. Using a small sharp knife, remove the fine digestive cord. Wash the prawns and pat them dry with paper towel.

For the Sauce, peel the lemon grass stalks to reveal the tender, whitish center and crush with the flat of a knife. Cut it into 3 inch (7.5 cm) pieces.

Reserve 1 tablespoon of the coconut milk and set aside. Bring the rest of the coconut milk to a simmer in the wok. Add the lemon grass stalks and simmer for 10 minutes.

Combine the chili, cilantro, garlic and shallots in a blender or food processor with the reserved coconut milk and the water and mix well. Add this paste to the simmering coconut milk together with the fish sauce, sugar and shrimp paste. Continue simmering for 2 minutes. Now add the prawns and continue to simmer for 3 minutes or until the prawns are cooked. Toss in the basil leaves and give the mixture several good turns. Serve at once.

FISH SAUCE AND SHRIMP PASTE are both fermented products. Fish sauce is a thin brown liquid made from fermented, salted fresh fish. Shrimp paste is made from ground shrimp. Neither add an especially "fishy" taste, but imbue your cooking with a deep richness and quality. Look for them in glass jars at the supermarket.

BROCCOLI *with* FRAGRANT WINE SAUCE

Serves 2 to 4

Broccoli is a vegetable of sturdy character. It has a rich color and a distinctive taste and texture that allows it to be paired with strong seasonings and flavors – for example, the ginger and Shaoxing rice wine of this dish. The recipe is of Shanghai origin. The justly famous yellow Shaoxing wine is produced in that region of China and quite understandably it has attained a prominent place in Shanghai cuisine. This is a quick, easy and fragrant wok dish that can serve as a perfect side dish or as a main vegetarian treat.

Separate the broccoli heads into small florets, then peel and slice the stems. Blanch the broccoli pieces in a large pan of boiling salted water for 3 minutes and then immerse them in cold water. Drain thoroughly.

Heat a wok or large frying pan over high heat until it is hot. Add the oil, and when it is very hot and slightly smoking, add the ginger shreds, salt, sugar and pepper and stir-fry for a few seconds. Add the blanched broccoli. Add the rice wine or dry sherry and continue to stir-fry over a moderate to high heat for 4 minutes or until the broccoli is thoroughly heated through. Add the sesame oil and continue to stir-fry for 30 seconds. Transfer to a warm plate and serve at once.

1 pound (450 g) fresh broccoli

1½ tablespoons peanut oil

2 tablespoons finely shredded fresh ginger root

1 teaspoon salt

½ teaspoon sugar

½ teaspoon freshly ground black pepper

5 tablespoons Shaoxing rice wine or dry sherry

2 teaspoons sesame oil

EGG FRIED RICE

Serves 2 to 4

1¾ cups long-grain
 white rice

2 eggs, beaten

2 teaspoons sesame oil

2½ teaspoons salt

2 tablespoons peanut oil

1 onion, coarsely chopped

½ teaspoon freshly ground
 black pepper

½ large cucumber, peeled,
 seeded and diced

¾ cup fresh or frozen corn
 kernels

1 teaspoon chili oil

The Chinese hate to waste anything. To throw away food is unconscionable. This is a lesson my mother taught me very well and, to this day, even in affluent and, I must say, wasteful America, I cannot bring myself to simply discard leftover food.

Fortunately, the wok is most useful when it comes to making the best of leftovers. The trick is to create tasty, nutritious meals by means of the wok stir-fry technique. Here I take bits of leftover cucumber and corn and blend them with spicy embellishments. You will enjoy a tasty treat and feel virtuous as well. Remember that your cooked rice should be very cold before you put it into the wok. If you want a vegan version, simply leave out the eggs.

Cook the rice according to the Steamed Rice recipe (see page 74) at least 2 hours in advance or the night before. Let cool thoroughly and then put in the refrigerator.

Combine the eggs with the sesame oil and ½ teaspoon of the salt.

Heat a wok or large frying pan over a high heat until very hot. Add the oil and, when it is very hot and slightly smoking, add the onions, remaining salt and the pepper and stir-fry for 2 minutes. Add the beaten eggs and stir-fry for 1 minute. Add the rice and continue to stir-fry for 3 minutes. Finally, add the cucumber, corn and chili oil and continue to stir-fry for 5 minutes. Transfer to a warm platter and serve hot or cold as a rice salad.

EAST-WEST FRIES

Serves 4

The wok is perfect for making potato fries, or chips as they are known in other parts of the world. Its round concave shape makes it ideal for deep-frying without wasting any oil.

The secret to making good chips lies in the cooking technique. First, chill the cut potatoes for several hours. This allows the natural starch to set so that when the chips hit the hot oil, they do not act like sponges and become greasy. They must then be dried thoroughly so they are without a trace of moisture. Then use the double-frying technique. The first quick-fry cooks them, then, after letting the chips drain and allowing the oil in the wok to regain the frying point, put the chips in for the second quick-fry. They cook to a crisp and golden perfection.

I then toss the chips in a tasty mix of salt, cayenne, five-spice powder and crushed Szechwan peppercorns. These chips are marvelous with grilled foods and as a snack they are unbeatable. They are a perfect vegetarian dish.

1¾ pounds (750 g) potatoes

3 cups peanut oil

FOR THE SEASONING MIXTURE

2 teaspoons salt

½ teaspoons cayenne pepper

½ teaspoon five-spice powder

½ teaspoon whole Szechwan peppercorns, roasted and finely ground (optional, see note)

½ teaspoon freshly ground black pepper

Peel and cut the potatoes into 3 inches x ½ inch (7.5 cm x 5 mm) strips. Put the strips into a large bowl, cover with cold water and chill for 2 hours or overnight.

Combine the ingredients for the Seasoning Mixture in a small bowl and set aside. Drain the potatoes in a colander, then spin them dry in a salad spinner or pat them dry with paper towel. The potatoes should be as dry as possible for the best results.

Heat a wok or large frying pan over a high heat until it is hot. Add the oil and, when it is very hot and slightly smoking, fry half of the potatoes for 8 minutes. Remove the potatoes with a slotted spoon and drain in a colander; then fry the second batch and drain.

When you are ready to serve them, reheat the oil until it is very hot. Fry half of the potatoes until they are crispy and golden brown. Remove and drain well on paper towel. Reheat the oil until it is very hot. Fry the other half and drain. Transfer the potatoes to a warm platter, toss with the seasoning mix and serve at once.

SZECHWAN PEPPERCORNS are reddish brown and milder than black peppercorns. If you can't find them, substitute ¼ teaspoon of black peppercorns, in addition to the ½ teaspoon of freshly ground black pepper.

To roast, heat a wok or heavy frying pan to medium heat. Add the peppercorns (you can cook about 5 ounces (150 g) at a time) and stir-fry for about 5 minutes, until they brown slightly and start to smoke. Remove the pan from the heat and let cool. Grind the peppercorns in a peppermill, clean coffee grinder or with a mortar and pestle. Seal the mixture tightly in a screw-top jar. Alternatively, keep the whole roasted peppercorns in a well-sealed container and grind when needed.

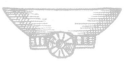

SIMPLE BEIJING-STYLE
MARINATED CUCUMBER SALAD

Serves 4

1¾ pounds (750 g) cucumbers

2 teaspoons salt

1 tablespoon chili bean sauce
(see note)

1 teaspoon light soy sauce

1 teaspoon sugar

½ teaspoon chili oil

2 teaspoons sesame oil

My good friend, Lillian Robyn, is originally from Beijing. Now married to an American and living in America, she still cooks in the Beijing style. A meal in her home is always a special treat for me. I have enjoyed this refreshing salad at her home many times. It can be prepared hours ahead and is thus perfect for multi-course meals or simply by itself with hot rice.

Cut the unpeeled cucumbers into 1 inch (2.5 cm) slices, sprinkle with the salt and put them into a colander to drain for 20 minutes. Squeeze the cucumber slices in a dish towel to remove any moisture. Blot them dry with paper towel.

In a small bowl, mix the chili bean sauce, soy sauce, sugar, chili oil and sesame oil. Toss the cucumber slices in this sauce and let them sit in the refrigerator overnight. Drain off any excess moisture before serving.

CHILI BEAN SAUCE IS A HOT AND SPICY SEASONING made from soy beans and chilies. Look for it at the grocery store in jars, where it might also be called hot bean paste, hot bean sauce or chili bean paste. It keeps for quite a long time when stored in the refrigerator. Don't confuse it with chili sauce, which is hotter and made without beans.

SPINACH *with* FRIED GARLIC

Serves 4

Inspired by one of the best Chinese restaurants in London, Fung Shing, this recipe is a delicious but simple method for cooking spinach. The garlic is slowly fried, removed and then the spinach is cooked in the flavor-infused oil. The garlic is then added as a crispy aromatic garnish. It is very simple to prepare and may be served hot or cold.

1¾ pounds (750 g) fresh spinach

1½ tablespoons peanut oil

1 teaspoon salt

2 tablespoons thinly sliced garlic (see note)

1 teaspoon sugar

Wash the spinach thoroughly. Remove all the stems, leaving just the leaves.

Heat a wok or large frying pan over a high heat until it is hot. Add the oil and reduce the heat to medium. Add the salt and garlic and slowly stir-fry for 2 minutes or until the garlic is golden brown and crisp. Remove the garlic with a slotted spoon and drain on paper towel. Add the spinach to the wok and stir-fry for about 2 minutes to coat the leaves thoroughly with the oil and salt. When the spinach has wilted to about one-third of its original size, add the sugar and stir-fry for 4 minutes. Transfer the spinach to a warm plate and pour off any excess liquid. Sprinkle with the fried garlic. Serve hot or cold.

THE CHINESE USE GARLIC IN NUMEROUS WAYS: whole, finely chopped, crushed and pickled. It is used to flavor oils as well as spicy sauces, and it is often paired with other equally pungent ingredients such as green onions, salted black beans and fresh ginger. Select garlic which is firm and preferably pink in color. It should be stored in a cool, dry place but not in the refrigerator.

STEAMED RICE

Serves 4

1¾ cups long-grain white rice

2 cups water

*S*teaming rice the Chinese way is simple, direct and efficient. I prefer to use long-grain white rice, which is drier and fluffier when cooked and gives the most authentic results in wok cooking. There are many varieties but I particularly like basmati or Thai fragrant rice which are widely available. Don't use pre-cooked or "easy cook" rice for Chinese cookery as both these types of rice have insufficient flavor and lack the texture and starchy taste fundamental to Chinese rice.

The secret of preparing rice that is not sticky is to cook it first in an uncovered pan at a high heat until most of the water has evaporated. Then the heat should be turned down to very low, the pan covered and the rice cooked slowly in the remaining steam. As a child I was always instructed never to peek into the rice pan during this stage or else precious steam would escape and the rice would not be cooked properly, thus bringing bad luck.

Here is a good trick to remember: if you make sure that you cover the top of the rice with about 1 inch (2.5 cm) of water, it should always cook properly without sticking. Many packet recipes for rice specify too much water and the result is a gluey mess. Never uncover the pan once the simmering process has begun; time the process and wait. Follow my method and you will have perfect steamed rice, the easy Chinese way.

Most Chinese eat quite large quantities of rice (about 5 ounces (150 g) per head, which is more than many Westerners are able to manage). This recipe allows about 13 ounces (37.5 g) dried weight, of rice for four people. If you want more than that, just increase the quantity of rice, but remember to add enough water so that the level of water is about 1 inch (2.5 cm) above the top of the rice.

Put the rice into a large bowl and wash it in several changes of water until the water becomes clear. Drain the rice and put it into a heavy pan with the water and bring it to the boil. Continue boiling until most of the surface liquid has evaporated. This should take about 5 minutes on high heat. The surface of the rice should then have small indentations like pitted craters. Another way to know it's ready is to cover it when it gives off a dry hissing sound from the water evaporating from the "rice craters." At this point, cover the pot with a very tight fitting lid, turn the heat down to as low as possible and let the rice cook undisturbed for 15 minutes. There is no need to "fluff" the rice. Let it rest for 5 minutes before serving.

THAI-STYLE CURRY RICE

Serves 4 to 6

The Thais are geniuses with spices – they can transform everyday recipes into glorious and tasty dishes. One I particularly enjoy eating in Thailand is curry rice. This popular platter is perfect for a quick snack which one can enjoy there from sidewalk vendors. It is simple to make and surely makes a change from ordinary plain rice. In fact, it is a meal by itself.

Cook the rice according to the Steamed Rice recipe (see page 74) at least 2 hours in advance or the night before. Allow it to cool thoroughly and then put it in the refrigerator.

Combine the eggs with the sesame oil and ½ teaspoon of the salt.

Cut the chicken into ½ inch (1 cm) dice.

Heat a wok or large frying pan over a high heat until it is hot. Add the oil and, when it is very hot and slightly smoking, add the garlic, onion, ginger, remaining salt and the pepper and stir-fry for 2 minutes. Add the chicken and stir-fry for 2 minutes. Add the steamed rice and continue to stir-fry for 3 minutes. Finally, add the bell peppers, corn, chili oil and curry powder and continue to stir-fry for 2 minutes. Add the egg mixture and continue to stir-fry for another minute. Transfer to a warm platter, garnish with the green onions and serve hot or cold as a rice salad.

1¾ cups long-grain white rice

2 eggs, beaten

2 teaspoons sesame oil

2½ teaspoons salt

8 ounces (225 g) chicken breasts

2 tablespoons peanut oil

2 tablespoons coarsely chopped garlic

1 small onion, finely chopped

1 tablespoon finely chopped fresh ginger root

½ teaspoon freshly ground black pepper

1¼ cups diced red bell pepper

¾ cup fresh or frozen corn kernels

1 teaspoon chili oil

1 tablespoon Madras curry powder

3 tablespoons finely chopped green onions, for garnish

POACHED GINGER PEARS

Serves 4

4 firm pears

1 lemon

6 tablespoons sugar

2 cups water

1 vanilla pod, split in half

8 slices fresh ginger root

In Chinese culture, pears are a traditional symbol of longevity and fidelity. Moreover, their appeal extends beyond the grave, to the dead who cannot forget the pleasure they brought. Thus, I was told as a child never to bring home pears on the fifteenth day of the seventh month, for at that time ghosts were roaming the earth seeking pears, among other things. So, on that day the pears might contain ghosts who would bring bad luck into the house. It was quite believable to me at the time.

Pears also traditionally bring happiness, and this means that they should be eaten whole, never divided. Chinese pears are quite different from Western ones, being round and crisp like apples, rather than the soft and pear-shaped fruit with which we are most familiar.

In Chinese cuisine, the pear is most often cooked and served as part of a soup. In this French-inspired recipe, however, the pears are poached with ginger resulting in a delicious, refreshing dessert. For a richer dessert, serve it with cream or a compatible ice cream.

In using a wok to make this dessert, switch to a non-reactive one, that is, a non-stick wok. A basic carbon steel wok will react to the acid from the lemon and may lose its seasoning.

Peel the pears and cut them in half. Remove the core and seeds. Cut the lemon in half, squeeze the juice on the pears and mix well. Combine the sugar, water, vanilla pod and fresh ginger in a non-stick wok and boil the mixture together until the sugar has completely dissolved. Add the pears, cover and simmer over a low heat for 20-25 minutes or until they are tender. The cooking time will depend on the ripeness of the pears.

When the pears are cooked, remove them with a slotted spoon together with the vanilla pod and ginger slices. Over a high heat, reduce the liquid to a syrup by boiling it fast. Discard the ginger slices, but keep the vanilla pod and, when it dries, put it in sugar to keep for future use.

Pour the syrup over the pears and serve at once. Alternatively, you can let the mixture cool, cover it with plastic wrap and chill until you are ready to serve it.

WARM BERRY COMPOTE *with* BASIL

Serves 4

This dessert is inspired by the English summer pudding I have enjoyed many times. It works to perfection only when berries are at their peak of flavor. It is a refreshing and simple dessert to make and is delicious served warm as well as cold. The touch of basil adds a piquant accent which balances the slight acidity of the berries. Any combination of berries in season will work well, and the more variety the better. I love it with vanilla ice cream. If you use a wok, make sure it is non-stick so that the acid of the berries does not react with the carbon steel.

Using a non-stick or coated wok, bring the sugar and water to a boil, add the vanilla pod and simmer for 10 minutes. Remove the vanilla pod and save for future use.

Add the berries and butter and simmer for 2 minutes, just enough to warm and not to cook them. Remove from the heat, add the basil and stir gently. Transfer to a warm bowl and serve at once.

½ cup sugar

⅔ cup water

1 vanilla bean pod, split in half

6 ounces (175 g) strawberries

6 ounces (175 g) raspberries

6 ounces (175 g) blueberries

2 tablespoons unsalted butter

3 fresh basil leaves, finely shredded

Madhur Jaffrey

SPICY FRESH CHEESE SNACK

Promila Kapoor's Paneer Chat - Serves 4

This absolutely delightful dish may be served as a snack, as an accompaniment for drinks or as a first course at a more formal meal. The cheese (paneer) is like the Italian mozzarella.

To make the Cheese, bring the milk to a boil in a heavy saucepan. As soon as it begins to froth, add 3 tablespoons of the lemon juice, stir it in and turn off the heat. The curds should separate from the whey – if they don't do so completely, bring the milk to a boil again and add another tablespoon or so of lemon juice. Stir and turn the heat off.

Line a strainer with a large, doubled-up piece of cheesecloth. Set the strainer over a large bowl. Pour the contents of the saucepan into the strainer. Let the whey drain away. Lift up the 4 corners of the cheesecloth. Using one of the corners tie up the cheese in the cheesecloth into a bundle. Put this bundle on a board set in the sink. Put a plate on the bundle. Now put a weight – such as a medium-sized pan filled with water – on top of the plate. Remove the weight after 3-4 minutes. Untie the bundle. The cheese is ready. It can be refrigerated if necessary.

For the Spices, combine in a bowl the ginger, onion, tomato, chilies, cilantro or mint, salt and black pepper, chaat masala and lemon juice. Toss. Taste for the balance of the seasonings. Cut the cheese into ⅛ inch (3 mm) thick slices. Arrange the slices in a single layer on a serving dish or on several individual plates. Put a generous dollop of the onion-tomato mixture on top of each piece and serve immediately.

FOR THE CHEESE

7½ cups whole milk
3-4 tablespoons lemon juice

FOR THE SPICES

1 (1 inch) (2.5 cm) piece of fresh ginger root, peeled and finely chopped
4 tablespoons finely chopped onion
4 tablespoons finely chopped tomato
1-2 fresh hot green chilies, finely chopped
2 tablespoons finely chopped fresh cilantro or mint
1 teaspoon salt
Freshly ground black pepper
½-1 teaspoon chaat masala (see below)
2-3 tablespoons lemon juice

Chaat Masala

Here is a Punjabi version of this spice mixture used throughout north India. Mix all the ingredients thoroughly, breaking up any lumps. Store in a tightly lidded jar.

4 teaspoons lightly roasted and ground cumin seeds
1½ tablespoons amchoor (see note)
2 teaspoons cayenne pepper
1 teaspoon finely ground black pepper
1 teaspoon finely ground black salt (see note)
1 teaspoon salt

AMCHOOR IS GREEN MANGO POWDER available in Indian grocery stores. Unripe green mangos are peeled, sliced and their sour flesh sun-dried and ground to make amchoor powder. (The dried slices are also used in Indian cooking but not needed for recipes here.) The beige, slightly fibrous powder, rich in Vitamin C, is tart but with a hint of sweetness and is used as lemon juice might be. It is particularly useful when sourness is required but the ingredients need to be kept dry, such as when sautéing spiced potatoes. As the powder can get lumpy, crumble it well before use.

BLACK SALT (KALA NAMAK) is a fairly strong-smelling rock salt used in many of north India's snack foods. It is sold both ground and in lump form by Indian grocers. If you buy the lump form, grind what you need in a clean coffee grinder. Store in a tightly lidded jar.

Opposite: Chettinad Pepper Chicken (page 88).

Amritsari Fish

Amritsari Macchi - Serves 4 to 6

2¼ pounds (1 kg)
  fish steaks, cut into
  ¾ inch (2 cm) pieces
  (use any fleshy fish
  such as salmon, trout
  or cod)

1 tablespoon salt plus
  2 teaspoons salt

3 tablespoons cider
  vinegar

1⅓ cups chick-pea flour

1½ tablespoons peeled
  and very finely grated
  fresh ginger root

1½ tablespoons crushed
  garlic

1 teaspoon cayenne
  pepper

½ teaspoon ground
  turmeric

½ teaspoon freshly
  ground black pepper

1½ tablespoons ajwain
  seeds (see note)

Oil for deep-frying

Lime wedges, for garnish

This is sold all over Amritsar: fish, either filleted or in steaks, that has been marinated, rubbed with a spicy chick-pea flour paste and then deep-fried. It is crunchy on the outside and very sweet and tender inside. Local river fish such as rahu, a kind of carp, or singhara, a slimmer long fish, are generally used but you may substitute fish such as salmon, trout or cod, which are superb cooked by this method.

Rinse the fish steaks in cold water and pat them dry with paper towels. In a shallow ceramic bowl mix the 1 tablespoon salt and the vinegar. Add the fish steaks in a single layer, turning them so that they are coated with this marinade. Marinate for 30 minutes. Remove the fish steaks from the marinade and place on paper towels to get rid of any excess marinade.

Put the chick-pea flour into a bowl. Slowly add 1¼ cups water to make a smooth paste of coating consistency. Add the ginger, garlic, cayenne pepper, turmeric, ajwain seeds, black pepper and remaining 2 teaspoons salt to the paste and mix them in. Rub the fish with this mixture and place in a flat dish in a single layer to marinate for 30 minutes.

Heat the oil in a wok or deep frying pan to 375°F (190°C). When hot, put in as many pieces of fish as will fit in a single layer. Fry for a minute and turn the heat down to medium-high. Cook, turning now and then, until the fish is golden-brown and cooked through. Remove with a slotted spoon and drain on paper towels. Do all the fish this way. Serve with the lime wedges.

AJWAIN SEEDS LOOK LIKE CELERY SEEDS but taste more like a pungent version of thyme. (A student of mine compared it to a mixture of anise and black pepper!) Used sparingly, as their flavor is strong, they are sprinkled into Indian breads, savory biscuits and numerous noodle-like snacks made with chick-pea flour. They also add a pleasant thyme-like taste to vegetables such as green beans and potatoes and to roast meats. Buy ajwain seeds in an Indian specialty store.

BOATMAN'S CURRY

Mr. Damodaran's Vallamkarnanda Meen Kootan - Serves 4

This recipe was taken from boatmen plying the inland waterways near Kumarakom. They make their living fishing and carrying goods – such as rice – and people. This is a dish they cook on their rice boats for themselves and any passengers. The fish used here was the very popular flat, freshwater karimeen but steaks from any firm-fleshed fish such as kingfish, cod, swordfish or salmon may be used. The karimeen are cleaned and then cut, crossways, into 2 or 3 pieces, head and all. Steaks will need to be cubed. This is one of the few times that I have reduced the amount of chilies. The boatman's curry was utterly delicious but incendiary! It may be worth noting that no oil is used in the cooking.

If you wish to substitute unsweetened, dried coconut for fresh coconut use 1 scant cup. Barely cover with warm water and leave for 1 hour, then proceed with the recipe.

Put all the ingredients for the Spice Paste into an electric blender. Add ½ cup water. Blend to make a smooth paste. Put the Spice Paste into a medium-sized heavy-bottomed pan. Add ½ cup water. Stir. The paste should have a similar consistency to that of a puréed soup.

For the fish, heat the spice paste over medium-low heat. Bring to a gentle simmer. Add the tamarind paste, green chilies, ginger, shallots and salt. Stir and simmer for 2-3 minutes. Slip in the fish. Stir once and cover. Simmer gently for 10-15 minutes until the fish is just cooked.

FOR THE SPICE PASTE

4-6 dried hot red chilies, soaked in hot water for 15 minutes

1 teaspoon cayenne pepper

1 tablespoon paprika

3 tablespoons ground coriander

1 teaspoon ground turmeric

1¼ cups freshly grated coconut

FOR THE FISH

2½ tablespoons tamarind paste (see note)

3-4 fresh hot green chilies, split into halves

1 (1 inch) (2.5 cm) piece of fresh ginger root, peeled and lightly crushed

4-5 shallots, peeled and lightly crushed

1½ teaspoons salt

1½ pounds (750 g) fish steaks, about ½ inch (1 cm) thick

THE FRUIT OF A TALL SHADE TREE, tamarinds look like wide beans. As they ripen, their sour green flesh turns a chocolate color. It remains sour but picks up a hint of sweetness. For commercial purposes, tamarinds are peeled, seeded, semi-dried and their brown flesh compacted into rectangular blocks. These blocks need to be broken up and soaked in water. Then the pulp can be pushed through a strainer. This is tamarind paste. You can find it at Indian specialty stores.

5 tablespoons oil

FOR THE SPICE PASTE

1½ tablespoons cumin seeds
  (see page 94)
8-10 dried hot red chilies,
  broken into halves
3 tablespoons coriander
  seeds
1½ teaspoons fennel seeds
1½ teaspoons black
  peppercorns
1½ teaspoons white poppy
  seeds (see note)
5 garlic cloves, peeled and
  coarsely chopped
1 (1½ inch) (4 cm) piece of
  fresh ginger root, peeled
  and coarsely chopped
½ teaspoon ground turmeric
1½-2 teaspoons salt

FOR THE CHICKEN

3 bay leaves
5 cardamom pods
  (see page 117)
1 (1 inch) (2.5 cm) cinnamon
  stick, broken in pieces
1 teaspoon fennel seeds
3 cloves
1½ teaspoons urad dal
  (see page 115)
15-20 fresh curry leaves,
  (optional) (see page 98)
2 onions, peeled and finely
  chopped
1 large tomato, chopped
1 (2¼ pound) (1 kg) chicken,
  skinned and cut into
  serving pieces

CHETTINAD PEPPER CHICKEN

From the home of A. C. Muthiah: Koli Milagu Masala - Serves 4 to 6

*A*nother exquisite dish from the Chettiar community, this is generally served with plain rice. What gives the dish a very special southern flavor is the use of fennel seeds, curry leaves and of course, the legume urad dal (see page 115). This is definitely a dish you'll want to make very frequently. (Illustrated on page 82.)

Make the Spice Paste: in a small frying pan, heat 1 tablespoon of the oil over medium-high heat. When hot add the cumin seeds, chilies, coriander seeds, fennel seeds, black peppercorns and poppy seeds. Stir and fry briefly until lightly roasted. Now, put these into a clean coffee grinder and grind to a powder. Empty into the container of an electric blender. Put the garlic, ginger, turmeric and salt into the blender as well, along with 6-8 tablespoons water. Process until you have a fine paste, pushing down with a rubber spatula if needed. Set aside.

For the Chicken, heat the remaining 4 tablespoons of oil in a large saucepan over medium-high heat. When hot, add the bay leaves, cardamom pods, cinnamon, fennel seeds, cloves and urad dal. Stir and fry briefly until the urad dal turns red, then add the curry leaves, if using. Stir once or twice and add the onions. Fry the onions until they are soft and just lightly colored. Now add the Spice Paste. Continue to stir and fry for about 4-6 minutes, adding a little water to prevent sticking. Add the tomato. Stir and fry for a further 3-4 minutes. Add the chicken pieces to the onion and spice mixture. Stir until they are well coated, then add 2½ cups water, just enough to cover. Bring to a boil. Turn the heat to low, cover and simmer until the chicken is almost cooked, about 20-25 minutes.

Using a slotted spoon, remove the chicken pieces. Turn the heat up to medium-high, and reduce the sauce until very thick. This should take about 6-8 minutes. Return the chicken to the pan, fold gently into the sauce and cook for a further 5 minutes before serving.

POPPY SEEDS CAN BE BLUE OR WHITE. India just happens to grow the white ones. These very tiny seeds are usually roasted first and then ground to make a nutty paste that is excellent in meat sauces. It thickens the sauces and provides a deeper flavor at the same time. When used in kebobs and meatballs, it adds a touch of firmness just as bread crumbs might.

CHICKEN *with a* ROASTED COCONUT SAUCE

Jude Sequeira's Xacuti - Serves 6

There are probably as many recipes for this as there are Goan homes. Here is a fairly traditional Catholic one. Xacuti (pronounced "sha-koo-tee") may be made out of rabbit, field heron, lamb or even with vegetables. What distinguishes a xacuti from other dishes is that all the seasonings in it are roasted before they are ground to a paste. It is supposed to be so spicy that it exorcises all sniffles and coughs in the rainy monsoon season when farmers spend long hours knee-deep in the paddy fields.

If you wish to substitute unsweetened, dried coconut for fresh coconut use 1¼ cups. Roast it in the same way as the fresh coconut, then soak it in ¾ cup water for 1 hour. Process the coconut and water together.

Make the Spice Paste: heat a cast-iron frying pan over medium-high heat. When hot, put in the coconut. Stir and roast until it is medium-brown. Add the turmeric and stir once or twice. Remove and set aside. Put the chilies, coriander seeds, cumin seeds, fennel seeds, peppercorns, cardamom pods, cloves, star anise, cinnamon, mace and nutmeg into the same hot pan. Stir until the spices are almost roasted. Add the poppy seeds. Keep roasting until the spices are lightly browned. Remove all the spices and let them cool slightly. Put the spices into a clean coffee grinder, in several batches if necessary, and grind to a fine powder.

Put the 1 tablespoon oil into the same pan and heat over medium-high heat. When hot, add the onion, ginger and garlic, and sauté until medium brown. Remove.

Put the coconut, ground spices and onion mixture in an electric blender. Add 1½ cups water or more and blend to a paste, in more than one batch, if needed.

For the Chicken, put the chicken pieces in a single layer on a large plate. Sprinkle on both sides with ¾ teaspoon of the salt and lemon juice. Rub this in. Set aside for 20 minutes.

Heat the 4 tablespoons oil in a wide, preferably non-stick pan over medium-high heat. When hot, put in the sliced onions. Stir and fry until browned. Put in the spice paste. Stir and cook for 2-3 minutes. Add the chicken and all accumulated juices as well as the remaining salt and 1¼ cups water. Stir and bring to a simmer. Cover, turn the heat to low and cook for about 25 minutes or until the chicken is tender. Add the curry leaves, if using, and stir well.

FOR THE SPICE PASTE

2 cups freshly grated coconut (see page 101)
½ teaspoon ground turmeric
5-6 dried hot red chilies
4 tablespoons coriander seeds
1 teaspoon cumin seeds (see page 94)
1 teaspoon fennel seeds
½ teaspoon black peppercorns
5-6 cardamom pods (see page 117)
½ teaspoon cloves
2 star anise
1 (2 inch) (5 cm) cinnamon stick, broken
A curl of mace
⅓ whole nutmeg
2 tablespoons white poppy seeds (see page 88)
1 tablespoon vegetable oil
1 onion, peeled and cut into half-rings
1 (2 inch) (5 cm) piece of fresh ginger root, peeled and thinly sliced
6-7 garlic cloves, peeled and coarsely chopped

FOR THE CHICKEN

3 pounds (1.5 kg) chicken, cut into small pieces
1½ teaspoons salt
2 tablespoons lemon juice
4 tablespoons vegetable oil
2 onions, peeled and sliced into half-rings
15-20 fresh curry leaves, (optional) (see page 98)

LAMB CHOPS MASALA

Mrs. Chadda's Chaamp Masala - Serves 3 to 4

1 (3 inch) (7.5 cm) piece of fresh ginger root, peeled and coarsely chopped

3 tablespoons peeled and coarsely chopped garlic

6-8 lamb chops (1¾ pounds) (800 g), each about ¾ inch (2 cm) thick

1 cup grated or finely chopped tomatoes

2 onions, finely chopped

1 tablespoon cayenne pepper

1¾ cups plain yogurt made from whole milk

1½ teaspoons salt, or to taste

1 teaspoon ground roasted cumin seeds (see note)

1-2 teaspoons Punjabi Garam Masala (see page 109)

3 tablespoons lemon juice

2-3 tablespoons chopped fresh cilantro

Serve this with Mustard Greens (see page 112) and any Punjabi bread such as Flat Corn Breads (see page 121) or Puffed Leavened Breads (see page 123). Note: In the Punjab tomatoes are grated to make a purée.

Put the ginger and the garlic into the container of an electric blender with 2-3 tablespoons of water and blend to a paste.

Put the chops, tomatoes, onions, cayenne pepper, yogurt, salt and the ginger-garlic paste into a large wok or large heavy-bottomed saucepan. Stir and bring to a boil. Turn the heat to low, cover and simmer for 50 minutes or until the chops are almost cooked. Add the ground roasted cumin seeds and simmer for 10-15 minutes or until the meat is tender and the sauce is thick. Stir in the garam masala and lemon juice. Sprinkle the fresh cilantro over the top and serve.

CUMIN SEEDS LOOK LIKE CARAWAY SEEDS but are slightly larger, plumper and lighter in color. Their flavor is similar to caraway, only gentler and sweeter. They are used both whole and ground. When whole, they are often subjected to the tarka (dry-roasting) technique, which intensifies their flavor and makes them slightly nutty. When ground, they are used in meat, rice and vegetable dishes. Cumin seeds can also be dry-roasted first and then ground. This version is sprinkled over many snack foods, relishes and yogurt dishes.

To roast cumin seeds, put 3-4 tablespoons of cumin seeds into a small, heated, cast-iron frying pan. Keep over medium heat. Stir the cumin until it is a few shades darker and emits a distinct roasted aroma. Grind in a clean coffee grinder and store in a tightly lidded jar.

Lamb Cooked *in* Milk *and* Yogurt

Mrs. Dasgupta's Rezala · Serves 4

Rezala, which can be made with both lamb and chicken, is a specialty of the Muslims of Bengal. It is eaten at celebratory meals. It is almost always made with rather fatty rib chops. I prefer to use boned lamb shoulder.

When the dish has almost finished cooking, many Muslim families add a sprinkling of kewra water. This has a marvelously flowery aroma. Most serious Indian grocers sell it. Use rose water or orange blossom water as substitutes.

Serve with naans, chapatis, pita breads or any rice dish of your choice.

For the Marinade, put the ginger and garlic into the container of an electric blender. Add 4 tablespoons water and blend to a fine, frothy paste. Put the paste into a large bowl. Add the remaining marinating ingredients and mix well. Add the lamb. Leave to stand unrefrigerated for 3-4 hours. (You may marinate the meat overnight. Cover and refrigerate and bring to room temperature before cooking.)

Remove the meat from the Marinade, reserving the meat and the Marinade separately.

To finish cooking the Lamb, heat the oil or ghee in a large, wide, preferably non-stick pan or wok over high heat. When hot, add the lamb, salt and sugar. Stir and fry for 8-10 minutes until the meat is lightly browned. Reduce the heat to very low. Add the Marinade. Cover and cook for 1 hour or until the meat is tender. Add the green and red chilies. Cook for a further 5-10 minutes. Add the kewra water, stir and serve.

FOR THE MARINADE

1 (3 inch) (7.5 cm) piece of fresh ginger root, peeled and finely chopped

8-9 garlic cloves, peeled and coarsely chopped

1½ cups plain yogurt, lightly beaten

1 cup milk

3-4 bay leaves

8-10 cardamom pods (see page 117)

8-10 cloves

1 teaspoon ground mace

½ teaspoon ground nutmeg

FOR THE LAMB

2¼ pounds (1 kg) boned lamb from the shoulder

1 tablespoon vegetable oil

3 tablespoons ghee (see note) or vegetable oil

1½-1¾ teaspoons salt

½ teaspoon sugar

10 fresh hot green chilies, each with a small slit at one end

6-8 dried hot red chilies, soaked in warm water for 10 minutes

1 teaspoon kewra water (see introduction)

GHEE IS BUTTER that has been so thoroughly clarified that it can even be used for deep-frying. As it no longer contains milk solids, refrigeration is not necessary. It has a nutty, buttery taste. All Indian grocers sell it and I find it more convenient to buy it. If, however, you need to make it, put 1 pound (450 g) unsalted butter in a pan over low heat and let it simmer very gently until the milky solids turn brownish and cling to the sides of the pot or else fall to the bottom. The time that this takes will depend on the amount of water in the butter. Watch carefully toward the end and do not let it turn. Strain the ghee through a triple layer of cheesecloth. Homemade ghee is best stored in the refrigerator.

½ eggplant, cut into ¾ inch x ½ inch (2 cm x 1 cm) sticks

2 small carrots, peeled and cut into ¾ inch x ½ inch (2 cm x 1 cm) sticks

1 cup peas

4 ounces (100 g) French beans, cut into 1 inch (2.5 cm) pieces

1 potato, peeled and cut into ¾ inch x ½ inch (2 cm x 1 cm) sticks

½ cup freshly grated coconut (see page 101)

4 fresh hot green chilies

2 tablespoons white poppy seeds (see page 88)

1¼ teaspoons salt

3 tomatoes, coarsely chopped

1 tablespoon plain yogurt

1 teaspoon Punjabi Garam Masala (see page 109)

2 tablespoons chopped fresh cilantro

MIXED VEGETABLE CURRY

Mrs. A. Santha Ramanujam's Kurma - Serves 4 to 6

Nothing could be simpler, or for that matter, more delicious. Vegetables, whatever happens to be in season, are lightly par-boiled or steamed and then "dressed" with a ground paste of fresh coconut, poppy seeds and green chilies. The dressing is not just poured over the top. Instead, it is cooked briefly with the vegetables so it is absorbed by them. This is best with plain rice. You could serve it by itself or as part of a larger meal.

If you wish to substitute unsweetened, dried coconut for fresh coconut use 5 tablespoons. Barely cover with warm water and leave for 1 hour, then proceed with the recipe.

Place the eggplant, carrots, peas, French beans and potato in a medium-sized saucepan. Add 1 cup of water. Bring to a boil. Cover, turn the heat to medium and cook for 4 minutes or until the vegetables are just tender.

Meanwhile, put the coconut, chilies, poppy seeds and salt into an electric blender. Add ⅔ cup water and purée to a fine paste.

Set aside. When the vegetables are cooked, add the spice paste and another ⅔ cup water. Stir and simmer gently for 5 minutes. Now add the tomatoes, yogurt and the garam masala. Stir gently to mix well. Bring to a boil and simmer gently for 2-3 minutes. Turn into a serving dish and garnish with the fresh cilantro.

PORK *with* VINEGAR *and* GARLIC

Jude Sequeira's Pork Vindalho · Serves 4 to 6

A dish of Portuguese ancestry, vindalho is made by Goan families on festive occasions – birthdays, weddings and even at Christmas. The dish, an unusual combination of a curry and a preserve, can be made up to a week in advance and often is. The vinegar acts as a preservative, making it an ideal party dish. Goans do take the precaution of bringing it to a boil once a day in the earthen vessel used for cooking. We in the West can also make it a few days in advance but I would keep it, well covered, in the refrigerator.

Sprinkle the pork with 1 teaspoon of the salt. Add 3 tablespoons of the vinegar. Rub in well and set aside for 2-3 hours.

Make the Spice Paste: combine the red chilies, paprika, cumin seeds, cinnamon, cloves, peppercorns and cardamom pods in a clean coffee grinder and grind as finely as possible. Put the 10-12 garlic cloves and the ginger in an electric blender along with 2 tablespoons of the vinegar and the turmeric. Blend well. Add the dry ground spices to the garlic mixture and blend again to mix. Rub the pork cubes with half of the spice paste, cover and refrigerate overnight. Cover and refrigerate the remaining spice paste.

To cook the Pork, heat the 3 tablespoons oil in a wide, preferably non-stick pan over medium-high heat. When hot, put in the 3-4 garlic cloves. Stir and fry until they begin to pick up a little color. Put in the onions and continue to fry until browned. Now add the tomatoes and 3 of the green chilies. Stir for a minute. Add the remaining spice paste, the sugar and the remaining 1 tablespoon vinegar. Stir and fry until the paste begins to brown a little.

Now add the marinated meat and all the spice paste clinging to it. Turn the heat to medium-low and cook, stirring, until the pork begins to exude its own liquid. Add 1¼ cups water and the remaining salt and bring to a boil. Cover, turn the heat to low and simmer gently until the meat is tender and the sauce has thickened somewhat, about 40 minutes.

If necessary, raise the heat to reduce the sauce to a medium-thick consistency toward the end. Add the remaining 3 green chilies and stir once.

FOR THE PORK

2¼ pounds (1 kg) boneless pork shoulder, cut into (2 inch) (5 cm) cubes

1½ teaspoons salt

6 tablespoons red wine vinegar

3 tablespoons vegetable oil

3-4 garlic cloves, peeled and lightly crushed

3 onions, peeled and finely sliced

2 large tomatoes, chopped

6 fresh hot green chilies, sliced in half lengthwise

1 teaspoon sugar

FOR THE SPICE PASTE

4-10 dried hot red chilies

1 tablespoon bright red paprika

½ teaspoon cumin seeds (see page 94)

1 (3 inch) (6 cm) cinnamon stick, broken up into smaller pieces

10-15 cloves

½ teaspoon black peppercorns

5-6 cardamom pods (see page 117)

10-12 garlic cloves, peeled

1 (1 inch) (2.5 cm) piece of fresh ginger root, peeled and coarsely chopped

½ teaspoon ground turmeric

SHARK *with* SPICES *and* FRESH CILANTRO

From the home of A. C. Muthiah: Sora Puttu - Serves 4 to 6

1 pound (450 g) shark, the younger the better, cut into thick steaks

2 teaspoons salt

1 teaspoon ground turmeric

5 tablespoons vegetable oil

1 (1 inch) (2.5 cm) cinnamon stick, broken

8-10 shallots, finely chopped

½ teaspoon fennel seeds

1 (1½ inch) (2 cm) piece of fresh ginger root, finely chopped or grated

4-5 fresh hot green chilies, cut into fine half-rounds

5 garlic cloves, finely chopped

20 fresh curry leaves (optional) (see note)

1 cup freshly grated coconut (see page 101)

2 tablespoons chopped fresh cilantro, plus extra for garnishing

2 teaspoons lemon juice

This recipe comes from the kitchen of a princely Chettiar home. The flaked flesh of baby sharks can be cooked so that it remains moist but it can also be stirred and stirred until the flakes turn crisp. This recipe is the second version. Generally, it is mixed with plain rice and eaten with a sambar (a South Indian dish of split peas with spices). If you cannot get shark, use fresh tuna or swordfish.

If you wish to substitute unsweetened, dried coconut for fresh coconut use ⅔ cup. Barely cover with warm water and leave for 1 hour. Squeeze dry and proceed with the recipe.

Put the shark, 1 teaspoon of the salt and the turmeric in a large saucepan with 4½ cups water. Bring to a boil over medium heat. Reduce the heat to a gentle simmer. Cook for 15-20 minutes until the shark is tender. Drain and allow to cool. Remove the skin and cartilage of the shark and flake. Put in a large bowl and set aside.

Heat the oil in a large frying pan over medium-high heat. When hot, add the cinnamon, shallots and fennel seeds. Stir and fry for 4-5 minutes or until the shallots are golden. Add the ginger, chilies and garlic. Stir and fry until lightly browned and softened. Add the remaining salt and the flaked shark. Stir and fry briskly for 10-15 minutes. Add the curry leaves, if using, and the 2 tablespoons cilantro. Cook until dry. Just before serving, add the lemon juice. Serve hot, garnished with the remaining cilantro.

CURRY LEAVES ARE HIGHLY AROMATIC LEAVES used in much Indian coastal and southern cookery. They are always used in their fresh form. They are now increasingly available in the West. You could use the dried leaf if the fresh is unavailable, but its aroma is very limited. Indian grocers sell both fresh and dried curry leaves. They come attached to stalks. They can be pulled off their stalks in one swoop. Keep curry leaves in a flat, plastic bag. They last for several days in the refrigerator. They may also be frozen, so when you do see them in the market, buy a lot and store them in your freezer.

SHRIMP CURRY

Sophie Gonsalves' Samar Codi - Serves 4

*W*hen I arrive in Goa, the first dish I order is this simple shrimp curry. It uses no oil as nothing in it requires frying or sautéing. In many ways, it is the humblest of curries and may be made with very cheap fish cut into chunks, fish steaks or fillet pieces.

I like it made with juicy shrimp, fresh from the sea. With a spicy, red coconut sauce flowing over a bed of white, pearly rice – what more can one want? I rarely order this dish in the hotel that I stay in. I find a small beach shack covered in palm thatching, generally owned by real fishermen, and order it there. All I need with it is a cold glass of beer.

If you buy un-peeled, headless shrimp or prawns, you will need 1½ pounds (675 g). Peel and devein them, then wash them and pat them dry.

In a bowl, combine 1¼ cups water with the cayenne pepper, paprika, turmeric, garlic and ginger. Mix well. Grind the coriander seeds and cumin seeds in a clean coffee grinder and add to the mixture.

Put the spice mixture into a pan and bring to a simmer. Turn the heat to medium-low and simmer for 10 minutes. The sauce should reduce and thicken. Add the coconut milk, salt, kokum or tamarind paste and bring to a simmer. Add the shrimp and simmer, stirring now and then, until they turn opaque and are just cooked through.

---

1 teaspoon cayenne pepper

1 tablespoon bright red paprika

½ teaspoon ground turmeric

4 garlic cloves, peeled and crushed

1 (1 inch) (2.5 cm) piece of fresh ginger root, peeled and grated to a pulp

2 tablespoons coriander seeds

1 teaspoon cumin seeds (see page 94)

1 (14 ounce) (397 g) can coconut milk, well stirred

¾ teaspoon salt

3 pieces of kokum (see note) or 1 tablespoon tamarind paste (see page 87)

1 pound (450 g) peeled and deveined, medium sized, uncooked shrimp or prawns

---

KOKUM IS THE PLIABLE, semi-dried, sour and astringent skin of a mangosteen-like fruit that grows along India's coast. It is used for souring, rather like lemon or tamarind. It can sometimes be a bit salty as well so use a little care. Store in an air-tight container to prevent drying out. When kokum is used in a dish, it is rarely eaten. It is left either in the pan or in the serving dish.

Split Peas *with* Shallots

¾ cup toovar dal, picked over
and washed in several
changes of water (see note)

3 tablespoons vegetable oil

1 fresh hot green chili, split
in half lengthwise

12-14 shallots, peeled

2 tablespoons tamarind paste
(see page 87)

2-2½ tablespoons Sambar
Powder (see following
recipe)

1½ teaspoons salt

½ teaspoon ground turmeric

½ teaspoon brown mustard
seeds (see page 105)

15-20 fresh curry leaves
(optional) (see page 98)

1 tablespoon finely chopped
fresh cilantro

*S*ambar and rice are the meat and potatoes of Tamil Nadu. Plain toovar dal (see note) is first boiled. It is then made deliciously sour with tamarind paste and exquisitely spicy with the addition of a special Sambar Powder that contains a mixture of roasted spices. This basic sambar can be varied daily with the addition of different vegetables. One of my favorites is shallot sambar. The shallots are lightly sautéed before being added to the sambar, giving them a sweet, glazed quality. Pickling onions may be substituted. Serve with plain rice or another Indian dish.*

Place the toovar dal in a medium-sized saucepan with 2½ cups water. Bring to a boil. Cover partially, turn the heat down to low, and simmer for 45 minutes to an hour or until the dal is tender. When cooked, stir with a spoon to mash up the dal. Heat 2 tablespoons of the oil in a medium-sized frying pan over medium-high heat. When hot, put in the chili. Stir for a few seconds until the chili softens. Add the shallots. Stir and fry until the shallots are very lightly browned. Turn the heat down and cook until the shallots soften and cook through.

Add the tamarind paste, sambar powder, salt, turmeric and 2 cups of water to the saucepan of toovar dal. Also add the contents of the frying pan. Mix and bring to a simmer. Simmer gently, uncovered, for 10 minutes, stirring now and then. Meanwhile, heat the remaining 1 tablespoon of oil in a small saucepan or small frying pan over medium high heat. When hot add the mustard seeds. As soon as the mustard seeds pop, a matter of seconds, throw in the curry leaves, if using. Stir once and quickly pour over the sambar. Sprinkle the fresh cilantro over the top.

Sambar Powder

This powder, which uses split peas as spices, is used to make the South Indian dish called sambar. It can be stored in a tightly closed jar for several months.

Heat the oil in a large, heavy frying pan or a heavy wok over medium heat. Add the coriander seeds, mustard seeds, moong dal, chana dal, urad dal, fenugreek seeds, black peppercorns, asafetida and cumin seeds. Stir and roast for 3-4 minutes. Add the curry leaves, if using. Stir and roast for another 5 minutes. Add the dried chilies and continue stirring and roasting for 2-3 minutes or until chilies darken. Remove spices to a plate. When the spices have cooled, put them into a coffee grinder in small batches and grind as finely as possible. Store in a tightly lidded jar.

1 teaspoon vegetable oil

5 tablespoons coriander seeds

*1 teaspoon mustard seeds
  (see page 105)*

*1 teaspoon moong dal
  (see note)*

*1 teaspoon chana dal
  (see page 115)*

*½ tablespoon urad dal
  (see page 115)*

*1 teaspoon fenugreek seeds
  (see note)*

1 teaspoon black peppercorns

*¼ teaspoon ground asafetida
  (see page 113)*

*1 teaspoon cumin seeds
  (see page 94)*

*20 fresh curry leaves,
  (optional) (see page 98)*

12 dried hot red chilies

Toovar dal (also called arhar dal) is a dull yellow split pea with an earthy taste. Indian grocers sell it in its plain form and in an "oily" form which is darker. The latter is rubbed with castor oil. This oil needs to be washed off.

Moong dal are yellow split beans that are sold both with and without skin by almost every Indian grocer. The skins are green, the flesh yellow.

Fenugreek seeds are angular, yellowish seeds that give many commercial curry powders their earthy, musky "curry" aroma. In most of northern India they are used mainly in pickles, chutneys and vegetarian dishes. In western, southern and eastern India, they are used in meat and fish dishes as well. They are part of the Bengali spice mixture, panch phoran.

TANDOORI CHICKEN

Serves 4

DRY SEASONINGS IN THE MARINADE

1½ tablespoons cumin seeds (see page 94)

1½ tablespoons black peppercorns

Seeds from 3 black cardamom pods (see page 117)

Seeds from 1 tablespoon green cardamom pods (see page 117)

1 teaspoon cloves

REMAINING SEASONINGS IN MARINADE

3 fresh hot green chilies, coarsely chopped

2 garlic cloves, peeled and coarsely chopped

1 (1½ inch) (4 cm) piece of fresh ginger root, peeled and coarsely chopped

1½ teaspoons salt

1 tablespoon Kashmiri chili powder (see note) or paprika

2 tablespoons heavy whipping cream

4 tablespoons vegetable oil

FOR THE CHICKEN

2¼ pounds (1 kg) chicken pieces, skinned

2-3 tablespoons melted unsalted butter or vegetable oil

1-2 tablespoons Chaat Masala (see page 83)

4 lime or lemon wedges

Surjit's Chicken House – in reality it is a tiny stall – is reputed to sell the best tandoori chicken in town and has become quite an institution in Amritsar. Over the last 40 years, I have watched and monitored the changes in this simple, oven-roasted chicken dish from the northwest frontier of what is now Pakistan. Originally, it had no seasonings other than the very simple ones in the marinade itself. Today, with north India's passion for sour and spicy foods, a great deal of the flavor comes from chaat masala, a mixture of seasonings used mainly for snack foods, which is sprinkled over the top. Chaat masala may be purchased from any Indian grocer or made at home using the recipe on page 83.

Here is the new version of the dish. For those of us who do not have clay tandoors (ovens) in our homes, it is best to use an oven heated to its maximum temperature. This chicken may be enjoyed with sliced white radishes and beer, as it is by the men of Amritsar, or eaten as part of a meal with a salad and any bread, Indian or Western.

Combine all the ingredients for the Dry Seasoning Marinade in a clean coffee grinder and grind to a powder. Combine the Remaining Ingredients for the Marinade and ½ cup of water in an electric blender and blend to a paste. Empty the dry marinade spices into the blender and blend to mix. Empty into a large bowl.

Cut deep, diagonal slits in the fleshy parts of the chicken pieces. Rub the marinade all over the chicken pieces, making sure that you go deep inside the slits. Put the chicken into the marinade bowl, cover and refrigerate overnight or for up to 48 hours. Remove the chicken pieces from the marinade. Shake off as much marinade as possible. If you have a tandoor, pierce the chicken pieces onto a sturdy skewer and cook for 15-20 minutes, depending on the thickness of the flesh. If you do not have a tandoor, put one shelf in the upper third of the oven and preheat the oven to its highest temperature. Lay the chicken pieces in a single layer in a very shallow baking tray. Brush with the butter or the oil. When the oven is very hot, put in the tray. The breast pieces will probably cook in 10-12 minutes. Take the chicken out of the oven, sprinkle with the chaat masala and lime or lemon juice and serve immediately.

KASHMIRI CHILI POWDER is a powder made from a long Kashmiri chili that is relatively mild in taste but which, like paprika, gives off a lovely deep red color.

Carrots Stir-Fried *with* Green Chilies

Kumud Kansara's Gajar Marcha No Sambharo - Serves 4 to 6

Gujaratis eat many vegetables that are very lightly stir-fried. The tarka technique, known by many other names such as baghaar, chhownk or "seasoning in oil" is quite unique to India. First, the oil has to be very hot. Then, spices such as mustard seeds or cumin seeds are dropped into it. Then, either the flavored oil is poured over cooked foods or foods are added to the oil and cooked in it. Any food cooked in this oil picks up the heightened flavor of all the spices.

Doing a tarka takes just a few seconds so it is important to have all spices ready and at hand. A tarka is sometimes done at the beginning of a recipe and sometimes at the end. Legumes, for example, are usually boiled with a little turmeric. When they are tender, a tarka is prepared in a small frying pan, perhaps with asafetida, cumin seeds and red chilies, and then the entire contents of the frying pan, hot oil and spices, are poured over the legumes and the lid shut tight for a few minutes to trap the aromas. These flavorings can be stirred in later. They pick up the boiled legumes and bring them to life. Sometimes tarkas are done twice, both at the beginning and end of a recipe.

Heat the oil in a large, wide, preferably non-stick pan or wok over medium heat. When hot, add the mustard seeds. As soon as they pop (a matter of seconds) add the asafetida. Stir to mix. Add the carrots, chilies, salt, turmeric, coriander and lime juice. Stir and fry for 2-3 minutes. Remove from the heat. The carrots should remain slightly crunchy.

3 tablespoons peanut or other vegetable oil

½ teaspoon brown mustard seeds (see note)

¼ teaspoon ground asafetida (see page 113)

1¼ pounds (550 g) carrots, peeled and very coarsely grated

6 fresh hot green chilies, slit in half and cut into long slivers

½ teaspoon salt

¼ teaspoon ground turmeric

½ teaspoon ground coriander

½ teaspoon lime juice

BROWN MUSTARD SEEDS – Of the three varieties of mustard seeds, white (actually yellowish), brown (a reddish-brown) and black (slightly larger brownish black seeds), it is the brown that has been grown and used in India since antiquity. To confuse matters, the brown seeds are often referred to as black. When shopping, look for the small, reddish-brown variety although at a pinch, any will do.

CASHEW NUTS *with* COCONUT

Jude Sequeira's Cashew Nut Bhaji - Serves 4 to 6

3 cups raw cashew nuts
2 tablespoons vegetable oil
1 teaspoon brown mustard
   seeds (see page 105)
1 teaspoon cumin seeds
   (see page 94)
1 teaspoon urad dal
   (see page 115)
2-3 dried hot red chilies,
   broken up
1½ teaspoons salt
½ teaspoon ground turmeric
1 cup freshly grated coconut
   (see page 101)
2 fresh hot green chilies,
   slit lengthwise
1 teaspoon Goan Five-Spice
   Mix (see below)
1 tablespoon chopped fresh
   cilantro

Goan Five-Spice Mix
*P*ut the ingredients in
a clean coffee grinder and
grind. Any leftovers you have
may be stored in a tightly
lidded jar.

10 cardamom pods
   (see page 117)
½ teaspoon cloves
1 teaspoon of cinnamon stick
   pieces
1½ teaspoons cumin seeds
1 teaspoon black peppercorns

*C*ashew nuts are grown all over the southwest coast of India. They are harvested in winter, roasted lightly to rid them of their reddish-brown skins and then eaten out of hand or used in hundreds of cakes, puddings and halvas. The Hindus of Goa also serve them as a vegetable. Indian breads are the traditional accompaniment to this bhaji. It is best to use fresh coconut for this.

Soak the cashew nuts in water for 8 hours or overnight. Drain.

Heat the oil in a large frying pan over medium-high heat. When hot, add the mustard seeds. As soon as they start to pop, a matter of seconds, add the cumin, urad dal and red chilies. Stir and fry for a few seconds until the dal turns reddish and the chilies darken. Add the cashew nuts and salt. Stir for a minute. Add the turmeric. Stir once and add ⅓ cup water. Cover and turn the heat to low. Simmer gently for 10 minutes. Remove the cover and add the coconut, green chilies and five-spice mix.

Mix well, sprinkle with the fresh cilantro and serve.

CAULIFLOWER ENCRUSTED *with* POPPY SEEDS

Maya's Phulkopir Posto ~ Serves 4 to 6

Eat this with Deep-Fried Stuffed Breads (see page 120) as a snack or at lunch time, or with any Indian meal. When cooking this dish, remember to dry up all the sauce. You may need to adjust your heat to achieve this.

Put the chilies and poppy seeds for the Spice Paste into a clean coffee grinder and grind to a fine powder. Put the powder into a small bowl, add 6 tablespoons of water, mix well and set aside.

For the Cauliflower, rub the turmeric, ½ teaspoon of the salt and ½ teaspoon of the sugar over the cauliflower florets and set aside.

Heat 4 tablespoons of the oil in a large, wide, preferably non-stick frying pan or wok over medium-high heat. When hot, add the cauliflower. Stir and fry for 4-5 minutes until the cauliflower just starts to brown. Remove the florets from the pan with a slotted spoon, leaving as much oil behind as possible. Gently shake the florets in paper towels to remove the excess oil. Set aside.

Add the remaining oil to the pan and set over medium heat. When hot, add the kalonji, bay leaves and chilies and stir once or twice. Quickly add the Spice Paste and stir and fry for 2-3 minutes or until the mixture turns a reddish-brown color. Add the cauliflower and the remaining salt and sugar. Stir gently to coat the cauliflower with the spices.

Add ⅔ cup water, stir to mix and bring to the boil. Cover, reduce the heat and allow to simmer gently for 10-12 minutes. Stir occasionally to prevent sticking, adding a sprinkling of water when necessary. The sauce should be absorbed and the florets should remain slightly crunchy and be evenly coated with the spices.

FOR THE SPICE PASTE

3 dried hot red chilies, roughly broken

5 tablespoons white poppy seeds (see page 88)

FOR THE CAULIFLOWER

½ teaspoon ground turmeric

1 teaspoon salt

1 teaspoon sugar

1 medium cauliflower, cut into chunky florets

7 tablespoons mustard oil (see page 92) or any other vegetable oil

½ teaspoon kalonji (see page 92)

2 bay leaves

3-4 dried hot red chilies

CREAMY SPICED BEANS

Ma Di Dal / Dal Makkhani - Serves 6

1 cup whole black urad
    beans (see note)

⅓ cup red kidney beans

4 teaspoons peeled and
    very finely grated fresh
    ginger root

4 teaspoons crushed garlic

2 tomatoes, finely chopped

2 teaspoons cayenne pepper,
    or to taste

2-3 teaspoons salt, or to taste

⅓ cup white butter or
    unsalted butter
    (see introduction)

½ cup whipping cream

2 teaspoons Punjabi Garam
    Masala (see following
    recipe)

FOR THE TARKA

3 tablespoons unsalted
    butter or vegetable oil

1 small onion, sliced into
    very thin half rings

1 teaspoon cayenne pepper

2-3 tablespoons chopped
    fresh cilantro

More than half of the Punjab's population is vegetarian and for them, after wheat, nothing is more important than beans. This dish in a simpler form (without the cream, garlic and tomatoes as well as the final tarka of onions) is served with plain breads (rotis) at Sikh gurdwaras (temples) to anyone who asks for food. In this simple form, it also bubbles away for hours in all dhabas (fast food joints), in monstrous, narrow-necked pots, stirred every now and then with huge paddles. It can be enriched as orders come in. This enrichment can consist of a simple tarka of onions and cayenne pepper in ghee (clarified butter), in which case it is called ma di dal with tarka or it can have cream added to it as well as the tarka or a generous dollop of butter, in which case it is called dal makkhani (buttery beans). White butter is butter that is churned at home or on farms and is without additives or coloring. Good, unsalted butter is the best substitute. Serve with a Punjabi bread, meat, vegetable, yogurt relish and a pickle or chutney.

Wash the 2 types of beans and drain. Cover with water and leave to soak overnight. Drain.

The day of serving in a large pan, combine the beans with 2½ quarts (5 pints) water and bring to a boil. Cover, turn the heat to low and simmer gently for 3-4 hours or until the beans are quite tender. With a potato masher, beat or mash about half the beans lightly until they form an exceedingly coarse purée. Half the beans should remain whole. Add the ginger, garlic, tomatoes, cayenne pepper, salt, butter, cream and Garam Masala.

Cook very gently for another 30 minutes, stirring occasionally. The beans may be served just this way with a final dollop of butter at the top. They are also very good with a tarka.

For the Tarka, heat the butter or oil in a frying pan over medium-high heat. Add the onion. When the onion is a rich reddish-brown color, add the cayenne pepper. Immediately lift up the pan and empty its contents into the pot with the beans. Garnish with the fresh cilantro before serving.

BLACK URAD BEANS are small black-skinned oval beans that are pale yellow inside. Their texture is somewhat glutinous. You can buy them from all Indian grocers. Ask for whole urad or sabut urad. In the Punjab, where they are very much loved, they are known as ma di dal.

Punjabi Garam Masala

Garam Masalas are spice combinations that vary in different parts of India. Here is a Punjabi version of this spice combination that is made in every Indian household.

Put the coriander and cumin into a cast-iron frying pan over medium heat. Stir until very lightly roasted. Empty onto a plate. Allow to cool slightly, then put the roasted spices and the remaining ingredients into a clean coffee grinder and grind as finely as possible. You may need to do this in more than one batch. Store in a tightly lidded jar.

5 tablespoons coriander seeds

3 tablespoons cumin seeds (see page 94)

2½ tablespoons black peppercorns

2½ tablespoons black cardamom seeds (see note)

1½ teaspoons green cardamom seeds (see note)

½ a cinnamon stick

4-5 cloves

About ⅙ whole nutmeg

CARDAMOM SEEDS that have been removed from their pods are sold separately by Indian grocers. If you cannot get them, take the seeds out of the pods yourself. The most aromatic pods are the ones that are green in color. White ones sold by supermarkets have been bleached and therefore have less flavor.

DRY SPLIT PEAS

Mrs. Kumud Kansara's Mugh Ni Dal - Serves 4

1 cup moong dal
   (see page 103)

5 tablespoons peanut or
   other vegetable oil

½ teaspoon cumin seeds
   (see page 94)

¼ teaspoon ground asafetida
   (see page 113)

4 fresh hot green chilies,
   finely chopped

¾ teaspoon salt

¼ teaspoon ground turmeric

½ cup water

The grains of moong dal cook quite separately here and look, to all intents and purposes, like rice. Gujaratis like to eat them with a chick-pea soup and plain rice. You may serve this with any Indian meal.

Wash the moong dal in several changes of water until the water runs clear. Drain. Soak in lukewarm water to cover by 1 inch (2.5 cm) for 3 hours. Drain.

Heat the oil in a heavy, medium-sized pan over medium-high heat. When hot, add the cumin seeds. Let them sizzle for 10 seconds. Add the asafetida. Stir once. Quickly add the moong dal, chilies, salt, turmeric and water. Stir to mix and bring to a boil. Cover very tightly, turn the heat to very, very low and cook for 15 minutes or until the water has been absorbed.

Mango Yogurt

Mrs. Kumud Kansara's Shrikhand · Serves 4

*I*n India, cooling yogurt is eaten throughout the year in different forms. Here it is transformed into a dessert. Shrikhand is generally served with the meal, although I actually prefer to serve it at the end.

Put a sieve over a small bowl. Line the sieve with a double layer of thin muslin or cheesecloth, large enough to tie into a bundle later.

Empty the yogurt into the sieve. Let the water drain into the bowl. Tie the corners of the muslin or cheesecloth tightly with string. Put a 4½ pound (2 kg) weight on top to extract the remaining water. Leave for 2 hours. You should end up with roughly 2½ cups (1 pint) drained yogurt. Discard the water.

Put the yogurt into a mixing bowl. Add the sugar. Beat for 4-5 minutes or until smooth and thick. Add the mango pulp. Mix well. Serve chilled.

2½ quarts (4 pints)
plain yogurt

1¾ cups sugar

1¼ cups mango pulp

MUSTARD GREENS

Jatinder Kaur's Sarson Da Saag - Serves 6

8 cups very finely chopped
spinach

8 cups very finely chopped
mustard greens

5 tablespoons coarsely
chopped garlic

4-6 fresh hot green chilies

1½-2 teaspoons salt

5-6 tablespoons cornmeal
flour (see note)

3 tablespoons vegetable oil
or ghee (see page 95)

1 onion, finely chopped

1 (2 inch) (5 cm) piece of
fresh ginger root, peeled
and cut into thin slivers

2 tomatoes, finely chopped

A dollop of unsalted butter

If you can imagine a buttery, meltingly soft, mustard-greens-flavored polenta, this is it. It is Punjab's very own winter specialty, made nowhere else in India. Something of a cross between a dish of greens and polenta, it is always eaten with Flat Corn Breads (see page 121) lathered generously with homemade white butter. If a Punjabi farmer comes in for lunch after a hard morning's work in the cold fields to find that his wife has prepared a big warming bowl of these greens, butter glistening at the top, a stack of flat corn breads and a tall glass of lassi (yogurt drink), he tends to return to the fields a very happy man.

The greens must cook slowly and for a long time. The fairly tough stems of the leaves need to turn very soft. If your greens are still a bit watery when you finish cooking them, you can increase the cornmeal flour by 1-2 tablespoons. The coarse purée of greens should be fairly thick, but still soft and flowing. It is best to use the cornmeal flour sold by Indian grocers. It has just the right texture for this dish and the breads. In the Punjab a special wooden tool is used to mash the greens in the pan in which they are cooked. Called a saag ghotna (greens masher), it looks somewhat like a wooden potato masher, with a long straight handle attached to a chunk of wood with a rounded base. A whisk, not an electric blender, is the best substitute.

Combine the spinach, mustard greens, garlic, chilies, salt and 3⅓ cups water in a large, heavy pan. Set over high heat and bring to a boil. Cover, turn the heat to low and simmer gently for 1¾ hours or until even the stems of the mustard green leaves have turned buttery soft.

With the heat still on, add 5 tablespoons of the cornmeal flour, beating constantly with a whisk or traditional greens masher. Using the same whisk or masher, mash the greens until they are fairly smooth (a little coarseness

is desirable). The greens will thicken with the addition of the cornmeal flour. If they remain somewhat watery, add another tablespoon or so. Leave on very low heat.

Heat the oil in a separate pan or wok over medium-high heat. When hot, add the onion. Stir and fry until it turns medium brown. Add the tomatoes. Stir and fry until the tomatoes have softened and browned a little. Now pour this mixture over the greens and stir it in. Empty the greens into a serving dish, top with the dollop of butter and serve.

THERE ARE MANY GRADES OF CORNMEAL FLOUR. The one used for tortillas is perhaps the closest to the Indian variety, but it is really best to buy this flour from Indian grocers.

PLANTAIN CHIPS

Mr. A. R. Sunil's Kaya Varathathu - Serves 4

Plantain chips, made from green cooking plantains, have always been sold all over India's south. (Today they are sold all over the north as well.) The best way to make them is to slice them directly into the hot oil using a mandolin or other slicing gadget.

Peel the plantains with a knife making sure that all the skin has been removed. Combine the tumeric, asafetida, salt and 2 tablespoons water in a small cup.

Heat the oil over medium heat in a wok or frying pan until it reaches 375°F (190°C). The oil is suitably hot if a cube of bread sizzles nicely and turns golden-brown. Slice the plantains directly into the hot oil. The chips must be thin and round. Make just enough to have one, slightly overlapping layer in the oil.

Quickly dip your fingers into the turmeric solution and sprinkle whatever liquid your fingers pick up over the chips. Stir and fry for 1-2 minutes, turning the chips half-way through this cooking time. Throw in a good pinch of the chopped chili and 2-3 curry leaves, if using. Fry for another few seconds and remove with a slotted spoon. The chips should remain yellow in color. Drain on paper towels. Make all the chips this way.

Leave to cool and store in an air-tight jar. They should last a good week.

2 green cooking plantains

½ teaspoon ground turmeric

¼ teaspoon asafetida (see note)

1¼ teaspoons salt

Oil for deep-frying

1 fresh hot green chili, finely chopped

15-20 fresh curry leaves (optional) (see page 98)

ASAFETIDA IS THE SAP FROM THE ROOTS AND STEM of a giant fennel-like plant. The sap dries into a hard resin. It is sold both in lump and ground form. Only the ground form is used here. It has a strong fetid aroma and is used in very small quantities both for its legendary digestive properties and for the much gentler, garlic-like aroma it leaves behind after cooking. (James Beard compared it to the smell of truffles.) Asafetida is excellent with dried beans and vegetables. Store in a tightly closed container.

Spinach *with* Coconut

Mrs. K. M. Matthew's Spinach Thoran · Serves 4

2 garlic cloves, peeled

1 small red onion or 2-3 large
  shallots, peeled and
  chopped

¼ teaspoon cayenne pepper

1 cup plus 1 tablespoon
  freshly grated coconut
  (see page 101)

1 teaspoon salt

9 cups washed and
  shredded spinach leaves

2 fresh hot green chilies,
  one finely chopped
  and one split in half

1 tablespoon coconut
  or other vegetable oil

½ teaspoon brown mustard
  seeds (see page 105)

1 teaspoon rice

2 shallots, finely sliced

15 fresh curry leaves
  (optional) (see page 98)

Thorans are generally cooked in woks. Vegetables, or shrimp, for that matter, are lightly sautéed or poached and then pushed to the edges of the wok. A mixture of fresh coconut and spices is placed in the center and covered over with the main ingredient. The wok is covered and the dish is allowed to cook gently. The results are light and delicious. Serve with any Indian meal. In this recipe, rice is used as a spice, adding an unusual nutty flavor.

If you wish to substitute unsweetened, dried coconut for fresh coconut use 10 tablespoons. Barely cover with warm water and leave for 1 hour, then proceed with the recipe.

Put the garlic, onion, cayenne pepper, coconut and salt into electric blender. Add 6 tablespoons water and blend to a smooth paste. Set aside.

Put the spinach in a wok or a large, wide, preferably non-stick frying pan over low heat. Sprinkle 3-4 tablespoons water over the top and cover. When steam begins to creep out the sides and the spinach has wilted, remove the lid. Make a well in the pile of spinach and spoon in the coconut paste and chopped chili. Cover with the spinach and replace the lid.

Again wait until steam appears, then remove the lid.

Meanwhile, heat the oil in a small pan over medium-high heat. When hot, add the mustard seeds and rice. As soon as the mustard seeds begin to pop and the rice expands, a matter of seconds, add the shallots. Stir and fry until the shallots start to turn golden. Add the split chili and the curry leaves, if using. Stir and fry for a second. Pour over the cooked spinach. Stir to mix.

STIR-FRIED CABBAGE *and* CARROTS

Mrs. A. Santha Ramanujam's Mutta Kose Kilangu · Serves 4

*S*trangely enough, when Tamils speaking English refer to a curry, they mean a dry dish, totally devoid of any sauce. This is one such "curry." You could cook the cabbage plain, or with carrots as I have done here, or with the addition of shelled peas. A similar dish can be made out of green beans, boiled beet roots and the pear-shaped green vegetable called chow chow and known more correctly as the chayote or sayote.

If you wish to substitute unsweetened, dried coconut for fresh coconut, use 5 tablespoons. Barely cover with warm water and soak for 1 hour, then proceed with the recipe.

Heat the oil in a large frying pan over medium-high heat. When hot, add the chana dal, urad dal and mustard seeds. Stir and fry until the mustard seeds pop and the dals turn reddish, a matter of seconds. Add the curry leaves, if using. Stir for a few seconds. Add the chilies and stir once. Now add the cabbage and carrots. Stir once to mix. Add the salt and mix again. Cover, turn the heat to low and cook for 5-6 minutes or until the cabbage is wilted and just tender.

Remove the cover. Add the coconut and mix it in with the cabbage, stirring vigorously for a minute or so.

Ingredients

- 3 tablespoons vegetable oil
- 1½ teaspoons chana dal (see note)
- 1½ teaspoons urad dal (see note)
- 1 teaspoon mustard seeds (see page 105)
- 20 fresh curry leaves (optional) (see page 98)
- 2-4 fresh hot green chilies
- 2½ cups finely shredded dark green cabbage
- 2 carrots, coarsely grated
- ¾-1 teaspoon salt
- ½ cup freshly grated coconut (see page 101)

CHANA DAL IS AN INDIAN VERSION OF YELLOW SPLIT PEAS but with better texture and a very nutty flavor. The peas come whole and split. Chana dal may be cooked by itself or it can be soaked and cooked with rice or vegetables or meat. In the south, it is used as a spice. It also goes into many Indian snacks of the "Bombay Mix" variety. Ask for it at any Indian grocery store.

URAD DAL IS A SMALL, PALE YELLOW SPLIT PEA that is used, among other things, to make all manner of South Indian pancakes. It has a slightly viscous texture. It is also used as a seasoning. It is south Indians who seem to have discovered that if you throw a few of these dried, split peas into hot oil, using the tarka method (see page 105), the seeds will turn red and nutty. Anything stir-fried in the oil afterwards will pick up that nutty flavor and aroma.

COCONUT PISTACHIO SWEETMEAT

Mrs. Kumud Kansara's Coco Pista Pasand - Makes 8 to 10 Sweets

FOR THE PISTACHIO FILLING

2 tablespoons shelled, unsalted pistachios

1 tablespoon powdered sugar

1 teaspoon white poppy seeds (see page 88)

½ tablespoon milk

FOR THE COCONUT CASING

⅔ cup sugar

5 cardamom pods, crushed in a mortar or ground in a clean coffee grinder (see page 117)

1½ cups unsweetened dried coconut

4 tablespoons canned condensed milk

Here is an Indian version of a sponge roll: the outside is sweetened coconut and the inside is pistachios.

To make the Pistachio Filling: put the pistachios into a clean coffee grinder. Grind to a coarse powder. Put the ground pistachios, sugar, poppy seeds and milk into a bowl. Mix to a paste. Set aside.

To make the Coconut Casing: put the sugar into a small heavy-bottomed pan. Add 4 tablespoons water. Stir and bring to a simmer. Cook over medium-high heat for 2-3 minutes until the syrup forms a single thread when a little is dropped from a spoon into a cup of cold water. Remove from the heat. Add the cardamom and coconut. Mix well. Add the condensed milk. Stir to mix.

Lay a 9 inch (23 cm) piece of plastic wrap on your work surface. While the coconut paste is still warm, roll it into a thick 9 inch (23 cm) cylinder. Put the coconut cylinder horizontally onto the center of the piece of plastic wrap and flatten it to form a rectangle about 3½ inches (9 cm) wide.

Roll the pistachio paste into a separate cylinder of the same length. Put the rolled pistachio cylinder on the coconut rectangle slightly below the center, a little closer to your end. With the aid of the plastic wrap, fold the coconut paste over the pistachio paste. Press down on the plastic wrap to firm up the roll. Now continue rolling, being careful to keep the plastic wrap on the outside of the roll, until you have a slim "Swiss Roll" or jelly roll. Press down evenly on the plastic wrap to get a neat roll. Let the roll cool and harden a bit. Remove the plastic wrap and cut crosswise into ½ inch (1 cm) thick slices.

PANCAKE CAKE

Bebinca - Serves 6 to 8

This is the festive cake Goans make for Christmas. Come December even the humblest of housewives sets about the task of making her bebinca. First one pancake is made. Then, batter for the second is poured over it and cooked from the top. Then comes the batter for the third and then the fourth ... and so on until she ends up with a caramelized confection that tastes like a rich, dense fruitcake. For anyone who wants high cakes of many layers, it can take all day. This particular cake has only 5-6 layers. A bebinca can be made several days in advance. Store, covered, in a cool spot.

1 cup brown sugar

5 cardamom pods, crushed (see note)

1 cup all-purpose flour

5 egg yolks

1 cup coconut milk

½ tablespoon ghee (see page 95) or melted butter

Make a syrup by putting the sugar and the crushed cardamom pods in a small pan and adding 1 cup water. Heat gently until all the sugar is dissolved and then allow to cool. Strain to remove the cardamom pods (it is fine if a few traces remain).

Combine the flour, egg yolks, coconut milk and cooled syrup in a medium-sized bowl. Beat well to make a smooth batter. Set aside to rest for 30 minutes.

Turn the grill (broiler) to high. Take an 8 inch (20 cm) crêpe pan or sturdy non-stick frying pan and set it on medium-high heat. Pour in the melted butter. When hot, ladle in ½ cup of the batter, making sure that it spreads to the edges by tilting the pan in all directions. Cook over medium heat until the bottom is golden.

Place the pan under the grill (broiler) and allow the pancake to turn golden brown on top. You may need to adjust your grill (broiler) by turning the heat down slightly. The pancake should not burn.

Now ladle a further ½ cup batter over the first pancake, spread it around and place under the grill (broiler) until the second layer, too, is golden brown. Continue this way until all the batter is used up. Allow the bebinca to cool overnight before turning it out of the pan.

GREEN CARDAMOM PODS are the small fruit of a ginger-like plant, holding clusters of black, highly aromatic seeds that smell like a combination of camphor, eucalyptus, orange peel and lemon. Whole pods are put into rice and meat dishes and ground seeds are the main flavor in garam masala. This versatile spice is the "vanilla" of India and is used in most desserts and sweets. It is also added to spiced tea and sucked as a mouth freshener.

BLACK CARDAMOM PODS are somewhat like the smaller cardamom in flavor, but have seeds with a cruder, heavier flavor and aroma.

Spongy, Spicy, Savory Diamonds

Mrs. Kumud Kansara's Khaman Dhokla - Makes 20 to 30 Diamonds

For the Batter

1 tablespoon peanut oil or any other vegetable oil

1¾ cups chick-pea flour, sifted

¼ cup plus 1 tablespoon sugar

2 teaspoons salt

½ teaspoon citric acid (see note)

1 teaspoon Eno's Fruit Salt (see note)

Dhoklas are spongy, savory cakes which can be cut into squares or diamonds. Belonging to the general family of dhoklas, this is known locally as just plain khaman. Wonderfully sweet, sour and slightly hot, all at the same time, they may be served as part of a meal or eaten as a snack with tea.

All dhoklas need to be steamed. It is important that you check your steaming apparatus before you start. A large wok, with a cover, is the ideal steaming utensil. The ideal steaming tray is an Indian thali, about 12 inches (30 cm) in diameter, with sides that are about 1½ inches (3 cm) high. The steaming time varies according to the size of the steaming tray and the thickness of the batter. If you are using a large wok for your steaming and your steaming tray is the thali suggested above, your steaming time will be about 30 minutes. However, if your steaming gadget is smaller and you can only fit in an 8 inch (20 cm) tray with 1 inch (2.5 cm) sides, the steaming would take about 15 minutes and you will have to steam in two batches. The way to test if a dhokla is done is to insert a toothpick into it as you would for a cake. If it comes out clean and the dhokla feels spongy and resistant, then it is ready.

If you are cooking a dhokla in two batches, divide all the ingredients in half. It is best to have two steaming trays. Make one batch and put it in to steam. Then make your second batch from scratch, beating in the water and the baking soda just before you are ready to steam.

To start with, measure out all your dry ingredients, as you would for a cake, and grease your steaming trays. Get the water boiling in your steaming utensil and have extra boiling water ready in case you need it to refill the utensil.

Get everything ready for steaming. Pour approximately 3 inches (7.5 cm) of water into the wok. You should be able to fit the thali or tray near the top of the wok. You may need to rest it on a small dish so that it is secure rather than wedged in. It should sit above the water level. Bring the water in the wok to the boil. Grease the tray or trays with the 1 tablespoon of oil.

If you are steaming the Batter in one batch, put the chick-pea flour, sugar, salt, and citric acid into a mixing bowl. Slowly add 1½ cups water as you beat the mixture to a thick, smooth batter. The color should become lighter and the mixture double in volume. Add the Eno's Fruit Salt. Gently beat for a further 1-2 minutes. The mixture should bubble.

Quickly pour the batter into the baking tray, place the tray in the wok, cover the wok and steam for 30 minutes or until a toothpick inserted into the cake comes out clean and the cake has a light, fluffy, sponge-like texture. Cut into 1 inch (2.5 cm) squares or diamonds.

If the dhokla is to be cooked in 2 separate batches, divide the flour mixture into 2 equal lots. Add only half the water to each lot and beat it in just before steaming it. Follow general directions.

Meanwhile, for the Spices, heat the 4 tablespoons oil in a small pan over medium-high heat. When hot, add the mustard seeds. As soon as they pop, a matter of seconds, remove the pan from the heat. Add the asafetida, chilies and ¾ cup plus 1 tablespoon water. Return the pan to medium-high heat. Add the sugar, citric acid and salt. Bring to a boil. Boil for 2 minutes or until you have a light syrup. Remove from the heat.

Pour the syrup evenly over the cooked dhokla. Sprinkle the fresh cilantro and dried coconut over the top.

For the Spices

4 tablespoons peanut oil or any other vegetable oil

½ teaspoon brown mustard seeds (see page 105)

¼ teaspoon ground asafetida (see page 113)

6 fresh hot green chilies, roughly chopped

1 tablespoon sugar

¼ teaspoon citric acid (see note)

½ teaspoon salt

2 tablespoons finely chopped fresh cilantro

1 tablespoon fresh or dried coconut (see page 101)

CITRIC ACID IS A WHITE, WATER-SOLUBLE POWDER which has a strong acidic taste. It occurs mainly in citrus fruits and it is obtained by fermentation of raw sugar or corn sugar. You can find it in Indian grocer shops or in some pharmacies.

ENO'S FRUIT SALT IS A WHITE POWDER ANTACID sold in small glass jars. It is made in India and available in Indian grocer shops.

DEEP-FRIED STUFFED BREADS

Sonali Basu's Koraishuti Kachori · Makes 15

≈

FOR THE STUFFING

1 cup shelled green peas or frozen, defrosted peas

1 (¾ inch) (2 cm) piece of fresh ginger root, peeled and finely sliced

2 fresh hot green chilies, roughly chopped

1½ teaspoons sugar

1 teaspoon salt

4 tablespoons vegetable oil

1 teaspoon ghee (see page 95) or vegetable oil

1½ tablespoons all-purpose flour

1 tablespoon cumin seeds

1 bay leaf

FOR THE DOUGH

2 scant cups all-purpose flour, plus extra for rolling

½ tablespoon vegetable oil

½ teaspoon salt

½ teaspoon sugar

A pinch of kalonji (see page 92)

Oil for deep-frying

Bengalis like their deep-fried breads made out of white flour. While other Northerners eat pooris made out of whole-wheat flour, Bengalis make very similar breads that they call loochis out of plain white flour. Sometimes, these loochis are stuffed with crushed peas. They are then called koraishuti kachori and are eaten at breakfast or as a mid-morning snack. I like this version of the bread.

For the Stuffing, put the peas, ginger, chilies, sugar and salt into the container of an electric blender. Add 3 tablespoons water and blend to a purée.

Heat the 4 tablespoons oil and the ghee in a large, wide, preferably non-stick pan or wok over medium heat. When hot, add the puréed peas. Stir and fry for 6-8 minutes. Add the 1½ tablespoons flour. Stir and fry for 2 minutes and remove from the heat.

Set a small pan over low heat. When hot, dry roast the cumin seeds and bay leaf for 2 minutes until the cumin seeds turn golden. Remove from the heat. Put the roasted cumin and bay leaves into a clean coffee grinder. Grind to a fine powder. Add the ground bay leaves and cumin to the puréed peas. Stir to mix. Set aside to cool.

For the Dough, put the flour, oil, salt, sugar, kalonji and ⅔ cup water into a bowl. Mix and knead, using your hands, for about 5 minutes to make a smooth dough. Divide the dough into 15 equal-sized balls. Flatten each ball to a 2 inch (5 cm) round. Put 1 teaspoon of the pea purée into the center of each round. Close the dough around the pea mixture and squeeze the edges to seal the opening well, so that no pea purée will escape. On a lightly floured surface, roll the stuffed dough balls to 5 inch (13 cm) circles.

Meanwhile, heat the oil for deep-frying in a wok or frying pan over medium heat. Let the oil get really hot. Drop in one of the breads carefully, making sure that it does not double over. It should start sizzling immediately. Baste the bread with quick motions, pushing it gently into the oil. It should puff up in seconds. Turn it over and cook for another 30 seconds. Remove with a slotted spoon. Make all the breads this way. Either eat them immediately or stack them on a plate and keep them covered with an inverted plate.

FLAT CORN BREADS

Makes 8 Breads

In the small towns and villages of the Punjab all the women and many of the men can form these flat corn breads by hand in seconds. For those not used to it, this is quite an art – but one well worth learning. I have described the method below. You may, if you prefer, roll them out with a rolling pin, just as you would any other Indian flat breads, into 6½ inch (16 cm) rounds. Just keep your rolling surface well dusted with flour. The edges of the breads may crack a little but that does tend to happen with the rolled version.

These breads are always served with Mustard Greens and are a winter delight. They are best enjoyed with a nice layer of butter slathered on them while they are still hot!

3 cups cornmeal flour
(see page 112)

1 teaspoon salt

About 1¾ cups plus
1 tablespoon warm water
(it should be just bearable
to the touch)

Unsalted butter for spreading
on breads (about 2-3
teaspoons per bread)

Mix the cornmeal and salt in a large, shallow bowl. Gradually add as much warm water as you need (aim for the texture of play-dough), mixing the water until it is incorporated into the flour. Knead for 10 minutes, or until the dough is pliable. Divide the dough into 8 equal portions and form into balls. Flatten the balls to form patties and keep them covered. Set a cast-iron frying pan or tava over high heat. Wait for it to get really hot.

Take one patty and dip it in the extra flour. Roll the edges of the patty in the flour as well, as if it were a wheel. Put the patty down on a floured work surface. Press down repeatedly on the patty with the palm of one hand while turning the patty a little. This will keep flattening it and thinning it out. Keep your other hand at the edge of the patty and push in slightly to prevent the edges from breaking. Dip the patty in the flour a second time if you need to.

When you have a disc about 6½ inches (16 cm) in diameter, lift it up carefully and slap it onto the hot frying pan or tava. Let it sit for 1 minute. Turn it over. Let it cook on the second side for 40 seconds. Turn it over again and cook for 30 seconds. This time, using a bunched-up cloth, press down on the bread in different spots to help it puff up slightly. Now turn it over. Cook for another 30 seconds, pressing down with the cloth. Turn it again and cook for 30 seconds. The bread should have attractive brown spots and be cooked through. If not, turn one more time.

Take it off the heat. Pinch it in a few spots and spread generously with the butter. Make all the breads this way. Keep them in a covered dish as you make them and eat them while they are hot with a slathering of unsalted butter.

GOAN BREAD

Poee - Makes 6 Breads

1 teaspoon sugar

1 teaspoon dried yeast

*3½ cups all-purpose flour,
plus extra for dusting*

Pinch of salt

*P*oee is somewhat like pita bread only it is butterfly-shaped and very spongy inside, full of large, airy holes. It can be bought in most Goan markets but it is best to go straight to the local baker and buy it just as it comes out of the oven.

There is one such bakery, with a huge beehive oven made of clay, glass pieces and salt, in the tiny town of Parra. Large wooden paddles push dough in and pull breads out. Breads line the room. Huge blobs of very soft dough rise in another room. The smell is heavenly.

Poees can be eaten with all Goan and many Indian meals.

Let the sugar dissolve in ½ cup warm water, then sprinkle over the dried yeast. Mix until smooth. Set aside for 10 minutes or until the yeast is frothy.

Place the flour and salt in a large bowl. Pour in the yeast mixture and 1½ cups water. Mix well, using your hands or a fork. When all the liquid has been incorporated into the flour, turn the dough out onto a well-floured board (it will be very soft) and knead well for 5 minutes, dusting with flour frequently to prevent it from sticking to the surface.

When it has become smooth and elastic, place it in a bowl and cover with a clean cloth. Put the bowl in a warm place for about an hour, or until the dough has doubled in size.

Preheat the oven to 425°F (220°C). Turn the dough out and knead briefly again on a well-floured board. Cut into 6 equal pieces and knead these into slightly flattened rounds (see drawing A). Slash each over the top in the center with a sharp knife (see drawing B) or blade and spread out both to the right and left, as if you were opening a book (see drawing C). Place the buns on a greased baking sheet and allow to rise for at least 30 minutes – they should now look like flat butterflies (see drawing D).

Sprinkle the breads with flour and place them in the oven for 15-20 minutes, or until they are golden brown.

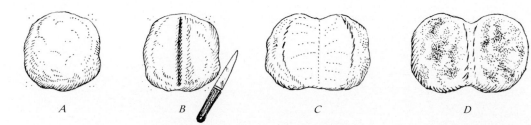

A   *B*   *C*   *D*

PUFFED LEAVENED BREADS

Bhatura - Makes about 18 breads.

Rather like North Indian pooris, these are puffed, deep-fried breads. The difference is they are made with white flour and have leavening and yogurt in the dough, which makes them slightly spongy. They may be eaten with any split peas, beans and vegetables and are also delightful with kebabs inside them.

In a large shallow bowl, mix together the flour, semolina, baking powder, baking soda and salt. Whisk the yogurt, ¾ cup water and sugar in a separate bowl. Make a well in the center of the flour mixture and slowly pour in the yogurt mixture, mixing as you do so, until it is fully absorbed. Knead this dough until it is pliable but firm. Cover with a damp cloth and let it stand for 15 minutes.

Melt the butter and mix it into the dough. Knead for another 5 minutes. Cover with a damp cloth and let the dough rest for 45 minutes. Break the dough into 1¼ inch (3 cm) wide balls. There should be about 18.

Heat the oil in a wok or large frying pan over high heat to 375°F (190°C). While it heats, dust your rolling surface with flour. Flatten one ball in the flour. Roll the ball out with a rolling pin, dusting it with flour when needed, until you have a disc about 5 inches (13 cm) in diameter.

Lift up the discs carefully, without allowing it to fold up, and slip it into the hot oil. It should sink to the bottom and rise immediately. Quickly flip it over. Keep tapping it lightly with a slotted spoon, pushing it down gently into the oil as you do so. It should puff up within seconds. Turn it over after 30 seconds and fry for a further 20-30 seconds or until it is golden and crisp. Remove with a slotted spoon.

Rest briefly on paper towels to drain and then put on a plate. Cover with a domed lid or inverted bowl. Make all the breads this way and serve immediately.

3 cups plus 2 tablespoons all-purpose flour, plus extra for dusting

½ cup semolina (sooji) (see note)

½ teaspoon baking powder

¼ teaspoon baking soda

1 teaspoon salt

2 tablespoons yogurt made from whole milk

2 teaspoons sugar

2 tablespoons ghee (see page 95) or unsalted butter

Vegetable oil for deep-frying

SEMOLINA (SOOJI) IS WHEAT ground to the texture of grain cornmeal or polenta. It is sold by Indian grocers as sooji and really has no good substitute. The supermarket semolina tends to be far too fine for Indian pilafs and halvas.

NICK NAIRN

Nick's television programs on Great Food are not whimsically named "Wild Harvest." This young rising star of Scotland uncovers for his viewers the "wild harvests" that Nick uses to create the acclaimed food that is served in his highly rated restaurant *Braeval,* near Aberfoyle.

Taking a ferry to the Isle of Skye, Nick goes fishing for squat lobster then cooks *Lasagna of Squat Lobster with Herbs and Tomato;* an organic lamb farmer helps Nick make *Roast Rump of Lamb with Crushed Potatoes and Olive Oil and Rosemary Sauce;* while the apple orchards of Kelly Castle yield the juicy treasures that are the tender morsels for apple pie.

"Traveling around Scotland has reaffirmed my faith – as if I ever needed it – in the strength of the natural produce available these days. I've hand-dived my own scallops, been up all night in search of a sea trout, and got down on my hands and knees in the forest foraging for wild mushrooms. People say that we have no legacy of fine dining in Scotland, yet I believe we have the finest raw ingredients in the world."

Nick Nairn's enthusiasm to create recipes that show off simple but high quality basic ingredients, started him on an unexpected course. Nick is a self-taught chef who has elevated himself from "not being able to boil an egg" to being the youngest chef to win a Michelin star in Scotland. This young and energetic man believes if he can do it, anyone can.

"I was a natural at mixing gin and tonics, but the rest didn't fall into place until much, much later. The thing was, I liked hanging out in the kitchen, but the aspiration to become a good cook was fueled by something else entirely. I was home on leave from the Navy and found that man does not live on canned spaghetti sauce alone.

"What I learned was there was no big mystery: it's just food, the simpler the better. With a good sharp knife and a chopping board, you're really halfway there. Time passes and tastes change. What's important is for people to believe that the best food in the world is on their own doorstep. Enjoy your own Wild Harvests."

ROAST SCALLOPS *with* COUSCOUS *and a* RICH SHELLFISH SAUCE

Serves 4

*S*callops are sweet and succulent and lend themselves to the neatest of presentations. The scallops Alan Peace provided for the filming of my television show on Great Food were delicious, plump and so fresh that they almost crunch in the mouth. The tomato liquid I use as a basis for the sauce is superb but you can substitute vegetable stock. The beautiful orange corals or roe sacs attached to the scallops, add a brilliant color and essential flavor to the sauce, while the couscous soaks it all up nicely.

The day before, put the tomatoes in a food processor with the basil, tarragon and salt and pepper to taste. Process for a few seconds until coarsely chopped but be careful not to purée them. Transfer into a muslin-lined sieve set over a large mixing bowl and let drain overnight in the refrigerator or a cool place. The following day you will have about ½ cup of light-colored but intensely flavored tomato juice.

The day of serving, detach the corals from the scallops, cut them into small dice and set aside for the sauce. Cut each scallop horizontally into 3 or 4 discs, depending on the thickness, and set aside.

Bring the Nage or fish stock to the boil in a large pan. Add the couscous in a slow, steady stream, stirring all the time. It should look like a thick porridge. Remove from the heat, cover with a tight-fitting lid and let sit for 5 minutes. Fluff up the grains with a fork and add the chopped green onions, chilies, pickled ginger, cilantro, mint, garlic and lime zest. Add 1 tablespoon of the lime juice, olive oil and salt and pepper to taste.

Cover and set aside. It can be reheated after it has cooled, if you wish.

For the shellfish sauce, put the tomato juice into a small pan and bring to the boil. Add the diced scallop corals and purée with a hand blender or in an electric blender. When smooth, return to the pan. Now add the cold diced butter, either by whisking in a few pieces at a time over a low heat or puréeing with the hand blender. Taste for salt and pepper and keep warm, but don't let it boil.

Heat a frying pan over a high heat. Add the Clarified Butter or sunflower oil and the scallop slices and cook for about 1 minute on just one side. Quickly transfer to a baking tray, cooked-side-up, sprinkle with the salt and pepper to taste and with a little of the remaining lime juice.

To serve, put a large biscuit cutter on each plate, pack in the couscous and remove the cutter (this gives a neat shape). Pour the sauce around and arrange the scallop slices on top of the couscous.

8 ounces (225 g) fresh, ripe plum tomatoes, quartered

A few fresh basil leaves

A few fresh tarragon leaves

8 large fresh scallops, with their corals, shelled (see introduction)

1⅛ cups Nage (see page 156) or fish stock

¾ cup couscous

4 green onions, finely chopped

2 fresh red chilies, seeded and finely chopped

2 tablespoons Japanese pickled ginger, finely chopped

2 tablespoons chopped fresh cilantro

1 tablespoon chopped fresh mint

1 garlic clove, crushed

Juice and finely grated zest of 1 lime

3 tablespoons olive oil

4 tablespoons cold unsalted butter, diced

1 tablespoon Clarified Butter (see page 154) or sunflower oil

Salt to taste

Freshly ground white pepper to taste

Opposite: Peppered Fillet of Beef with Straw Sweet Pototoes (page 134).

Lasagna *of* Squat Lobster *with* Herbs *and* Tomato

3 pounds (1.5 kg) live squat
   lobsters, lobsters or
   langoustines

8 dried lasagna noodles,
   broken in half

4 cups Nage (see page 156)

½ cup very finely diced
   mixed vegetables, such
   as leek, carrot, celery
   and fennel

¼ cup olive oil

2 tablespoons Tomatoes
   Concassées (see page 151)

2 tablespoons chopped
   mixed fresh herbs,
   such as chervil,
   chives and parsley

1 tablespoon lemon juice

Salt to taste

Freshly ground white pepper
   to taste

Sprigs of fresh chervil, for
   garnish

Squat lobsters are too often overlooked in favor of larger shellfish, such as langoustines, which can command higher prices from restaurants. They are, however, a true bargain, and though they might be a bit fiddly, their sweet delicate flavor makes this my favorite of all the dishes we cooked on this series of television shows for Great Food.

First cook the live squat lobsters, lobsters or langoustines. Have some salted water at a full boil in a pot large enough to take all the lobsters. Plunge them in, cover and let the water come back to the boil. Now cook for 2 minutes, then take the lobsters out of the pan and immediately put them into cold water. This stops the cooking process. Remember, the biggest sin you can commit with any kind of fish is to overcook it. Leave it as late as you can before you take them out of the shells, otherwise the meat will dry out, but don't leave them lying around for more than 24 hours.

Cook the lasagna in boiling salted water until al dente and drain. Now pour the Nage into a wide shallow pan and boil until reduced by half. Add the mixed vegetables and simmer for 3-4 minutes, then add the shelled lobster tails, olive oil, Tomato Concassées, chopped herbs and cooked lasagna noodles. Season with salt and pepper, add the lemon juice and warm through for about 30 seconds.

Divide among shallow serving bowls, giving everybody equal amounts of lasagna noodles, lobsters and sauce. Take a bit of care here and you'll have quite an impressive assortment of colors and textures. Decorate with the sprigs of chervil.

Pan-Fried Mallard *with* Stir-Fried Greens *and a* Whiskey, Soy, Honey *and* Lemon Sauce

Serves 4

*T*he secret of success here is to get the sweet and sour balance in the sauce just right. Mallard is smaller than farmed duck, but leaner and much tastier. If you can't get mallard, use four small female duck breasts.

Boil the stock vigorously until reduced to ½ cup. Add the whiskey, honey, soy sauce, lemon juice, and seasoning and set aside.

Season the breasts well. Heat a large frying pan until very hot, add a good splash of sunflower oil, then the breasts, skin-side-down. Cook for 4-5 minutes until crisp and brown. Cook the other side for 2 minutes, leaving the centers pink. Remove and leave in a warm place for 10 minutes. Add a little oil if necessary, add the green onions, beans, asparagus and peas and sir-fry over a high heat for 1-2 minutes. Season well. Bring the sauce back to the boil, lower the heat and whisk in the butter. Check for seasoning.

To serve, carve each breast diagonally into slices. Put the vegetables on warm serving plates, arrange the mallard on top, then pour the sauce around.

Variation

Roast the mallard bones for 30 minutes. Brown ¼ cup each of chopped shallots, mushrooms, carrot and celery in 2 table-spoons sunflower oil. Add 1 tablespoon tomato paste. Deglaze with ⅔ cup port. Add 1⅛ cups beef stock, 2 cups chicken stock and bones. Simmer for 1 hour, strain and chill overnight. Lift off the fat and boil vigorously until reduced to ⅔ cup. Add 1 tablespoon chives, 1 ounce (25 g) finely chopped summer truffle and seasoning. Cook the mallard as above and serve on ½ pound (225 g) spinach that has been wilted, Mini Potato Fondants (see page 143) and the sauce.

2 mallard ducks, breasts removed and carcasses used to make 2 cups stock (or use 2 cups chicken stock)

2 tablespoons whiskey

1 tablespoon good honey

1 tablespoon light soy sauce

2 tablespoons lemon juice

Sunflower oil

6 green onions, cut in strips

¾ cup fine green beans, halved and blanched

¾ cup asparagus, blanched

¾ cup sugar snap peas, blanched

2 tablespoons butter, cubed

Salt to taste

Freshly ground white pepper to taste

Peppered Fillet *of* Beef *with* Straw Sweet Potatoes *and a* Salad *of* Herbs

Serves 4

3 tablespoons black
    peppercorns

4 (6 ounce) (175 g) beef fillet
    steaks

4 teaspoons Dijon mustard

Salt to taste

1½ pounds (750 g) sweet
    potatoes, cooked as
    for Straw Potatoes
    (see page 144)

2 tablespoons Clarified
    Butter (see page 154)

4 tablespoons unsalted
    butter

¼ cup Armagnac or Cognac

¼ cup beef stock

3 tablespoons heavy
    whipping cream

1 tablespoon olive oil

Herb Salad (see page 142)

Freshly ground white pepper
    to taste

This is a simple dish but a real masterpiece. The pale pinky-orange color of the sweet potatoes gives it a welcome twist. The steak is carefully fried then coated in buttery, meaty juices. Just that. Heaven. (Illustrated on page 128.)

Coarsely crush the peppercorns in a coffee grinder. Tip the pepper into a fine sieve and shake out all the powder. This is very important because the powder will make the steaks far too spicy. Now spread the peppercorns over a small plate. Smear both sides of the steaks with the Dijon mustard and coat them in the crushed peppercorns. Only now season with the salt, because salting first would prevent the pepper sticking to the meat. Set aside.

Cook the sweet potatoes as for Straw Potatoes.

Heat a large frying pan until hot. Add the Clarified Butter and then the steaks and cook for about 2 minutes on each side (a bit longer if you don't like your meat rare). Do not move them around once they are in the pan or the peppercorn crust will fall off.

The aim is to produce a good crust coating on each surface. Now add the unsalted butter to the pan and let it cook just until it turns a nut brown color, spoon the steaks with the buttery juices as you cook. Transfer the steaks to a baking tray and leave in a warm place.

Add the Armagnac or Cognac to the pan and boil over a high heat for 1 minute. Add the beef stock, bring back to the boil and pour in the cream. Scrape the bottom of the pan and stir any gooey bits into the sauce. It is now ready to serve.

Dress the Herb Salad. Pour any juices from the steak baking tray back into the sauce. Place a steak on each plate with a pile of the Herb Salad and the Straw Potatoes. Spoon the sauce over the steaks and serve.

SADDLE *of* HARE *with* WILD RICE, GAME SAUCE *and* RED ONION MARMALADE

Serves 4

Each saddle of hare gives two loins and one loin is sufficient for one portion. Get your butcher to bone out the saddles and trim up the loins. He can then also hack up the bones for the stock while he's at it.

Preheat the oven to 475°F (240°C). For the sauce, put the reserved bones (see introduction), bay leaf, thyme, shallots, garlic, mushrooms, olive oil and juniper berries in a small roasting pan. Roast for 35-45 minutes, stirring now and then until well browned. Add the port and scrape up all the bits from the bottom of the pan. Pour everything into a saucepan, add water to cover, bring to the boil and simmer for 1 hour. Pour into a conical strainer or a fine sieve set over another pan and press out all the liquid with the back of a ladle or wooden spoon. Boil vigorously, skimming off any scum, until reduced to ½ cup.

For the Rice, put the rice into a large pan with the water, onion, carrot, bay leaf and thyme. Add salt and pepper to taste, bring to the boil, cover and simmer for about 35 minutes, until tender. Some of the grains will burst but that's O.K. Drain, remove the aromatics, cover and keep warm.

Sprinkle the hare with the salt and pepper to taste. Heat a frying pan until very hot, add the sunflower oil, half the butter and the hare and cook for 2-3 minutes on each side until well browned but still pink in the center. Remove from the heat and let rest in a warm place for 10 minutes.

To serve, gently warm the Red Onion Marmalade in a small pan. Cut the hare into thin slices. Put the rice on 4 warmed plates and arrange the hare on top. Bring the sauce to the boil and whisk in the remaining butter. Check the seasoning and then pour the sauce around the rice and drizzle with the olive oil, if you wish. Spoon the marmalade on top and garnish with the Deep-Fried Parsley.

2 prepared saddles of hare, bones reserved separately (see introduction)

1 bay leaf

1 sprig fresh thyme

2 shallots, roughly chopped

1 garlic clove, crushed

¾ cup button mushrooms, roughly chopped

2 tablespoons olive oil

6 juniper berries, crushed

⅔ cup ruby port

1 tablespoon sunflower oil

4 tablespoons butter

4 tablespoons Red Onion Marmalade (see page 155)

Olive oil to taste

Salt to taste

Freshly ground white pepper to taste

Deep-Fried Parsley, for garnish (see page 155)

FOR THE RICE

1½ cups wild rice

3 cups water

1 small onion, quartered

1 carrot, sliced

1 bay leaf

1 sprig fresh thyme

ROAST RUMP *of* LAMB *with* CRUSHED POTATOES *and* OLIVE OIL *and* ROSEMARY SAUCE

Serves 4

1 tablespoon olive oil, plus
   extra to serve (optional)

1 pound (450 g) rump bottom
   round of lamb, plus
   4 ounces (100 g) of fat
   trimmings

1 small onion, finely sliced

1 garlic clove, crushed

1 tablespoon tomato paste

1 (8 ounce) (225 g) can
   chopped tomatoes

1¼ cups red wine

1¼ cups beef stock

1¼ cups chicken stock

1 tablespoon sunflower oil

1 tablespoon softened butter

1 teaspoon finely chopped
   fresh rosemary or basil

6 plum Tomatoes Concassées
   (see page 151)

Salt to taste

Freshly ground white pepper
   to taste

Rosemary, garlic and tomato are lamb's traditional allies but it's a versatile meat and can successfully take on so many other flavors – anything and everything except lurid shop-bought mint sauce, really. It doesn't like heavy sauces, however, so I've given this one a refined, classic treatment. The olives and anchovies in the crushed potatoes work particularly well with the tender, pink meat.

I recommend asking your butcher to seam-bone your lamb. Seam boning is mainly a European practice but, like many traditional butchery techniques, it should be more widely used. It splits the meat of a leg down into individual muscles, of which, the rump is one, which gives you no gristle and an even texture.

Try to make the sauce the day before, as this is complicated special-occasion cookery. It also makes it much easier to skim off the fat, which will have solidified on top.

Heat a large frying pan. Add the olive oil and the lamb trimmings and stir-fry for about 5 minutes, until well browned. Add the onion and garlic and cook for 5 minutes. Add the tomato paste and the canned tomatoes, turn up the heat and boil off any liquid. Add the red wine and boil for about 15-20 minutes, until thick. Add the beef and chicken stock, bring to the boil, then reduce the heat and simmer rapidly for another 20 minutes. Pour the sauce into a fine sieve set over a bowl and use the back of a wooden spoon to force it through. You should be left with about 1¼ cups sauce, so reduce further, if necessary. Let cool and then chill. Skim off any solidified fat from the top.

The day of serving, preheat the oven to 425°F (220°C). Cook the potatoes in boiling salted water until tender. Drain and set aside. While the potatoes are cooking, heat an ovenproof frying pan until very hot. Sprinkle the lamb with salt and pepper to taste. Add the sunflower oil to the pan, then the lamb and the butter and cook over a high heat for 2-3 minutes on each side, until well browned. Then place the pan in the oven for 7-12 minutes, depending on how rare you like your meat. Transfer to a warm place.

Return the potatoes to their cooking pot and crush coarsely with the back of a fork. Add the pan juices from the lamb, the diced olives, anchovies and basil, mix well and taste for salt and pepper.

Now reheat the skimmed sauce. Stir in the chopped rosemary or basil and the Tomatoes Concassées. Bring back to the boil, taste for salt and pepper, and it's ready.

To serve, place a 3 inch (7.5 cm) pastry cutter in the center of one serving plate and fill with the potatoes. Lift off the ring and repeat with the other plates. Pour the sauce around. Carve the lamb and place 3 to 4 slices on top of the potatoes. Now, if you like, pour a little olive oil around the edge of the sauce in a nice puddle. And that's it – done!

FOR THE CRUSHED POTATOES

1 pound (450 g) new potatoes, scrubbed

12 black olives, pitted and diced

1 tablespoon finely diced anchovy fillets

1 tablespoon roughly chopped fresh basil

SEARED MACKEREL FILLETS *with* STIR-FRIED VEGETABLES *and a* FROTHY BUTTER SAUCE

Serves 4

½ cup fine green beans, halved

½ cup asparagus, cut into 2 inch (5 cm) lengths

4 green onions, cut into 2 inch (5 cm) lengths

1 small zucchini, cut into 2 inch (5 cm) sticks

9 ounces (250 g) egg thread noodles

1-2 tablespoons sunflower oil

4 (5 ounce) (150 g) mackerel, monkfish or herring fillets

Juice of ½ lime

Chili Oil to taste (see page 152)

1 teaspoon Thai fish sauce (nam pla)

½ recipe Nage Butter Sauce (see page 157)

½ cup loosely packed fresh finely chopped cilantro leaves

¼ cup heavy whipping cream, lightly whipped

Salt to taste

Freshly ground white pepper to taste

This is my favorite way to enjoy mackerel. One of my favorite memories of filming Wild Harvest for Great Food on the Isle of Skye is fishing for mackerel with Jerry Cox. Great shoals of mackerel filled the bay and we were able to walk out of Jerry's front door, straight onto his boat and catch our supper.

Bring a pan of salted water to the boil. Add the green beans and bring back to the boil. Add the asparagus and bring back to the boil. Add the green onions and zucchini, bring back to the boil and drain immediately. Refresh under cold running water to arrest the cooking and set the color. Leave to drain on a dish towel.

Bring a pan of salted water to the boil. Drop in the noodles, then remove the pan from the heat, cover and leave for 4 minutes. Drain and set aside. Toss with a teaspoon of the sunflower oil so the noodles don't stick together.

Heat a frying pan until really hot, add about a teaspoon of the sunflower oil, then the fish fillets, skin-side-down, and cook for 4 minutes. Turn over and fry for 2 minutes.

Transfer to a plate, pour over half the lime juice, sprinkle with the salt and pepper to taste and keep warm.

Heat a little more of the sunflower oil in the pan, add the cooked vegetables and stir-fry for just 1 minute. Add the Chili Oil, Thai fish sauce, remaining lime juice and salt and pepper to taste. Remove from the heat and set aside.

Now warm through the Nage Butter Sauce and whisk until light and frothy. Add the cilantro and whisk again, then whisk in the lightly whipped cream.

To serve, divide the noodles among 4 warmed bowls. Spoon the vegetables on top then crown with the fish, skin-side-up. Whisk the sauce until frothy and spoon around the edge of the bowls.

Seared Sea Trout *with* Zucchini Relish *and* Herb *and* Saffron Oil

Serves 4

Cooking fresh fish is a doddle: definitely not something to be scared of. A good sea trout combines the best qualities of both salmon and trout but is better than either. Expect a glossy, firm fish with a delicate flavor, so keep things as simple and panic-free as possible. The relish is sweet and aromatic with a wonderful warm flavor.

If you haven't already, make the Herb and Saffron Oils the day before.

The Zucchini Relish can be made in advance on the day you want to serve it. Cook the onions and garlic in the olive oil for 5 minutes, until softened. Add the sugar, tomato paste, balsamic vinegar, Worcestershire sauce and Tomato Concassées and simmer for 20 minutes, until very thick, then remove from the heat.

Cook the zucchinis in small batches over a very high heat, using about 1 tablespoon of the olive oil per batch, cooking for about 1 minute until lightly browned. This is very important for if you cook too many of the zucchini at a time over too low a heat they will release their liquid, which will make the relish go runny. Sprinkle with the salt and pepper to taste and then stir them into the cooked onions. Leave for at least 2 hours.

To finish the dish, put the Relish in a saucepan and cook over low heat until warmed through. Heat a frying pan over a high heat. Add a little of the sunflower oil, then add the trout fillets, skin-side-down, and cook for about 2 minutes until crisp and golden. Turn over and cook the other side for about 1 minute. Sprinkle with a little of the salt and pepper to taste and remove from the heat

To serve, place a pile of the warm Relish in the center of each plate. Drizzle the Herb and Saffron Oils over the rest of the plate, then put the trout, skin-side-up, on top of the Relish.

4 tablespoons Herb Oil
   (see page 153)

4 tablespoons Saffron Oil
   (see page 152)

Sunflower oil to taste

4 (5 ounce) (150 g) sea trout
   fillets, skin on

Salt to taste

Freshly ground white pepper
   to taste

FOR THE ZUCCHINI RELISH

1 small onion, sliced

1 garlic clove, crushed

2 tablespoons olive oil,
   plus extra for frying
   the zucchini

3 tablespoons soft light
   brown sugar

1 teaspoon tomato paste

¼ cup balsamic vinegar

1 tablespoon Worcestershire
   sauce

2 plum Tomatoes Concassées
   (see page 151)

1 pound (450 g) zucchini,
   cut into ½ inch (1 cm)
   dice

SPAGHETTI *with* CRAB, CHILI, GARLIC, PARSLEY *and* LEMON

Serves 2

1 (3 pound) (1.5 kg) crab
(see recipe) or 8 ounces
(250 g) white crab meat

FOR THE
COURT-BOUILLON

1 celery stick, coarsely
chopped

1 small onion, coarsely
chopped

1 carrot, coarsely chopped

1 garlic clove, lightly crushed

1 bay leaf

1 small bunch of fresh
parsley or herb stalks

FOR THE SPAGHETTI

⅓ cup olive oil

1 small fresh red chili, seeded
and very finely chopped

1 garlic clove, finely chopped

Juice and shredded zest of
1 lemon

8 ounces (225 g) spaghetti
or linguine

2 tablespoons chopped fresh
parsley

Salt to taste

Freshly ground white pepper
to taste

If you go to the trouble of cooking your own crab, make sure it's as big and firm as possible. Brown crabs are best, preferably ones that have big claws and feel heavy when you pick them up. The bigger they are, the easier it is to ferret out the delicious sweet flesh. I cook crabs in an unfashionable court-bouillon, or flavored cooking liquid, as I think it improves the taste. I also cook them for a much shorter time than most people, who recommend 20 minutes or more. You could use frozen or pasteurized crab meat but for a dish as simple as this, fresh is best.

Make sure the crab is alive when you buy it, then ask the fishmonger to kill it for you. If you cook it alive, the legs will fall off and overcook. Place the crab in a large pan with all the court-bouillon ingredients. Cover with cooled water and bring to the boil over a high heat. Once boiling, simmer for 2 minutes and then turn off the heat. Leave the crab to cool in the cooking water. It will be just cooked, and the meat nice and moist.

Remove the crab and discard the cooking water. Place the crab face down on a chopping board and give its back a slap with the heel of your hand. This should open it up. Pull off the claws and give them a bash with the back of a heavy knife or an old rolling pin. Pick out all the white meat from the claws, legs and body (the handle of a small teaspoon is useful for this). I usually stop there, as I'm not a great fan of the brown meat. You should have about 8 ounces (225 g) of white crab meat.

For the Spaghetti, place the olive oil, chili, garlic and lemon zest in a large saucepan and warm through until just simmering. Remove from the heat and let stand for 10 minutes (or you can let it cool completely and reheat it when you're ready to serve).

Meanwhile, cook the spaghetti in a large pan of boiling salted water until al dente and then drain. Add the lemon juice to the olive oil and chili mixture and salt and pepper to taste. Add the pasta and toss well, cooking until just warmed through, about 3 minutes. Add the crab meat and toss well, then the chopped parsley, tossing again. Heat until piping hot and divide among 4 warm serving bowls. I love this with Herb Salad (see page 142) and a glass of chilled Sancerre on the side.

GARLIC MUSHROOMS *on* TOAST

Serves 4

I use wild mushrooms on the Great Food television show, but this is a good opportunity to use big open-cup mushrooms. I'm assuming hungry people, so I'm allowing two per person. Real garlic lovers would add an extra clove or two, but don't sit next to me on the train!

Preheat the oven to 450°F (230°C). Remove the stalks from the mushrooms and chop coarsely. Now heat a frying pan until hot, add 1 tablespoon of the olive oil and put in the bacon. Stir-fry it until crisp. Add the mushroom stalks, onion, garlic and butter, reduce the heat and cook for about 7 minutes, until softened. Sprinkle with salt and pepper to taste, then add the parsley and bread crumbs and mix well. Remove from the heat and set aside.

Lightly brush a baking tray with the olive oil and put the mushroom caps on it, round-side-down. Brush the caps with about 3 tablespoons of the olive oil, then sprinkle with salt and pepper to taste and a good squeeze of the lemon juice. Now divide the filling between the mushrooms. If they look a bit dry, drizzle with a little more of the olive oil. Bake for 12-15 minutes.

Cut 8 (¾ inch) (2 cm) slices diagonally off the baguette and lay them on a baking tray. Brush generously with the olive oil. Sprinkle lightly with the salt and pepper and put them in the oven with the mushrooms. The bread will take about 7 minutes. Put the toasted bread on 4 serving plates, top each with a mushroom, then garnish with a sprig of the parsley and a drizzle of the olive oil.

8 large open-cup mushrooms, such as button or cremini mushrooms

6 tablespoons olive oil, approximately

4 slices smoked bacon, diced

1 small onion, finely chopped

2 garlic cloves, crushed

4 tablespoons butter

3 tablespoons chopped fresh flat leaf parsley

1 cup fresh white bread crumbs

Juice of ½ lemon

1 baguette (loaf of French bread)

Salt to taste

Freshly ground white pepper to taste

4 fresh parsley sprigs, for garnish

Herb Salad

Serves 4

1 cup loosely packed mixed
fresh herbs

Salt to taste

Freshly ground white pepper
to taste

1 tablespoon olive oil

1 teaspoon lemon juice

This turns up everywhere in my restaurant and is probably my favorite side dish of the moment. The fresh flavors of the herbs are far better than boring salad leaves. The secret is to divide the herbs into nice sprigs and keep them in a mixing bowl covered in plastic wrap in the refrigerator until you are ready to add the dressing. But do serve them the second the dressing goes on as they lose their texture and color rapidly. You can vary the herbs to suit each dish but I always return to the following combinations: basil, flat leaf parsley and arugula (rocket); chervil, tarragon and fennel; and chives, dill and chervil.

Season the herbs with a pinch of the salt and 4 turns of the white pepper in a pepper mill. Drizzle over the oil, add the lemon juice and gently toss the leaves to coat. Divide into 4 neat piles to serve, and that's it.

MINI POTATO FONDANTS

Serves 4

These potatoes are awash with butter but a little richness goes a long way. At Braeval we use the little French 'mids' but any new potato about 2-2½ inches (5-6 cm) in length will do. We usually allow four per portion but people invariably want more. The term, "fondant," refers to the classic French method of cutting potatoes in the form of long olives and cooking very gently until golden on the outside but still soft inside.

16-20 new potatoes

12 tablespoons unsalted
   butter

Salt to taste

Freshly ground white pepper
   to taste

Preheat the oven to 375°F (190°C). You need an ovenproof frying pan, preferably non-stick, which will hold all the potatoes in a single layer. First slice the tops and bottoms off the potatoes, which should leave you with unpeeled cylinders around 1 inch (2.5 cm) high. Now cut the butter into strips about ⅛ inch (3 mm) wide and line the base of the frying pan with them. Set the potatoes cut-face-down on top of the butter to fill the pan. Season well. Put the frying pan over a low to medium heat and keep an eye on it as the butter melts. It should just bubble gently but don't allow it to get too hot or you'll burn the bottoms of the potatoes. They should be nicely browned after about 35-40 minutes, so then put them into the oven for 10-15 minutes, to cook.

Take them out and let them stand in a warm place until you're ready to serve. They need about 10-20 minutes for the butter to be absorbed but will keep well for 1½ hours. To serve, lift them out of the pan, turn them over and place on the plate with the richly colored-side-up.

STRAW POTATOES

Serves 4

1 pound (450 g) potatoes,
  peeled

Sunflower oil for deep-frying

Salt to taste

Freshly ground white pepper
  to taste

Straw potatoes are thinner and crisper than regular French fries, and are great with a peppered steak and some salad. You can use all sorts of potatoes, even sweet potatoes. You really need a mandolin grater to get the right shape. I use the medium blade on my Japanese mandolin. A wok is good for deep-frying the potatoes as its shape helps prevent the oil from boiling over.

Use a mandolin to cut the potatoes into very narrow strips, about ⅛ inch (3 mm) thick. Wash them in cold water, then put them in a clean dish towel and wring out as much moisture as you can.

Pour 1 inch (2.5 cm) of the oil into a large deep saucepan or a wok and heat to 350°F (180°C) (you could, of course, use a deep-fat fryer). Drop the potatoes into the hot oil a few at a time. Don't cook all of them at once or the oil will boil over. Fry them, stirring from time to time, until pale golden, about 5-6 minutes. Drain on paper towel, season with the salt and pepper and serve. You can keep these warm in a low oven for 30 minutes.

Apple Soufflés *with* Apple Sorbet

Serves 6

*T*hese are two very different flavors at work here. The intense, cooked flavor of the soufflé and the light zing of the sorbet. The apple sorbet is one of the easiest puddings you'll ever have to make, and probably the cleverest. Leave the skins on the Granny Smiths and it will have a lovely pastel color.

First make the Apple Sorbet. Toss the apple pieces in 1 tablespoon of the lemon juice and then spread them over a baking tray and freeze for about 1 hour, until hard. Remove from the freezer and let thaw slightly at room temperature for 10 minutes. Transfer to a food processor, add the remaining lemon juice and the Stock Syrup and purée until smooth. Transfer the mixture to a plastic container, cover and freeze for 4 hours, until firm.

For the Apple Soufflés, put the diced apples, cider and Calvados into a saucepan and cook over a low heat for about 30 minutes, beating with a wooden spoon now and then if necessary, until most of the liquid has evaporated and you are left with a very thick purée. Set aside.

Preheat the oven to 425°F (220°C). Lightly butter 6 (3 inch) (7.5 cm) ramekins, dust with a little of the sugar and set aside in the refrigerator. If your sorbet is frozen, transfer it to the refrigerator to soften slightly.

Bring the milk to the boil in a pan. While the milk is heating, beat the egg yolks, half of the sugar, the cornstarch and flour together in a bowl until smooth. Whisk in the hot milk, then return the mixture to the pan and bring back to the boil, stirring. Reduce the heat and simmer gently for about 10 minutes. Pour into a large mixing bowl and stir in the apple purée.

Whisk the egg whites to soft peaks, then very gradually whisk in the remaining sugar to make a soft meringue. Stir a quarter of the meringue into the apple custard to loosen the mixture slightly, then very gently fold in the remainder. Spoon the mixture into the prepared ramekins and bake for 13 minutes, until brown but still slightly wobbly. The mixture won't double in height because of the extra weight of the apple. Serve immediately, with a scoop of the apple sorbet.

The sorbet keeps well in the freezer for up to 2 weeks. Leave in the refrigerator for 10 minutes before eating.

For the Apple Sorbet

4 Granny Smith apples, cored and diced

Juice of 1 lemon

⅓ cup Stock Syrup (see page 154)

For the Soufflés

4 apples, peeled, cored and diced

½ cup hard cider (see note)

2 tablespoons Calvados (apple brandy)

1¼ cups milk

3 egg yolks

⅓ cup sugar plus extra for dusting

1 tablespoon cornstarch

1 tablespoon all-purpose flour

4 egg whites

*I*N THIS BOOK, WHERE CIDER IS LISTED IN THE INGREDIENTS, it is referring to what we here in the U.S. know of as hard cider. It is being found more and more in grocery stores next to the beer. Some hard ciders contain up to 8% alcohol.

Caramel Mousse Brûlée

Serves 8

⅔ cup + 1½ tablespoons
    granulated sugar

½ vanilla pod, split open

⅓ cup water

2 teaspoons gelatin powder

5 eggs

¼ cup heavy whipping cream

Confectioners' sugar for
    dusting

This is just one of the many great puddings originated by my friend Jim Kerr, formerly of the Rogano restaurant in Glasgow. It's actually quite a light pudding that has all the flavor of caramel without any of the sticky sweetness.

To make the caramel, put the ⅔ cup of granulated sugar, vanilla pod and half the water into a heavy based pan. Leave over a low heat until the sugar has completely dissolved and the liquid is clear. Increase the heat and boil until the liquid turns a very dark caramel color. Quickly remove the pan from the heat, stand back and add the remaining water – it will hiss and splutter, but don't worry. Return the pan to a low heat until all the hardened pieces of caramel have dissolved.

Meanwhile, soak the gelatin powder in 1 tablespoon cold water for 5-10 minutes. Take the caramel off the heat and leave to cool for 2 minutes. Add the soaked gelatin and stir gently until dissolved.

Meanwhile, separate the eggs into 2 large, clean bowls. Add the remaining 1½ tablespoons of sugar to the yolks and whisk with an electric beater until the mixture is very pale and thick – it should leave a visible trail for a few seconds. Pour in the caramel, whisking constantly, then whisk for another 3 minutes.

Whisk the egg whites into soft peaks: the tips of the peaks should just flip over, not stand upright. Whip the heavy whipping cream softly. Gently fold the egg whites into the caramel mixture, followed by the cream. Pour the mousse into 8 (3 inch) (7.5 cm) ramekins, making sure it comes right up to the rim. Leave overnight in the refrigerator.

To serve, dust the tops of the mousses heavily with confectioners' sugar. Heat several long skewers in a gas flame until red hot and rest them lightly on the sugar to brand it in a criss-cross pattern and serve.

CARRAGHEEN PUDDING *with* BLAEBERRIES

Serves 4

There are still many surprise pleasures to be found on the Scottish beaches. Carragheen seaweed is the setting agent in this pudding. It was traditionally used as a restorative on the Isle of Skye, so I was expecting an unpleasant medicinal taste. But after trying it I can vouch for its rightful presence in the modern kitchen. If you can't gather your own, buy it dried and follow the instructions for use. This dish looks like an exotic mixture but both the primary ingredients were actually found almost side-by-side at the ocean. Blueberries would do instead of blaeberries.

If using fresh carragheen, leave in a tray in a sunny position for 2-3 days or bake overnight on a low heat in the oven to dry it out.

When ready to prepare the pudding, soak the carragheen in plenty of warm water for 10 minutes, then drain and squeeze dry. Pour the milk into a pan, add the carragheen and bring to a simmer. Simmer for 5 minutes, or until the mixture becomes gelatinous and thick. Pour into a sieve set over a large bowl and drain. You may have to work the milky mixture through gently with a wooden spoon. Whisk in the sugar then pour the mixture into 4 (½ cup) dariole molds. Leave in the refrigerator until set, preferably overnight.

For the Blaeberries, put the water and sugar into a pan and leave over a low heat until the sugar has completely dissolved. Bring to the boil and boil for 5 minutes. Add the berries and gin, bring back to the boil, then transfer into a bowl and let cool. Leave in the refrigerator overnight.

To serve, dip the dariole molds into hot water for a few seconds to release the puddings. Unmold into the center of each serving plate and spoon around the berries and gin syrup.

2½ ounces (65 g) fresh or ¾ ounce (20 g) dried carragheen (see introduction)

2 cups milk

⅓ cup sugar

FOR THE BLAEBERIES

⅔ cup water

⅔ cup sugar

6-8 ounces (175-225 g) blaeberries or blueberries

2 tablespoons gin

CHERRY *and* ALMOND TART

Serves 8 to 10

1 recipe Sweet Flan Pastry
   (see page 149)

1 cup plus 2 tablespoons
   softened unsalted butter

1¼ cups sugar

2 tablespoons all-purpose
   flour

2 cups ground almonds

4 eggs

1 (18 ounce) (600 g) can
   pitted black cherries,
   drained

3 tablespoons apricot jam

This has been one of our most successful desserts at my restaurant, but don't make the mistake I made during the filming of Wild Harvest for Great Food, when I mistook a bowl of salt for sugar. The tart should be eaten warm, when the pastry will still be crumbly and light. Brambles or other soft fruit could be substituted for the cherries. Serve with whipped cream, or with Vanilla Ice Cream (see page 150).

Use the Sweet Flan Pastry to line a 10 inch (25 cm) flan ring and bake blind as instructed in the recipe.

Reduce the oven to 325°F (160°C). Cream the butter and sugar together in a large mixing bowl until very pale and thick. Beat in the flour and a quarter of the ground almonds until smooth, then beat in the eggs, one at a time. Fold in the remaining ground almonds. You can freeze the mixture at this stage if you wish.

Spread the almond mixture in the flan case and then dot the cherries here and there over the top. Protect the edge of the pastry with very thin strips of foil and bake the tart for 1 hour or until risen and golden.

Put the apricot jam into a small pan and melt over low heat. Add a little water if it is very thick. Press it through a sieve to remove any lumps and then brush it liberally over the top of the tart to glaze. Serve warm with whipped cream or Vanilla Ice Cream (see page 150).

Sweet Flan Pastry

Makes 1 (10 inch) (25 cm) Flan

There are a multitude of fillings you can use with this crust. Let your imagination run wild.

Cream the butter, sugar and salt at a medium speed in a food processor. Add ½ cup of the flour. With the mixer on a lower speed, add the egg yolk and the remaining flour, a tablespoon at a time. When the flour is fully incorporated, add the water and mix for 15 seconds.

Transfer the dough to a floured surface and, with floured hands, gently knead 3 or 4 times until it comes together. Wrap in plastic wrap and refrigerate for at least 3 hours.

Preheat the oven to 400°F (200°C). Place the dough on a floured surface. Roll out until about ⅛ inch (3 mm) thick. Cut into a circle slightly larger than a 10 inch (25 cm) loose-based flan ring.

Press the pastry down into the flan ring, folding the edges over the top of the ring, and place on a baking sheet. Line with aluminum foil and fill with dried beans. Refrigerate for 15 minutes. Remove and bake in the oven for 11 minutes.

Remove from the oven, discard the aluminum foil and beans, and then bake for 9 more minutes, until lightly browned. Remove, neatly trim away overhanging pastry and cool.

12 tablespoons unsalted butter

¼ cup sugar

Pinch of salt

2 cups all-purpose flour

1 egg yolk

1 tablespoon cold water

Savory Flan Pastry

Makes 1 (10 inch) (25 cm) Flan

The pastry can be baked blind, and the filling made a day in advance. Assemble the flan just before baking.

To make the pastry, rub the butter, flour and salt together in a mixing bowl until it has the consistency of fine bread crumbs. Add the egg and bring together into a dough. Knead lightly 3 or 4 times with floured hands. Cover in plastic wrap and refrigerate for an hour.

Preheat the oven to 400°F (200°C). Roll the pastry out ⅛ inch (3 mm) thick and line a greased 10 inch (25 cm) metal flan pan, 1¼ inches (3 cm) deep. Fill with greaseproof paper and baking beans and bake for 11 minutes. Remove the beans and paper and bake for another 8-9 minutes, until lightly golden.

12 tablespoons butter

1¾ cups flour

1 teaspoon salt

1 egg, beaten

Vanilla Ice Cream *with* Deep-Fried Fruit Cheese

Serves 6

2 cups milk

2 split vanilla pods

6 egg yolks

⅓ cup sugar

1 cup heavy whipping cream

For the Deep-Fried Fruit Cheese

3 ounces (75 g) fruit cheese (see introduction)

Sunflower oil for deep-frying

1 cup flour

¼ cup sugar, plus extra for dredging

⅔ cup lager-style beer

Fruit "cheese" is a Scottish delicacy you might have seen made on the Great Food television show. It is actually puréed fruit that is packed into molds and has a dense, gelatinous texture. Outside of Scotland, you might try this recipe by frying fruit-flavored cream cheese.

Put the milk and the vanilla pods into a pan and bring slowly to the boil. Take off the heat and leave for 20 minutes to allow the flavor of the vanilla to infuse.

Whisk the egg yolks and sugar together in a bowl until pale and creamy. Bring the milk back to the boil, lift out the pods and whisk the milk into the egg yolks. Return the mixture to the pan and cook over a gentle heat, stirring constantly, until it thickens enough to coat the back of the wooden spoon lightly. It shouldn't take more than 3 minutes. Stir in the double cream and leave to cool. Cover and place in the refrigerator until well chilled.

Now you can either churn the mixture in an ice cream maker or pour it into a shallow plastic box and freeze until almost firm. Scrape the mixture into a food processor and whiz until smooth. Pour it back into the box and repeat once more. Return the ice cream to the freezer and freeze until firm.

If the ice cream has been made in advance, transfer it from the freezer to the refrigerator about 30 minutes before serving to allow it time to soften slightly.

For the Fruit Cheese, cut the cheese into ½ x ¾ inch (1 x 2 cm) blocks. Heat some oil for deep frying to 350°F (180°C). Sift the flour and sugar into a bowl and whisk in the beer until smooth. Dip the fruit cheese pieces into the batter and deep fry a few pieces at a time until crisp and golden. Drain on kitchen paper, dust with sugar and serve with the ice cream.

Variation

Make the ice cream as above, substituting 1½ lightly crushed cinnamon sticks for the pods. Whisk the yolks with ⅓ cup sugar, and stir in only ½ cup heavy whipping cream before freezing. Serve with Cherry and Almond Tart (see page 148).

BALSAMIC REDUCTION

This intensifies the flavor of the vinegar and also makes it thick and syrupy so it looks great when drizzled onto a plate, especially along with oils. It is excellent drizzled over roasted vegetables, Parma ham, salad, arugula or anything Italian. When you're preparing this, make sure that the kitchen is well ventilated – the fumes make your eyes nip! Stay middle-of-the-road; don't use the best 10-year-old balsamic vinegar for this!

1 (32 ounce) (1 l) bottle
balsamic vinegar

Bring the balsamic vinegar to the boil and simmer until reduced by half. Leave to cool.

We store ours in small squeeze bottles for convenience.

TOMATOES CONCASSÉES

Skinned, de-seeded and with the acidic water removed, these small sweet cubes of tomato can be used for sauces and salads. Like everything else, the success of even such a basic preparation depends on the use of the best quality ingredients. Make with any quantity of tomatoes – even just one!

Plum tomatoes, ripe
(minimum quantity – 1)

Remove the skin from the tomatoes. To do this, you can either:

A) Slit a small cross at the bottom of the tomatoes with a sharp knife. Pop them into boiling water and leave for a minute before removing with a slotted spoon. The skin should now peel off easily.

OR (MY PREFERRED METHOD):

B) Use a blow torch. First, spear one of the tomatoes with the tip of a sharp knife. Light your blow torch and apply the flame to the tomato skin, moving on as the skin blisters. This has the same effect as the first method, but is much more fun.

Once peeled, cut the tomatoes into quarters, scoop out the seeds and set aside. Cut the flesh into ¼ inch (5 mm) dice. It is best used immediately, but will keep for a maximum of 14 hours. Freeze the discarded tomato pulp, seeds and water, for use in stocks and sauces.

CLARIFIED BUTTER

Makes about 1 cup.

*2 sticks (½ pound) (250 g)
plus 2 tablespoons
unsalted butter*

Clarified butter is just the oil part of the butter, without the buttermilk. It is essential for frying potatoes, to give them a rich, buttery flavor. You can buy it already prepared in Indian delicatessens as ghee.

In a small saucepan, melt the butter on a low heat. Allow it to stand for a few minutes until all the oil rises to the top. Skim off the oil and transfer into a sealable plastic container. It will keep for 2 months. If you have a microwave oven, put the butter into a microwaveable container and cook on a high heat for 1 minute. If it is not completely melted, heat again for 30 seconds. Do not allow it to boil. Continue as above, discarding the watery buttermilk.

STOCK SYRUP

Makes 4 Cups

5½ cups sugar

3½ cups water

Used in desserts, this is a 50/50 mix of sugar and water. It keeps for eight weeks in the refrigerator, so make it well in advance and you'll always have it handy. It's good for poaching fruit and can be flavored with cinnamon, vanilla, lemon, orange – you name it!

Put the sugar and water in a medium saucepan and bring to the boil, stirring from time to time. Simmer for 5 minutes then remove from the heat. Skim off any impurities that may have risen to the surface. Let cool completely then store in the refrigerator. And that, as they say, is that.

DEEP-FRIED HERBS

Deep-fried herbs are very trendy at the moment. Quite rightly, since deep-frying improves the texture of the herbs and concentrates the flavor. You can use any herbs you like, but my favorites are flat leaf and curly parsley, sage, arugula, basil, tarragon and chives. Chervil, however, tends to go a bit gooey. This also works for celery leaves.

1 cup loosely packed fresh herbs

Sunflower oil for deep-frying

Salt to taste

Divide the herbs into large sprigs but not down to individual leaves. Have ready a plate lined with a double layer of paper towel on which to drain the herbs. Heat the oil to 350°F (180°C); it shouldn't be too hot. Drop the herbs into the oil in 2 batches and turn with a slotted spoon during cooking. They are ready once they stop sizzling, which shouldn't take more than 2 minutes. Drain and season with a tiny amount of the salt.

RED ONION MARMALADE

Makes about 1 pound (450 g).

The natural sweetness of red onions gives this a mellower flavor than ordinary onions, plus they're not that much more expensive. The marmalade is great with cold meats game, chicken livers and bacon. Or add a tablespoon to a meat gravy to make a rich onion gravy.

⅓ cup olive oil

3 pounds (1.5 kg) red onions, finely sliced

½ cup best-quality sherry vinegar, or even better, Cabernet Sauvignon vinegar

2 tablespoons crème de cassis

Salt to taste

Freshly ground white pepper to taste

Heat the oil in a large saucepan over a medium heat. Add the sliced onions, stir well to coat with the oil and then season. Cook slowly, uncovered, stirring from time to time, until the onions are very soft and the sugary juices have caramelized. This should take about 1-1½ hours and the onions should look thick, dark and sticky.

Now add the vinegar and cassis and cook for another 10 minutes or so, until all the harsh vinegar has been boiled off and the marmalade has a glossy texture. Leave to cool and then store in a jar in the refrigerator. If you pour in a tablespoon of olive oil to seal the top it should keep for 6-8 weeks.

NAGE

Marinated Vegetable Stock - Makes 4 Cups

1 large onion

1 leek

2 sticks celery

1 fennel bulb (optional)

4 large carrots

1 head garlic, sliced in half
across its equator

8 white peppercorns, crushed

1 teaspoon pink peppercorns

1 teaspoon coriander seeds

1 star anise

1 bay leaf

1½ cups loosely packed
mixed fresh herbs

1¼ cups white wine

This stock is essential to the making of Nage Butter Sauce, which crops up regularly throughout my recipes, so make big batches of this when you can. It freezes well and the ingredients are always reasonably easy to get. Freeze in cup size plastic containers, and defrost as needed.

Chop all of the vegetables into ½ inch (1 cm) dice, place in a pot and cover with water. Add the garlic, peppercorns, coriander seeds, star anise and bay leaf, bring to a boil and simmer for 8 minutes. Add the fresh herbs and simmer for 3 minutes.

Now add the white wine and remove from the heat. Leave covered to marinate for 48 hours in a cool place.

Once marinated, strain the stock through a fine sieve. It can be used immediately or frozen for up to 6 weeks.

Nage Butter Sauce

Makes about 1¼ cups.

This sauce is my favorite and the one I use most in my cooking. It is a delightful, fresh, buttery sauce on its own, but with the addition of other ingredients (freshly chopped herbs, chili, Pesto, tomato, shellfish ... you name it) it can become anything you desire.

It is easy to make, and the base ingredients are easily obtainable. The one item of equipment that is essential in the making of this sauce though, is a hand-held blender. Without one, it is difficult to obtain the light, smooth quality that makes it so versatile.

A word on "splitting." This is an emulsified sauce, a combination of fat and liquid, so if you don't give it sufficient heat and keep it moving, then it will split – you will end up with big globs of butter floating on the top – not dissimilar to a commercial salad dressing.

2 cups Nage (see page 156)

14 tablespoons unsalted butter, chilled and diced

1 teaspoon lemon juice

Salt to taste

Freshly ground white pepper to taste

Pour the Nage into a small, straight-sided saucepan, filling slightly more than half the pan. Place on a high heat and bring to the boil. Reduce down to roughly one-fifth of the original volume. It turns dark and looks thick and sticky!

Turn the heat to low and add the butter. Stick in a hand-held blender or put in an electric blender and purée until all the butter has been melted and the texture is light and frothy. Add the lemon juice, salt and pepper, tasting as you season, and keep warm (but don't let it boil) until it's needed.

If you let this sauce go cold and it solidifies, you can bring it back again by melting the sauce. The sauce will separate and the butter will float to the top. Now boil ⅓ cup of heavy whipping cream in a small saucepan. When it's boiling, use the hand blender to whisk it and, at the same time, pour the hot separated sauce into the saucepan in a steady stream. It is now ready to use.

GARY RHODES

WHENEVER A CHEF MAKES HIS ENTRANCE INTO A TELEVISION SHOW DRIVING A CANARY YELLOW LOTUS CAR, you know you're in for a different kind of culinary ride. But the surprise is even greater when your cheeky driver announces your culinary tour is around the tradition-laden food of England.

Indeed, Gary Rhodes is an unlikely combination: a charming young man with a decidedly modern hair style and attitude who delights in re-creating the most classic British dishes.

"Traveling around Britian to make the television shows for Great Food has given me lots of new experiences: from being serenaded over cod, chips and mushy peas by the Nolan Sisters to cooking on an oil rig, to mixing with ostriches, singing to pigs, meeting in lighthouses and even being Gary Glitter's 'Leader of the Gang.'

"But what's really great is meeting so many different people who get really excited about good, simple British dishes. Giving people tastes and textures that they have never experienced and a style that's new is a great feeling, but what excites me even more is cooking dishes which evoke half-remembered taste sensations. I cook for the people, giving them food they are going to enjoy and not being afraid of serving anything, because I have confidence in British cooking and the cooking styles we have to offer."

If restaurant-goers to *The Greenhouse* restaurant in London, where Gary is chef, are the ultimate food critics, then his cooking is getting rave reviews. The Greenhouse was awarded a Michelin star in 1997.

So get ready for a unique tour with Gary Rhodes around Britain – yellow Lotus-style.

Fillets *of* Smoked Eel *on a* Warm Potato, Onion *and* Beet Salad

Serves 4

The potato, beet and onion salad eats very well with the smoked eel. This dressing also tastes good with the addition of 2 teaspoons of horseradish, but I'm keeping this fairly simple to make.

To caramelize the onions, simply place them in a pan with the tablespoon of water and cook, uncovered, over a low heat for about 2 hours until all the natural juices and sugars from the onions begin to color to a rich, golden brown. This can be done in advance.

Cut the smoked eel into 2-3 inch (5-7.5 cm) slices, allowing 3 or 4 slices per portion. While the new potatoes are still warm, leave the skin on and cut them in half. Add three-quarters of the Basic Vinaigrette and the cooked onions and continue to warm in the pan. Add the beet, making sure that it's carefully mixed in and not coloring all the potatoes. Check for seasoning with the salt and pepper. Add the chopped fresh parsley. Season the remaining Vinaigrette and add to the salad leaves. Divide the potato and beet salad between 4 plates. Sit the leaves on top of the salads and lay the smoked eel on top and serve.

4 large onions, sliced

1 tablespoon water

1-1½ pounds (450-675 g) smoked eel fillets or smoked mackerel or trout

½ pound (225 g) new potatoes, cooked

½-¾ cup Basic Vinaigrette (see page 187)

1 large cooked beet, sliced

Salt to taste

Freshly ground black pepper to taste

1 tablespoon chopped fresh parsley

Mixed salad leaves, such as arugula, baby spinach, curly endive

Opposite: Honey Apples with Toffee Cream (page 178).

POTTED SALMON

Serves 4

1 pound (450 g) salmon fillet

1¼ cups Clarified Butter
(see note)

2 shallots, finely chopped

1 small garlic clove, crushed

½ teaspoon ground mace

½ teaspoon salt

Freshly ground white pepper
to taste

1 tablespoon chopped fresh
parsley

1 tablespoon chopped fresh
tarragon

1 cup loosely packed salad
leaves, for garnish

1 lemon, cut into wedge,
for garnish

Warm toast slices, to serve

This is a good summer dish which can be made and set in a serving dish and used as a starter or main course. Always be careful when cooking salmon as the fish is delicate. It needs very little cooking and should always be pink in the center to keep it moist and succulent. You can make the salmon pots a few days in advance, but always serve them at room temperature. This will allow the butter to become softer and a lot tastier.

Trim the salmon fillet and cut into ½ inch (1 cm) cubes. Warm the clarified butter to the simmering point and add the chopped shallots. Cook for a few minutes until the shallots have softened. Add the garlic, mace, salt and pepper. Carefully spoon the salmon into the butter and turn to a low heat. The salmon can now only be stirred very carefully to avoid breaking. As soon as the salmon has a light opaque color, about 5-6 minutes, remove it from the heat and let cool. Sprinkle on the chopped parsley and tarragon.

Spoon the cooled salmon into individual 3 inch (7.5 cm) serving molds, making sure that the shallots and herbs are evenly distributed among the molds. Top with the remaining butter. You may find that you have some butter left. This can be used for cooking fish, or frozen for a future use. Cool and then chill the molds in the refrigerator, until set.

Remove from the refrigerator and let return to room temperature. Turn out of the molds onto plates and garnish with the salad leaves and the lemon wedges. This dish is excellent served with warm thick toast slices.

To make Clarified Butter, simply melt 3 sticks (350 g) of unsalted butter until it foams. Don't allow it to brown. Remove from the heat and let stand until the milky residue sinks to the bottom. Strain off through muslin.

BOILED COLLAR *of* BACON *with* HOMEMADE SAUERKRAUT

Serves 4 to 6

Sauerkraut is a warm pickled cabbage. I used it a lot when I lived in Amsterdam in the late 1970's and also when visiting my brother who lived in Germany. We would always have grilled bratwurst sausage with sauerkraut in a roll. I think these were the German answer to hot dogs and ketchup! Sauerkraut is often cooked with bacon to help the flavor. I decided to keep the sauerkraut "vegetarian." Serve it with the boiled bacon and mustard seed sauce.

Pork shoulder is the best substitute for bacon collar. It's highly marbled in fat and very good for braising or boiling. If you do use the pork shoulder, you do not need to soak it like the bacon. You can ask your butcher to do the boning, rolling and tying required in the recipe.

Two days before serving, start the Sauerkraut. Place the shredded cabbage in a bowl with the wine and vinegar. Tie the bouquet garni ingredients in a square of muslin and add to the bowl. Let marinate for 48 hours, turning occasionally to make sure all the cabbage is marinated. This will give it a good pickly texture and taste.

One day before serving, soak the bacon in water for 24 hours. Soaking the bacon releases excess salt content, leaving a better and less salt taste. If you are using the pork shoulder, omit the soaking step.

The day of serving, remove and wash the collar. Place the prepared meat in a pan with the vegetables, bay leaf and stock or water. Bring to the simmer and simmer for 1-1½ hours. Remove from the heat and let the meat rest in the liquor for 20 minutes to relax the meat and make it more tender.

To make a mustard seed sauce, take 2 cups of the cooking liquid and boil until reduced by half. Add the cream and cook for 10 minutes. Add the butter and mustard seed to taste. Check for seasoning with the salt and pepper. Remove from the heat and set aside.

To finish the Sauerkraut, drain off the liquid and reserve the cabbage and liquid separately. Melt the butter in a pan and add the sliced onions. Cook on medium heat until slightly softened, but not brown. Add the white cabbage, bouquet garni and 2-3 tablespoons of the marinating liquid and cover with a lid. Cook on medium heat, stirring from time to time. Check the liquid level, adding more a little at a time until the cabbage becomes tender, but still has a slight crunch, about 20 minutes. Taste and season with salt and pepper.

To serve, spoon some of the Sauerkraut on each plate. Remove the meat from the liquid and carve, giving one thick or two thinner slices per person. Sit the meat on top of the Sauerkraut and spoon some liquid over to add some extra moisture to the meat. Serve with the mustard seed sauce.

FOR THE SAUERKRAUT

1 medium white cabbage, finely shredded

⅔ cup white wine

⅔ cup white wine vinegar

1 bouquet garni (2 teaspoons pickling spice, 2 teaspoons lightly crushed juniper berries, pinch of thyme, tied in muslin)

2 tablespoons unsalted butter

3 onions, sliced

FOR THE BACON

2-3 pounds (.9-1.5 kg) bacon collar or pork shoulder (see introduction), boned, skinned, rolled and tied

1 onion, coarsely chopped

2 carrots, coarsely chopped

2 celery sticks, coarsely chopped

1 bay leaf

Chicken stock or water to cover the bacon

⅔ cup heavy whipping cream

2 tablespoons unsalted butter

1-2 teaspoons mustard seed

Salt to taste

Freshly ground white pepper to taste

1 recipe Short Crust Pastry
   (see page 185)
4 (5 ounce) (125 g) mackerel,
   monkfish or herring fillets,
   skinned and trimmed
2 tablespoons Basic
   Vinaigrette (see page 187)
A few drops of balsamic
   vinegar
2 teaspoons fresh chives,
   snipped into ½ inch
   (1 cm) pieces

FOR THE ONIONS
AND PEPPER

4 large onions, sliced
1 tablespoon water
1 large red bell pepper,
   cut into strips
1 tablespoon olive oil
Salt to taste
Freshly ground black pepper
   to taste

FOR THE SOUSING
LIQUID

2 teaspoons olive oil
½ onion, coarsely chopped
1 small carrot, coarsely
   chopped
1 celery stick, coarsely
   chopped
1 sprig fresh thyme
1 sprig fresh tarragon
1 bay leaf
1 star anise (optional)
2 teaspoons pickling spice
⅓ cup white wine
⅓ cup white wine vinegar
2 cups water
A pinch of salt
Juice of ½ lemon

FILLET of MACKEREL with CARAMELIZED ONIONS and SWEET PEPPERS

Serves 4

*I*n this recipe, the mackerel is "cooked" in a sousing liquid made with white wine, white wine vinegar, water, pickling spices, star anise and herbs. The combination of the sharp, soused taste and the sweetness of the onions and peppers works really well. I like to present this dish on very thin short pastry discs. This gives the dish another texture, almost like eating an open flan. Monkfish and herring are fine substitutes for the mackerel.

Preheat the oven to 375°F (190°C). Roll out the pastry very thinly and cut into 3-4 inch (7.5-10 cm) discs and leave to rest in the refrigerator for 10 minutes. Bake in the preheated oven for about 10 minutes until cooked through and crisp. Set aside.

For the Onions and Pepper, place the onions in a pan with the water and cook over a low heat, uncovered, for about 2 hours until the color turns a rich, golden brown. This can be done in advance.

Cook the red pepper in the olive oil for 2-3 minutes until softened. Add to the caramelized onions and season with the salt and pepper to taste.

For the Sousing Liquid, warm the olive oil and add the onion, carrot, celery, thyme, tarragon, bay leaf, star anise (if you wish) and pickling spice and cook for 3 minutes until the vegetables begin to soften. Add the white wine, wine vinegar, water, salt and lemon juice, bring to the simmer and cook for 15 minutes. Strain into a bowl and set aside.

In a large frying pan cook the mackerel fillets in the warm Sousing Liquid and bring almost to the simmer just to warm through.

Sweeten the Basic Vinaigrette dressing with a little of the balsamic vinegar and add the chives.

To serve, place a pastry disc on each plate. Spoon the warm Onions and Pepper on the pastry and top with the fish. Spoon the dressing over and around the fish.

IF YOU HAVEN'T GOT ENOUGH TIME to make the caramelized onions, simply cook 2 or 3 sliced onions in butter until golden brown and almost burnt. This will give a more bittersweet taste that will become a lot sweeter when added to the red pepper.

GRILLED CHICKEN BREAST *with* BRAISED PEARL BARLEY, LEMON *and* THYME

Serves 4

This really is a simple dish: not too many ingredients but packed with textures and tastes. Instead of simmering the barley on the stove, it cooks evenly if you put it in a preheated oven at 350°F (180°C).

In a medium saucepan, bring 2 cups of the chicken stock to the boil, add the leek and cook for 30 seconds. Strain, reserving both the stock and leek separately.

In a large frying pan over medium high heat, cook the chopped onion in 4 tablespoons of the butter, without coloring, until softened. Add the pearl barley and cook for 1-2 minutes. Add the reserved stock and bring to the simmer. Cover and cook over a low heat, stirring continuously, until the barley becomes tender, about 30-40 minutes. Add more stock if the barley becomes dry. Add 1 tablespoon of the remaining butter and the reserved leeks and warm through. If there is still a lot of excess chicken stock, simply pour it off. Remove from the heat and keep warm.

The remaining chicken stock should be boiled and reduced by half to leave you with a good, strong stock.

While the chicken stock is reducing, cook the chicken breasts in your preferred style: roasting pan, barbecue, pan-fried or under the broiler. They will take about 15 minutes.

Also while the chicken stock is reducing, mix 8-10 tablespoons of the remaining butter with the thyme and lemon juice in a small bowl. This can be made at any time and will keep in the refrigerator for as long as the butter will last. When the chicken stock is reduced by half, gradually whisk in enough of the lemon and thyme butter until you have a smooth sauce consistency. Taste and add salt and pepper.

To serve, spoon the barley onto the center of a warmed serving plate and pour the sauce around. Slice the chicken breast through the middle and place on top of the barley.

3 cups chicken stock

1 leek, sliced or diced

1 large onion, finely chopped

12-16 tablespoons unsalted butter, softened but not melted

½ cup pearl barley

1 teaspoon chopped fresh thyme

Juice of 1-2 lemons

4 chicken breasts

Salt to taste

Freshly ground black pepper to taste

LEEK *and* MUSTARD CRUMBLE *on* CHEESY MASHED POTATOES

Serves 4 to 6

8 tablespoons unsalted
   butter

2 onions, sliced

⅔ cup vegetable stock

1-1½ pounds (450-675 g)
   leeks, split and sliced

2 teaspoons chopped fresh
   parsley

2 teaspoons chopped fresh
   tarragon

1 recipe Basic Crumble Mix
   (see page 183)

2 teaspoons grainy mustard

2-3 cups or ½ recipe
   Mashed Potatoes
   (see page 174)

1-2 cups grated cheddar
   cheese

Salt to taste

Freshly ground white pepper
   to taste

This recipe can be adapted to so many dishes, plus it's a complete vegetarian meal on its own. You can even make it without the Cheesy Mashed Potatoes and still have a great accompaniment to many simple meat or fish dishes.

Preheat the oven to 400°F (200°C). Melt 2 tablespoons of the butter in a pan. When the butter begins to bubble, add the onions and cook for 5 minutes, until slightly softened. Add the stock and bring to the boil. Add the leeks, return to the boil and cook for 30 seconds. Strain, reserving the stock and leeks and onions separately. Return the stock to the pan and boil until reduced by half.

Put the Basic Crumble Mix in a large bowl and stir in the chopped parsley, tarragon and mustard. Mix well and set aside.

Warm the Mashed Potatoes with about 1 cup of the cheddar cheese until the cheese is all melted. Taste and add more cheese, salt and pepper to taste.

Spoon the Mashed Potatoes into a large baking dish. Warm the onion and leeks in a teaspoon of the vegetable liquid, then spoon over the potatoes, and finish with the mustard seed crumble mix. Bake in the preheated oven or under a hot broiler for about 10 minutes until the crumble is golden and crunchy.

To make the sauce, reheat the reduced vegetable liquid and vigorously whisk in the remaining butter to give an almost creamy consistency. If you have an electric hand blender, this will really bind the sauce. Season to taste with the salt and pepper and serve with the crumble.

MUSHROOM RISOTTO *with* CRISPY BLACK PUDDING

Serves 4 to 8

*M*ushrooms and black pudding sausage are a traditional British combination, usually served at breakfast. They work together very well in this recipe, contrasting the creaminess of the risotto with the crispy, rich black pudding. The best mushrooms to use in this recipe are Portobello. These have an almost meaty texture and a much better flavor.

Melt the butter with the olive oil in a large pan. Add the chopped onions and chopped bone marrow, if using, and cook without coloring for 2-3 minutes.

Meanwhile, bring the stock to the boil. Add the sliced mushrooms to the onions, increasing the heat of the pan, and cook for 2-3 minutes. Add the rice and continue to cook over a medium heat for a further minute. Add the hot stock a ladle at a time, allowing it to become absorbed in the rice and evaporate before adding another ladle.

Continue this process, stirring almost continuously to keep an even cooking. This will take 20-30 minutes. When the risotto is almost cooked, the black pudding can be either pan-fried until crispy or cooked under the broiler.

Once the risotto is cooked, add some of the grated Parmesan and check the consistency is of a rich creamy texture. Season with the salt and pepper and spoon onto a plate or into bowls. Sprinkle with the Parmesan flakes, crispy black pudding and a few drops of olive oil.

8 to 12 tablespoons unsalted butter

1 tablespoon olive oil

2 onions, finely chopped

1 to 2 ounces (25-50 g) bone marrow, chopped (optional)

4 cups vegetable or chicken stock

8 to 12 ounces (225-350 g) Portobello mushrooms, sliced

1½ cups arborio rice

12 ounces (350 g) black pudding sausage or pork sausage cut into ½ inch (1 cm) dice

1 to 2 tablespoons freshly grated Parmesan cheese

Salt to taste

Freshly ground black pepper to taste

Parmesan cheese flakes, for garnish

Ox Cheek Stew *with* Neeps *and* Tatties

Serves 4 to 6

For the Stew

2½-3 pounds (1.1-1.5 kg) ox cheeks or chuck steak, trimmed of all fat and sinew

Salt to taste

Freshly ground black pepper to taste

2 tablespoons olive oil

2 large onions, sliced

1 small garlic clove, crushed

1 sprig fresh thyme

1 bay leaf

1 bottle red wine

3-4 cups veal or beef stock

1 pound (450 g) shallots

2 tablespoons unsalted butter

For the Neeps and Tatties

1 pound (450 g) turnips

1 pound (450 g) potatoes

½ cup (8 tablespoons) unsalted butter

Ox cheeks are an unusual cut of beef with a good, open texture which is ideal for braising or stewing as it enables the beef to absorb all the sauce and liquid. If you can't find a butcher to offer you the cheeks, then just use large pieces of chuck steak. This is similar in texture and will work well in this recipe.

And for your peace of mind, "neeps and tatties" is a slang term for "turnips and potatoes."

For the stew, sprinkle the ox cheeks or chuck steak with the salt and pepper. Preheat a frying pan and add a little cooking fat. Fry the meat until well colored on all sides. Remove from the pan and drain off the excess fat or juices. Cook the sliced onions in a large frying pan until very brown. Add the garlic, thyme, bay leaf and half the red wine. Bring to the boil and boil until reduced to almost dry. Add the veal or beef stock and meat and bring to the simmer. Cook the meat slowly for 1½-2 hours until tender.

While the meat is cooking, split the peeled shallots in half lengthwise and cook in a very little butter until very brown, almost burnt. Add the remaining red wine and boil until reduced to almost dry.

Also while the meat is cooking, make the Neeps and Tatties. Cook the turnips and potatoes separately in boiling salted water until tender. Drain and return to the pot, to dry for a few minutes. Lightly mash the vegetables or stir with a wooden spoon to give a coarse purée. If you prefer a smoother finish push the vegetables through a sieve. Stir in the butter and season with the salt and pepper to taste.

Once the meat is cooked, remove it from the sauce and set aside. Drain the sauce through a sieve and return to the pan. Reheat the meat in the finished sauce until warmed through.

To serve, spoon the meat into serving bowls. The shallots can be mixed with the sauce or sprinkled on top as garnish. Serve with the turnips and potatoes on the side.

ROAST COD *on* POTATOES *with* FRIED ANCHOVIES

Serves 4

*T*his has to be my favorite fish dish. As with most of the recipes, another fish can be used or you can leave the fish out and serve it as a warm potato salad with crispy anchovies. Marinated anchovies are sold loosely, not in cans. Because I'm roasting this cod, I want to keep the skin on. When shallow-fried then roasted, cod skin comes up very crisp and tasty – good enough to eat on its own!

Preheat the oven to 400°F (200°C). Cook the new potatoes, then peel off the skin. Cut into ¼ inch (5 mm) slices while still warm, then sprinkle to taste with the salt and pepper. Add 1-2 tablespoons of the Vierge Dressing or olive oil and the juice of ½ lemon. Sprinkle again with the salt and pepper to taste and keep warm.

Melt the butter and oil in a hot pan. Season the cod with salt and pepper and place in the pan skin-side-down. Cook until a deep brown, then turn over and finish cooking in the oven for 5-8 minutes, depending on the thickness of the cod.

Split the anchovies through the center. Mix the flour with the cayenne and a pinch of the salt. Dip the anchovies in the milk, then roll in the cayenne flour. Deep-fry in hot oil until very crispy. If you don't have a deep-fat fryer, cook them in about ¼ inch (5 mm) of hot oil in a frying pan, but don't let it get so hot that the oil smokes, and keep turning the fish in the pan until they are crispy.

To finish the dish, warm the remaining Vierge Dressing or olive oil and add the capers and shallots or onion with a squeeze of the remaining lemon juice and the herbs. Season with the salt and pepper to taste. The dressing should be served warm.

To serve, spoon some potatoes onto plates and top with a few of the green salad leaves, if you wish. Spoon the dressing all around and sit a few fried anchovy fillets on top of the dressing. Finish the dish with the roasted cod fillet on top with the crispy skin-side showing. Brush with a little butter to finish.

1 pound (450 g) new potatoes

Salt to taste

Freshly ground white pepper to taste

⅔ cup Vierge Dressing (see page 187) or olive oil

Juice of 1 lemon

2 tablespoons unsalted butter

2 teaspoons cooking oil

4 (6-8 ounce) (175-225 g) cod fillets

12 marinated anchovies

1 teaspoon flour

¼ teaspoon cayenne

2-3 tablespoons milk

Oil for deep-frying

1 tablespoon fine or chopped capers

2 shallots or ½ onion, very finely chopped

½ teaspoon chopped fresh parsley

1 teaspoon chopped fresh cilantro

1 teaspoon chopped fresh tarragon

1 teaspoon chopped fresh basil

4-5 ounces (125-150 g) green salad leaves (mesclun) (optional)

Sautéed Scallop *and* Fennel Salad

Serves 4

4 fennel bulbs

Juice of 1 lemon

1 star anise (optional)

3 cups water

Salt to taste

Freshly ground white pepper
to taste

4-6 tablespoons unsalted
butter

1 tablespoon olive oil

12 large scallops, trimmed
and roes removed

4-5 ounces (125-150 g) green
salad leaves (mesclun)

Basic Vinaigrette
(see page 187)

1 tablespoon snipped fresh
chives

Scallops are available fresh from many fishmongers, or you may find some good quality scallops frozen.

Trim the top and bottom off the fennel. Using a small knife, remove the core from the base of each fennel. Add the lemon juice and star anise, if you wish, to the water with a pinch of the salt and bring to the boil. Add the fennel, cover and simmer over a medium heat for 15-20 minutes until just tender.

Pour off half of the cooking liquid and boil it until reduced to about ½ cup. This will increase the flavor of the fennel. Add the butter and whisk vigorously until light and smooth. An electric hand blender makes an even lighter and smoother sauce. This sauce can be kept warm and reheated and whisked before serving.

Slice the fennel ¼ inch (5 mm) thick lengthwise. Heat a frying pan and add a teaspoon of the olive oil to the pan. Fry the fennel slices on both sides until golden brown. Season with the salt and pepper to taste, remove from the heat and set aside.

To cook the scallops, heat a frying pan with a few drops of the olive oil and a tablespoon of the butter. It is very important to cook scallops in a hot pan, to give good color and seal them quickly. If the pan is only warm, the scallops begin to poach in their own juices, creating a different texture and taste. Once colored and seasoned on both side, the scallops are ready. They should cook about 2-3 minutes, depending on size.

To serve, lay the fennel slices on the center of a warmed serving plate and spread the scallops on top. Mix the salad leaves with a little of the Basic Vinaigrette and place them in the center of the scallops. Add the chives to the rewarmed sauce and spoon around the plate.

SEARED SPICY PORK BELLY

Serves 4

Pork belly is quite a cheap cut of meat and, I think, highly under rated. Belly slices are wonderful roasted or barbecued, they have a great balance of meat and port fat content which helps them "crisp up" during cooking.

Well, for this recipe I'm not using the strips but instead squares of belly that have all bone and skin removed. It should be no problem to ask the butcher to cut some for you, but make sure they do remove all skin and bone. The squares you need should be about 3 inch (7.5 cm).

Teriyaki marinade is available in most large supermarkets; you'll find it near the soy sauce. The pork almost tastes Chinese; it has a good spicy flavor and eats very well with just buttered noodles or with Stir-Fried Spinach, Mushrooms and Bean Sprouts (see page 175).

The day before serving, score the pork belly squares diagonally on the fat side about ⅛ inch (3 mm) deep. They should also be scored very lightly underneath. The pork is now ready for marinating.

To make the Marinade, simply mix all the ingredients together. Reserve 3 tablespoons to use in the finished dressing, then pour the rest over the pork, turning from time to time. The pork only needs to marinate for 24 hours before cooking. It can, of course, be left longer but this will increase the taste of the spices which could become too strong.

The day of serving, preheat the oven to 400°F (200°C). To cook the pork, remove the pork from the Marinade, reserving both separately. Heat the olive oil in a roasting pan and add the pork fat-side-down, over a medium heat. The fat will start to color almost immediately, giving a rich roasted/ seared color. Continue to color until quite dark. Turn the pork and cook in the pre-heated oven for about 15-20 minutes. The cooking time will really depend on the thickness of the belly.

Once cooked, spoon the honey on top and glaze under a hot grill. Remove the pork and leave to rest for a few minutes. Mix any excess honey in the pan with the reserved marinade and the Vinaigrette dressing and strain through a sieve. Cut the green onions into small, thin oval pieces. Slice the pork into thin slices and sit in the bowl. Spoon the Marinade dressing over and sprinkle with the green onions.

4 pork belly squares
(see introduction)

1 tablespoon olive oil

4 teaspoons honey

4-5 tablespoons Basic
Vinaigrette (see page 187)

4-6 green onions

FOR THE MARINADE

⅔ cup teriyaki marinade

⅓ cup soy sauce

1 teaspoon Tabasco sauce

3 tablespoons Worcestershire
sauce

2 garlic cloves, sliced

1 tablespoon grated
ginger root, finely diced
or grated

MASHED POTATOES

Serves 4 to 6

2 pounds (900 g) potatoes,
 peeled and quartered

Salt to taste

Freshly ground white pepper
 to taste

½ cup unsalted butter

½ cup heavy whipping cream
 or milk

Freshly grated nutmeg

I find Russet are one of the best varieties for making mashed potatoes – then all you need to add is a little care.

Boil the potatoes in salted water until tender, about 20-25 minutes, depending on the size. Drain off all the water and replace the lid. Shake the pan vigorously, which will start to break the potatoes. Add the butter and cream or milk a little at a time, while mashing the potatoes. Season with the salt, pepper and nutmeg to taste. The potatoes will be light, fluffy and creamy.

STIR-FRIED SPINACH,
MUSHROOMS *and* BEAN SPROUTS

Serves 4

*T*his eats well on its own but is even better with the Seared Spicy Pork Belly (see page 173).

First remove the stalks from the spinach and tear the leaves carefully into small pieces. Wash the leaves and leave to dry.

Heat a wok or frying pan and add the olive oil and butter. Add the mushrooms and toss for 30 seconds. Add the bean sprouts and continue to cook for 2 minutes. Add the spinach and continue to stir for 30 seconds. Add the seasoning and lime juice and cook for about 30 seconds more until the vegetables are just tender.

1½-2 pounds (750-900 g) spinach

1-2 tablespoons olive oil

2 tablespoons unsalted butter

½ pound (225 g) mushrooms, sliced

½ pound (225 g) bean sprouts, blanched in hot water

Salt to taste

Freshly ground black pepper to taste

Juice of 1 lime

BLACKBERRY JAM TART

Serves 4 to 6

6-8 ounces (175-225 g)
 refrigerated puff pastry

12 tablespoons unsalted
 butter

¾ cup sugar

1⅓ cups ground almonds

⅓ cup all-purpose flour

3 eggs

¾ cup Homemade Black-
 berry Jam (see page 184)

I used to love jam tarts as a child: just sweet pastry tartlet molds filled with jam. I thought they were really delicious. Well, this recipe is for a jam tart with a difference. I have always felt that a jam tart needed another texture, so read on and you'll see exactly what I mean!

For this recipe I'm going to use four individual tartlet cases, but an 11 inch (28 cm) flan case will be fine. If you use a large flan case, the pastry can be left raw before adding the almond mix than all baked at the same time, in which case it will need 1-1¼ hours.

The jam tart eats well just with thick or clotted cream. I also like to serve home-made custard sauce, cold or warm, or sometimes flavored with Calvados.

Preheat the oven to 350°F (180°C). Roll out the pastry thinly and line the flan cases, leaving any excess pastry hanging over the edge of the rings. This will prevent the pastry from shrinking back into the mold during baking. Let rest for 20 minutes. Line the pastry with greaseproof paper and fill with baking beans or rice and bake in the preheated oven for 15-20 minutes, until the pastry is cooked and set. Remove the paper and beans and cut off any excess pastry hanging over the flan cases. To do this, simply take a sharp knife, position it at the top of the tart ring and cut all the pastry away. By cutting this way the pastry will be neatly flush with the tart case.

You can make the filling in a food mixer or processor. Beat the butter and sugar together until well creamed. Fold in the almonds and flour. Beat in 1 egg at a time, making sure they are well mixed. Spoon the almond filling into the flan case, leaving it about ⅛ inch (2 mm) from the top. If you find you have some mix left over, then chill it in the refrigerator where it will keep for up to 1 week.

Bake the tarts in the preheated oven, allowing 30-35 minutes for the small tarts or 45-60 minutes for a large flan case. When cooked, the tarts will be firm to the touch and a knife inserted in the center will come out almost clean.

To serve, check to see if the almond sponge mix has risen slightly. This can simply be sliced off the top to expose the sponge. While the tart is still warm, spoon some of the jam over the tarts until just covered. Return to the oven for 1-2 minutes by which time the jam will be making its way through the sponge. To serve, simply remove the flan case and eat hot or cold.

GYPSY TART

Serves 6

This is a recipe I had been searching for, for years. It's a dessert I remember from school days and it was my favorite. When I found somebody who knew the dish and was given the recipe I couldn't believe how simple it is – and it still tastes great.

Preheat the oven to 400°F (200°C). Roll out the Short Crust Pastry and line a 10 inch (25 cm) flan ring. Line with greaseproof paper and baking beans and bake in the preheated oven for 15-20 minutes. Remove from the oven and let cool.

Whisk the evaporated milk and sugar together in a food processor or blender for 10-15 minutes until thick and creamy. The mix should be coffee colored. Pour the mix into the pastry case and bake in the oven for 10 minutes. The gypsy tart will now have a slightly sticky surface but will not set completely until it has been cooled. Serve cold. I told you this recipe was easy.

About ⅔ recipe Short Crust Pastry (see page 185)

1 (14 ounce) (400 g) can evaporated milk

2¼ cups dark brown sugar

Vanilla Ice Cream

Serves 4 to 8

1¼ cups heavy whipping
    cream

1¼ cups milk

1 vanilla pod or a few drops
    of vanilla extract

6 egg yolks

¾ cup sugar

This is the base ice cream which you can vary in an infinite number of ways.

Mix together the cream and milk in a pan. Split the vanilla pod lengthwise and scrape the inside into the milk and cream, then add the scraped pod. Bring to the boil.

While the milk is heating, beat the egg yolks and sugar together until pale and light. This can be done in a food mixer. Pour on the milk and cream, stirring all the time until well blended. Stir from time to time until the ice cream mix has cooled. Remove the vanilla pod.

Once cooled, the mix is ready to be churned in the ice cream maker. If you have made the full recipe, you'll need to churn it in 2 batches. Pour the mix into the machine and begin to turn. The ice cream will take about 20-30 minutes and will have thickened and increased in volume. Don't leave the mix turning until completely frozen and set as this will be over-churned and slightly grainy in texture. Take out when thick and

starting to freeze and then finish in the freezer. This will give you a lovely silky smooth texture.

If you don't have an ice cream machine, simply turn the mixture into a freezer tray or bowl and freeze, turning regularly until set.

Variations

For Lemon Curd Ice Cream, mix 1 (12 ounce) (350 g) jar of lemon curd with 2 large tablespoons crème fraîche (see note) or heavy whipping cream and 1 large tablespoon of plain yogurt and churn. It's as simple as that!

For Marmalade Ice Cream, follow the recipe for the Vanilla Ice Cream, made without the vanilla pod. Stir the boiled cream and milk into the egg yolks and sugar, then add 1 (12 ounce) (350 g) jar coarse marmalade and then continue to follow the method.

Crème Fraîche is available at specialty food stores. If you're unable to find it, you can make your own. You can make as much or as little as you want by simply mixing together equal amounts of heavy cream and plain yogurt or sour cream. Put in a glass container, covered, and let it thicken at room temperature for several hours or overnight. Place in the refrigerator to chill. It will keep in the refrigerator for up to 1 week.

STEAMED LEMON and RHUBARB SPONGE

Serves 4 to 6

Using the red currant jelly with the rhubarb is an optional extra that helps enrich the juices from the sugared rhubarb. If eaten cold, the mixture will almost set to jam. The beauty of the recipe is that so many other flavors work with it. A little ginger may be added or you can use other fruit, such as blackberries or blueberries. The rhubarb recipe can also be cooked a little more and then puréed and turned into a sorbet or ice cream.

You can make individual puddings or one large one. The flavors of the rhubarb and lemon work really well together, and you can serve the dessert with Vanilla Ice Cream (see page 180).

For the Lemon Sponge, lightly butter and flour 4 (½ cup) molds or 1 (3 cup) mold. Beat the butter and sugar together until almost white in color and the sugar has dissolved. This is easily achieved in an electric mixer. It does, however, take a little while to cream to this stage. Beat in one egg at a time, making sure after each egg is added that the mix is beaten until completely mixed and fluffy again. Once both eggs have been added, continue with the same process for the egg yolk.

Most recipes will tell you now to fold in the flour slowly and carefully. Well, I want you to do almost the opposite. Add the lemon zest and flour and beat until all the flour has completely creamed into the mix, but do not over-work. Fold in the lemon juice and a little milk if necessary.

For the Rhubarb, peel any coarse skin from the rhubarb stalks; young tender rhubarb will not need to be peeled. Cut the rhubarb into ¾ inch (2 cm) pieces. Melt the butter in a pan until it begins to bubble. Add the rhubarb and stir gently for 1-2 minutes. Add the sugar and bring to the simmer. As the rhubarb is warming it will also be cooking. When it becomes tender, after 4-5 minutes depending upon the size and ripeness, remove from the heat. Stir in the red currant jelly, if using. Remove from the heat and let cool.

Spoon 4-5 tablespoons of the rhubarb into the large mold or 1 tablespoon into the individual molds, cover with the lemon sponge mix filling three-quarters full. Cover with lightly buttered squares of aluminum foil, just lightly folding the foil over the rims so the sponge can rise and push up the foil during cooking. Steam the sponges over boiling water, allowing 35-40 minutes for individual puddings or 1¼-1½ hours for the larger mold. Add more boiling water as necessary during cooking.

FOR THE LEMON SPONGE

½ cup unsalted butter

⅔ cup sugar

2 eggs

1 egg yolk

Finely grated zest and juice of 1 lemon

1½ cups self-rising flour (see page 182)

1-2 drops of milk, if needed

FOR THE RHUBARB

1 pound (450 g) fresh rhubarb

2 tablespoons unsalted butter

1 cup sugar

1 tablespoon red currant jelly (optional)

Gary Rhodes 181
Desserts

STEAMED SPONGE PUDDING

Serves 4 to 6

½ cup unsalted butter

⅔ cup sugar

2 eggs

1 egg yolk

1½ cups self-rising flour
(see note)

1-2 drops milk, if needed

These puddings are real homey classics – just the sort of pudding to finish your meal, especially for a Sunday lunch. Steamed sponges seem to be playing a big part in The Great British Revival. In fact, steamed lemon sponge was one of the, if not the, first pudding that I made. The sponge can be so light and fluffy to eat and will take on to many other flavors, many of which I am featuring here.

To make it a lot easier to turn out the puddings, use plastic molds which hold up very well to steaming, and when lightly pressed, the sponge should fall out easily.

Please note this basic sponge recipe should always be served with additional flavor enhancements. Golden Syrup Sponge is always a favorite. Add a generous spoon of syrup to the sponge mixture and pour some more into the base of each mold and then steam. Pour a little more syrup on top before serving. Check imported food specialty stores to find golden syrup or substitute light molasses.

To make Steamed Lemon Sponge, add the finely grated zest of 1 lemon at the same time the flour is to be added and mixed. Fold in the juice of 1 lemon and a little milk, if necessary. The sponge is now ready for steaming.

Lightly butter and flour 4 (½ cup) molds or 1 (3 cup) mold. Beat the butter and sugar together until almost white in color and the sugar has dissolved. This is easily achieved with an electric mixer. It does, however, take a little while to cream to this stage. Beat in one egg at a time, making sure after each egg is added that the mix is beaten until completely mixed and fluffy again. Do the same with the egg yolk.

Most recipes will tell you now to fold in the flour slowly and carefully. Well, I want you to do almost the opposite. Add the flour and beat until all the flour has completely creamed into the mix, but do not over-work. Add a little milk, if necessary.

Spoon the mixture into the molds, filling three-quarters full. Cover with lightly buttered squares of aluminum foil, just lightly folding the foil over the rims so the sponge can rise and push up the foil during cooking. Steam the sponges over boiling water, allowing 35-40 minutes for individual puddings or 1¼-1½ hours for the larger mold. Add more boiling water as necessary during cooking.

IF YOU ARE UNABLE TO FIND SELF-RISING FLOUR in the grocery store, here is the formula for making your own. Make up as much or as little as you need and store in an airtight container.
1 cup all-purpose flour · 1½ teaspoons baking powder · ½ teaspoon salt

BASIC CRUMBLE MIX

Serves 4

This recipe really couldn't be simpler. It's just two ingredients held together with butter and, of course, seasoned with salt and pepper. The nicest thing about it is that it lends itself to so many flavor combinations: from parsley and lemon to horseradish or mustard and herbs. If you are using additional flavors, add them before stirring in the shallot butter. All these flavors work well with fish, meat or vegetarian dishes.

It's best to use sliced bread that is 24 hours old, as this will firm the bread slightly and prevent the crumbs from becoming doughy.

6-8 slices day old bread

2-4 tablespoons unsalted butter, melted

2 large shallots or ½ onion, finely chopped

Salt to taste

Freshly ground black pepper to taste

Remove and discard the crusts from the bread and cut into quarters. The quickest way to turn these slices into crumbs is to chop in a food processor. If you don't have a food processor, simply push the slices through a metal sieve.

Melt the butter with the chopped shallots and bring to the simmer, remove from the heat and let cool.

Gradually spoon some of the shallot butter into the crumbs, mixing all the time. The mix will be ready when it holds once pressed together, but it should still stay free-flowing.

Use the crumble as directed in recipes.

Homemade Blackberry Jam

Makes about 2 pounds(900g).

2 pounds (900 g) blackberries

1 pound (450 g) or 2 pounds
(900 g) sugar with pectin
(see introduction)

Juice of 1 lemon

In this recipe there are two alternatives for the quantity of sugar, but both work by the same method. The difference is quite simple. If equal amounts of sugar and fruit are used, more syrup is made from the sugar. Also, by using a preserving sugar containing pectin, the jam is guaranteed to set. By using half the sugar content, less syrup is made and so consequently a thicker more "jammy" texture and not quite as sweet taste is the result. I prefer to make the jam with half of the sugar content to achieve a stronger natural taste of the fruits, although jam made in this way will only last for a maximum of two weeks.

This is a basic recipe which can be applied to most soft fruits such as raspberries, strawberries and cherries. However, sharp, firmer fruits, such as black currants, will require more sugar to balance the acidity. These berries obviously have seeds so if you prefer to make jam without them, simply strain through a sieve once.

If you intend to eat the jam within a week or two, simply allow the jam to cool, place in warmed jam jars, leave to cool, then chill. The sugar and pectin are both natural preservatives so the jam will keep perfectly fresh.

If you want to store the jams for longer, you'll need to sterilize them. Sterilize the jars first by covering them with cold water in a large pan, then bringing the water to the boil. Leave to boil for 10-15 minutes, then remove and dry. The glass should be warm before adding the hot jam to prevent the jar from shattering. Once the jars are filled, covered and sealed, you can sterilize them further by sitting the jars on a wire rack or cloth in a large pan and almost covering with water. Bring the water to the boil, then repeat the process. Store the jam in a cool, dark place, or chill it; it will last almost indefinitely.

Carefully rinse the blackberries, making sure you do not damage the fruits. Warm the sugar in a large, heavy-based pan over a low heat; this will take 1-2 minutes. Add the fruits and the sugar will begin to dissolve.

Once some liquid is forming, turn up the heat and bring to the boil, stirring gently. Stir in the lemon juice. As the mix is heating, some froth and impurities will begin to rise to the top. This froth should be skimmed off.

Once boiling rapidly, continue to cook for about 6-7 minutes. The jam should have reached the temperature of 220°F (105°C). With the pectin in the sugar this will be at setting point.

If you don't have a sugar thermometer, simply sit a spoonful of mix on a saucer and set in the refrigerator. Once cold and touched, the jam should have a jellied, wrinkled texture and is now ready to pour into the jars and cover with waxed paper. Allow to cool before closing the lids. The jam should be kept in a dark, cool place or chilled for extra life.

Short Crust *and* Sweet Crust Pastry

Makes about 14 ounces (400g).

This recipe is really short, in both ingredients and in texture. This quantity is really the minimum amount to make for a good texture. The beauty of this pastry is that it freezes well to be used later. This pastry works very well with the Fillet of Mackerel with Caramelized Onions and Sweet Peppers (see page 166) or as a savory or sweet flan base. To make sweet pastry, simply add ½ cup sifted confectioners' sugar to the flour.

1½ sticks (12 tablespoons) unsalted butter, chopped

2 cups all-purpose flour

4 tablespoons cold water

Rub the butter into the flour until a crumble effect is achieved. Add the water and fold in very lightly until the pastry is only just beginning to form and bind. Press the pastry between 2 sheets of plastic wrap. It will have a marbled look.

SODA BREAD

Serves 4

2⅔ cups all-purpose flour

1 level tablespoon baking
 soda

A good pinch of salt

1¼ cups buttermilk

This is a recipe I tried in Ireland – another easy recipe with great results. The first time I ate soda bread, it was filled with bacon and fried egg with a big mug of tea for breakfast – it was lovely. So if you want to have a go at making your own bread for your next "full Irish/ English" breakfast, follow this recipe.

If you can find traditional Irish self-rising soda bread flour, all you need to add is the salt and buttermilk, but this recipe works just as well.

Preheat the oven to 375°F (190°C). Sift the flour, baking soda and salt together. Make a well in the center and pour in the buttermilk. Mix gently to form a dough.

Dust a flat work surface with flour and knead until smooth without overworking. Lightly dust the work surface again with flour then roll out the dough to a circle about ¾ inch (2 cm) thick. Cut the circle into quarters. Place on a baking sheet and bake for 30-40 minutes until golden brown and hollow-sounding when tapped.

To cool and keep crispy, stand the bread on a wire rack. If you prefer a softer bread, wrap in a cloth to cool.

VARIATIONS

You can cook the bread on a griddle or frying pan. Heat the pan over a medium heat. To test the temperature, sprinkle a little flour on the pan; it should turn slightly off-white. Sit the bread into the pan and cook for 12-15 minutes on each side.

BASIC VINAIGRETTE

Makes 2 Cups

This recipe is very convenient: once made, it can sit in your refrigerator and be used at any time and for any dish you might fancy. The vinegar just gives a very slight sweetness to the taste.

Warm the olive and peanut oils together. Place all the remaining ingredients into a 2½ cup bottle. Pour the warmed oils into the bottle and close with a cork or lid.

For the best results, let marinate for a week. Shake the bottle once a day. Taste for salt and pepper before using.

1¼ cups extra-virgin olive oil, preferably French or Italian
1¼ cups peanut oil
2 tablespoons balsamic vinegar
1 bunch fresh basil
½ bunch fresh tarragon
¾ sprigs fresh thyme
12 black peppercorns, lightly crushed
3 shallots, finely chopped
2 garlic cloves, crushed
1 bay leaf
1 teaspoon coarse sea salt

VIERGE DRESSING

Makes 2 Cups

This dressing has a very different flavor and lends itself best to fish dishes. I was first inspired to make it while staying at La Côte St. Jacques in Joigny, France, in the mid 1980's when it was served with a red mullet dish. That restaurant now has three Michelin stars.

Warm the olive oil with the coriander seeds. Place the remaining ingredients in a 2 cup screw-top jar and pour the oil and coriander on top. Screw on the lid and let marinate for 1 week, shaking the bottle daily.

2 cups extra-virgin olive oil, preferably French or Italian
2 tablespoons coriander seeds, crushed
1 bunch fresh tarragon
12 black peppercorns, crushed
4 shallots, chopped
2 garlic cloves, crushed
A pinch of sea salt

DELIA SMITH

IT IS ONLY IN AMERICA WHERE DELIA SMITH NEEDS ANY SORT OF INTRODUCTION, FOR DELIA IS A BRITISH PHENOMENON – her books have sold millions of copies, her BBC specials have endeared her to thousands of viewers, and her name is as recognizable as Julia Child's.

And it only takes one viewing of her television show to understand why: Delia Smith cooks the food that people really want to eat. Looking for the perfect recipe to impress the boss? Or just the right sweet finish to serve after dinner for your closest friends? From the sunny portico of her home, in a style that is both elegant, knowledgeable and unpretentious, Delia calmly shows us just the right recipe, proceeding with clear instruction that inspires even the most inexperienced cook.

These recipes from *Delia's Winter Collection* glow with the pleasures of a warm house on a winter's night. "Surely it is in winter that food comes into our lives with an even sharper focus," muses Delia. Because it's then that we all need to be warm, cozy and comforted. In winter, cooking and eating are a much more serious affair – and here in the following pages, I have attempted to offer what I hope is a strong case for reviving this idea."

Simple methods show how to release the fullest flavors of even the simplest creations, such as *Black Bean Chili with Avocado Salsa* and *Beef in Designer Beer*. Finally, Delia enchants us with an array of truly indulgent desserts, such as *Chocolate Bread and Butter Pudding* and *Apple Crêpes with Calvados*.

Oh, did you think that soufflés and crepes were too complicated? Read on, and be convinced with what so many readers already know – with Delia, many things are possible.

With more than 10 million copies of her books in print, Delia is Britain's all-time best-selling cookbook author. She is the food editor of one of England's most prestigious periodicals, Sainbury's *The Magazine*, and lives with her husband in Suffolk, England.

APPLE *and* CIDER SALAD *with* MELTED CAMEMBERT DRESSING

Serves 6 as a starter or 2 as a light lunch.

*W*hen I wrote the Summer Collection I felt I'd got Caesar salad as perfect as it could be, but then I ate so many Caesar salads that I began to get bored. If this has happened to you too, then let me tell you that this makes an absolutely brilliant alternative, especially in the winter months. It does need ripe Camembert, but if you don't live near a supplier, a supermarket Camembert will have an expiration date that shows when it will have fully ripened, so you can gauge the best time to make the salad. The piquancy of the apple combined with cheese is absolutely superb.

You can, if you want, prepare the dressing ahead, then just gently melt it again before serving.

First make the Garlic Croutons. Then, for the Dressing, cut the cheese in half and use a small, sharp knife to peel it carefully like a potato, paring the skin away from the soft cheese. Place the cheese in a small saucepan. Add the crème fraîche and set aside.

For the Salad, mix the romaine and arugula salad leaves together, breaking up the larger ones into manageable pieces, and arrange on serving plates. Slice the apple, leaving the skin on, and put the slices in a small bowl. Sprinkle with a little of the cider – just enough to cover the slices. Pat them dry and arrange over the salad leaves.

To finish the Dressing, place the saucepan over a gentle heat and whisk the cheese and crème fraîche together for about 3-4 minutes or until the mixture is smooth. If the cheese is very ripe and runny, you may not need to add the rest of the cider, but if the center is less ripe, you will need to add it to keep the mixture smooth. The main thing is to melt the cheese just sufficiently for it to run off the whisk in ribbons, while still retaining its texture. Don't allow the cheese to overheat or it may go stringy – it needs to be melted rather than cooked.

Next, using a small ladle, pour the Dressing equally over the salad and finish with a scattering of the Garlic Croutons. Alternatively, you can hand the Dressing around the table and let your guests help themselves.

1 recipe Garlic Croutons
(see following recipe)

FOR THE DRESSING

9 ounces (250 g) round, ripe, unpasteurized Camembert, chilled

½ cup crème fraîche

FOR THE SALAD

1 head romaine lettuce

½ bunch arugula leaves

1 medium apple, such as Granny Smith or Braeburn

1-2 tablespoons dry cider (if Camembert isn't quite ripe) (see recipe)

Opposite: A Return to the Black Forest (pages 256-257).

Garlic Croutons

Serves 4

2 ounces (50 g) white bread,
cut into small cubes

1 garlic clove, crushed

1 tablespoon olive oil

Preheat the oven to 350°F (180°C). Place the cubes of bread in a bowl together with the garlic and oil and stir them around so that they get an even coating. Transfer to a baking sheet and bake on the high rack of the oven for 10 minutes or until they are crisp and golden.

One word of warning: do use a kitchen timer for this operation because it's actually very hard to bake something for just 10 minutes without forgetting all about it. I have baked more batches of charcoal-colored croutons than I care to remember! Allow them to cool, at which point you can use them immediately, or store in a screw-top jar.

ITALIAN STUFFED EGGPLANT

Serves 2 as a light supper dish or 4 as a starter.

Apart from tasting superb, this is particularly pretty to look at. I like to serve it as a first course, but with a salad and some good bread it would make a lovely supper dish for two people. Vegetarians can replace the anchovies with an extra teaspoon of capers.

Preheat the oven to 350°F (180°C). First of all wipe the eggplant and trim off the stalk end, then using the very sharpest knife you have to cut it lengthwise into 8 thin slices about ¼ inch (6 mm) thick. When you get to the bulbous sides these slices should be chopped into small pieces and kept aside for the filling. Now arrange the slices of eggplant in rows on a large solid baking sheet 16 x 12 inches (40 x 30 cm), lightly oiled, then brush each slice lightly with olive oil and season with the salt and pepper. Pop them into the oven on the high rack and let them precook for 15 minutes, by which time they will have softened enough for you to roll them up easily.

Next pour boiling water on the tomatoes and after 1 minute drain and slip the skins off. Then cut the tomatoes in half and, holding them in the palm of your hand, gently squeeze them until the seeds come out – it's best to do this over a plate or a bowl! Next using a sharp knife, chop the tomatoes into approximately ¼ inch (5 mm) dice. Now heat 1 tablespoon of the oil in a large solid skillet and fry the onion, chopped eggplant and garlic for about 5 minutes. Then add the chopped tomatoes, torn basil leaves and sun-dried tomato paste and continue to cook for about another 5 minutes. Give everything a good seasoning and add the chopped anchovies and the capers. Then remove the skillet from the heat and let the mixture cool slightly.

Now chop the mozzarella into very small dice. As soon as the eggplant slices are cool enough to handle, sprinkle each one with chopped mozzarella, placing it all along the center of each slice. On top of that put an equal amount of stuffing ingredients, leaving a border all around to allow for expansion. Roll up the slices and put them in a baking dish 16 x 12 inches (40 x 30 cm) also oiled, making sure the overlapping ends are tucked underneath. Finally brush each one with oil, combine the fresh bread crumbs and Parmesan, sprinkle the mixture over the eggplant, pop a basil leaf on top of each, then bake (same temperature) for about 20 minutes and serve immediately.

1 (12-14 ounce) (350-400 g) eggplant

2-3 tablespoons olive oil

Salt to taste

Freshly ground black pepper to taste

3 large ripe tomatoes

1 medium onion, finely chopped

1 large garlic clove, crushed

1 tablespoon torn fresh basil leaves

2 teaspoons sun-dried tomato paste

6 drained anchovy fillets, chopped

2 tablespoons drained small capers

5 ounces (150 g) mozzarella

A scant ¼ cup fine fresh bread crumbs

3 tablespoons freshly grated Parmesan cheese, preferably Parmigiano-Reggiano

8 fresh basil leaves, lightly oiled

Baked Eggs in Wild Mushroom Tartlets

Serves 6 as a starter.

For the Pastry

¾ stick butter, softened

1⅓ cups flour, sifted

½ cup finely grated
  Parmesan cheese,
  preferably Parmigiano-
  Reggiano

For the Filling

1 ounce (25 g) dried
  porcini mushrooms

¾ stick butter

2 small red onions,
  finely chopped

2 garlic cloves, chopped

6 ounces (175 g) button
  mushrooms

6 ounces (175 g) portobello
  mushrooms

Sea salt to taste

Freshly ground black pepper
  to taste

2 teaspoons lemon juice

1 heaping tablespoon
  chopped fresh parsley

6 large eggs

⅓ cup freshly grated
  Parmesan cheese,
  preferably Parmigiano-
  Reggiano, for sprinkling
  over the tarts

It's quite a long time since I made a large quiche or tart for entertaining. I feel that individual tarts are prettier and more practical, and people seem to enjoy them. This recipe, with a base of a concentrated mixture of fresh mushrooms and dried porcini, is a delight coupled with a softly baked egg and crisp pastry.

Begin by placing the porcini for the Filling in a bowl. Pour ¾ cup boiling water over them and leave to soak for 30 minutes.

Now make the Pastry. This can easily be done in a food processor or by rubbing the butter into the flour and stirring in the grated Parmesan and sufficient water (approximately 3 tablespoons) to mix to a soft but firm dough. Place the dough in a plastic bag and leave in the refrigerator for 30 minutes to rest. This Pastry will need a little more water than usual as the cheese absorbs some of it.

For the Filling, heat ½ stick of the butter in a heavy-bottomed skillet, add the onions and garlic and fry until they are soft and almost transparent (about 15 minutes). While that's happening, finely chop the button and portobello mushrooms. When the porcini have had their 30 minutes soaking, place a sieve over a bowl and strain them into it, pressing to release the moisture. You can reserve the soaking liquid and freeze it for stocks or sauces if you don't want to throw it out.

Then chop the porcini finely and transfer them with the other mushrooms to the skillet containing the onions. Add the remaining ¼ stick of butter, season with the sea salt and pepper and cook till the juices of the mushrooms run, then add the lemon juice and parsley. Raise the heat slightly and cook the mushrooms without a lid, stirring from time to time to prevent them from sticking, until all the liquid has evaporated and the mixture is of a spreadable consistency. This will take about 2 minutes.

While the mushrooms are cooking, preheat the oven to 400°F (200°C). Now roll out the Pastry to a thickness of ⅛ inch (2 mm) and cut out 6 rounds with a 5½ inch (14 cm) plain pastry cutter, rerolling the pastry if necessary.

Grease 6 tart pans with removable bottoms with a little melted butter and line each with the Pastry, pushing it down from the top so the Pastry will not shrink while cooking. Trim any surplus Pastry from around the top and prick the base with a

fork. Now leave this in the refrigerator for
a few minutes until the oven is up to temperature.

Now place the tart pans on a solid
baking sheet and bake on the middle rack of
the oven for 15-20 minutes until the pastry
is golden and crisp. Remove them from the
oven and reduce the temperature to 350°F
(180°C).

Divide the Filling between the tarts,
making a well in the center with the back
of a spoon. Then break an egg into a saucer
or a small ramekin, slip it into the tart and
scatter a little of the Parmesan over the top.
Repeat this process with the other 5 tarts
and return them to the oven for 12-15
minutes until they are just set and the yolks
are still soft and creamy. Serve immediately,
because if they wait around the eggs will go
on cooking.

PRAWN COCKTAIL 2000

Serves 6

2 pounds (900 g) large
    prawns or jumbo shrimp,
    in their shells (see recipe)

1 head crisp-hearted lettuce,
    such as romaine

½ bunch (1 ounce) (25 g)
    arugula leaves

1 ripe but firm avocado

Cayenne pepper to taste

1 lime, cut into 6 wedges

FOR THE COCKTAIL
SAUCE

1 recipe Homemade
    Mayonnaise
    (see following recipe)

½ tablespoon Worcestershire
    sauce

A few drops Tabasco sauce

½ tablespoon lime juice

2 tablespoons ketchup,
    preferably organic

Salt to taste

Freshly ground black pepper
    to taste

This recipe is part of my "sixties" revival menu. In those days it used to be something simple but really luscious, yet over the years it has suffered from some very poor adaptations, not least watery prawns and inferior sauces. So here, in all its former glory, is a starter quite definitely fit for the new millennium!

The very best version of this is made with prawns (either fresh or frozen in their shells) that you have cooked yourself. Failing that, buy the large cooked prawns in their shells, or if you can only get shelled prawns cut the amount to 1 pound (450 g).

If frozen, put the prawns in a colander and allow to defrost thoroughly at room temperature for about 1 hour. After that, heat a large solid skillet or wok and dry-fry the prawns for 4-5 minutes until the gray turns a vibrant pink. As soon as they're cool, reserve 6 in their shells for a garnish and shell the remainder. Then take a small sharp knife, make a cut along the back of each shelled prawn and remove any black thread. Place the prawns in a bowl, cover with plastic wrap and keep in the refrigerator until needed.

To make the Cocktail Sauce, prepare the Homemade Mayonnaise. Add the rest of the ingredients, stir and taste to check for seasoning. Keep the Sauce covered with plastic wrap in the refrigerator until needed.

When you are ready to serve, shred the lettuce and arugula fairly finely and divide them among 6 stemmed glasses. Peel and chop the avocado into small dice and scatter this in each glass among the lettuce. Top with the prawns and the Sauce. Sprinkle each with a dusting of the cayenne pepper and garnish with 1 section of the lime and 1 of the unpeeled prawns per glass. Serve with brown bread and butter.

HOMEMADE MAYONNAISE

Yields about 1¾ cups.

Homemade mayonnaise made by the traditional method is unbeatable. First a couple of tips: use a small bowl with a narrow base – a 2½ cup mixing bowl is ideal. Place the bowl on a damp towel so it will remain steady and leave your hands free: one to drip the oil, the other to hold the mixer.

First of all put the egg yolks into a bowl, add the crushed garlic, mustard, salt and a little of the freshly ground black pepper and mix well. Then, holding the peanut oil in a pitcher in one hand and an electric beater in the other, add 1 drop of oil to the egg mixture and beat it in.

However stupid it may sound, the key to a successful mayonnaise is making sure each drop of oil is thoroughly beaten in before adding the next drop. It won't take all day, because after a few minutes – once you've added several drops of oil – the mixture will begin to thicken and go very stiff and lumpy. When it gets to this stage you need to add the teaspoon of vinegar, which will thin the mixture down.

Now the critical point has passed, so you can begin pouring the oil in a very, very thin but steady stream, keeping the mixer going all the time. When all the oil has been added, taste for salt and pepper. If you'd like the mayonnaise to be a bit lighter, at this stage add 2 tablespoons of boiling water and beat it in.

Mayonnaise only curdles when you add the oil too quickly at the beginning. If that happens, don't despair. All you need to do is put a fresh egg yolk into a clean bowl, add the curdled mixture to it (drop by drop), then continue adding the rest of the oil as though nothing had happened.

The mayonnaise should be stored in a screw-top jar in the bottom of the refrigerator for no longer than a week.

2 large egg yolks

1 garlic clove, crushed

1 heaping teaspoon ground mustard

1 teaspoon salt

Freshly ground black pepper to taste

1¼ cups peanut oil

1 teaspoon white wine vinegar

WARM LENTIL SALAD *with* WALNUTS *and* GOAT CHEESE

Serves 4

1 tablespoon extra virgin
   olive oil

⅓ cup walnuts,
   roughly chopped

1 small red onion,
   finely chopped

1 large garlic clove, crushed

1½ cups raw Puy lentils

1 bay leaf

1 heaping teaspoon fresh
   thyme leaves, chopped

Salt to taste

½ bunch arugula,
   leaves torn in half

4 ounces (100 g) firm
   goat cheese

FOR THE DRESSING

1 large garlic clove

1 teaspoon sea salt

2 teaspoons ground mustard

2 tablespoons balsamic
   vinegar

2 tablespoons walnut oil

¼ cup extra virgin olive oil

Freshly ground black pepper
   to taste

I think we should all be eating more legumes, so the more recipes that include them the better. In this warm salad, I've chosen the tiny black-gray Puy lentils, but the green or brown variety will work just as well, given slightly less cooking time.

First you need to cook the walnuts. To do this, heat the oil in a medium saucepan and when it's hot, lightly fry the chopped walnuts for about 1 minute. Remove them with a slotted spoon to a plate and keep them aside for later.

Now to the oil left in the saucepan, add the onion and crushed garlic and let these cook over medium heat and soften for about 5 minutes. Stir in the lentils, bay leaf and thyme and stir well to make sure they all get a good coating of the oil. Add 1¼ cups of boiling water, cover, reduce the heat to a gentle simmer and let the lentils cook for 30-40 minutes or until they're tender and all the liquid has been absorbed. You really need to bite one to test if they're done.

While the lentils are cooking, you can prepare the Dressing. Use a mortar and pestle to crush the garlic with the salt until it's creamy, then add the mustard and work that into the garlic paste. Whisk in the balsamic vinegar, followed by the two oils. Season well with the freshly ground black pepper.

As soon as the lentils are cooked, add salt to taste. Empty them into a warm serving bowl and while they're still hot, pour the Dressing over. Give everything a good toss and stir, then crumble the goat cheese all over and add the arugula. Give everything one more toss and stir, and serve immediately with the walnuts scattered over.

WARM POACHED EGG SALAD *with* FRIZZLED CHORIZO

Serves 4

This makes a fun starter for four people, or a zappy light lunch or supper dish for two. For poaching you need very fresh eggs, so watch the expiration date on the carton when you buy them and, to be absolutely sure, pop them into a glass measuring cup filled with cold water. If the eggs sit horizontally on the bottom they're very fresh. A slight tilt is acceptable, but if they sit vertically your supplier's dates are in doubt.

Chorizo is a spicy Spanish pork sausage made with paprika. At specialty food shops you can also buy chorizo piccante, a spicier version, which gives the whole thing a wonderful kick. You can also make this with red wine and red wine vinegar or white wine and white wine vinegar for a little variety.

First make the Croutons by following the basic recipe, but omit the garlic and sprinkle the paprika over the bread cubes before the olive oil.

When you're ready to make the salad, start with the eggs. A useful way to poach 4 eggs without any last-minute hassle is to pour boiling water straight from the kettle into a medium frying pan. Place it over a heat gentle enough for there to be the merest trace of bubbles simmering on the bottom of the frying pan. Now carefully break the 4 eggs into the water and let them cook for just 1 minute. Remove the skillet from the heat and leave the eggs in the hot water for 10 minutes, after which time the whites will be set and the yolks creamy.

Now arrange the salad leaves on 4 plates. In another skillet, heat 1 tablespoon of the olive oil until it's very hot. Add the chorizo and cook for 2-3 minutes. Add the onion, garlic and bell pepper, stirring to keep the ingredients on the move. Cook for about 6 minutes until the ingredients are toasted around the edges, turning down the heat if it gets too hot. Now add the sherry, sherry vinegar and the remaining 2 tablespoons of the olive oil. Let it all bubble a bit and season with the salt and pepper.

To remove the eggs from the first frying pan, use a slotted spoon with a wad of paper towels underneath to absorb the moisture. Place them centrally on the salad leaves on the serving plates, pour the warm chorizo dressing over everything, and finally sprinkle on the croutons. We eat this with olive bread to mop up the juices – a wonderful accompaniment.

1 recipe Garlic Croutons (see page 194), minus the garlic and plus 1 tablespoon hot paprika

4 very fresh large eggs

3 ounces (75 g) assorted green salad leaves

3 tablespoons extra virgin olive oil

6 ounces (175 g) chorizo sausage, skinned and cut into ¼ inch (5 mm) cubes

1 medium onion, finely chopped

2 garlic cloves, finely chopped

1 red bell pepper, seeded and chopped small

3 tablespoons dry sherry

1½ tablespoons sherry vinegar

Salt to taste

Freshly ground black pepper to taste

FOR THE CRUST

2 cups white bread crumbs

⅔ cup finely grated Pecorino
   Romano cheese or
   Parmigiano-Reggiano

¼ stick butter, melted

Freshly ground black pepper
   to taste

FOR THE FILLING

3 large eggs

1 cup farmer cheese

½ cup fromage blanc (8% fat)

Salt to taste

Freshly ground black pepper
   to taste

1½ cups coarsely crumbled
   Roquefort cheese

2 tablespoons snipped
   fresh chives

4 scallions, finely sliced

FOR THE PEARS IN
BALSAMIC VINAIGRETTE

4 firm but ripe pears

1 large garlic clove

1 teaspoon sea salt

2 teaspoons ground mustard

Freshly ground black pepper
   to taste

1 tablespoon balsamic
   vinegar

⅓ cup extra virgin olive oil

WARM ROQUEFORT CHEESECAKE *with* PEARS *in* BALSAMIC VINAIGRETTE

Serves 8

*T*his savory cheesecake includes a clever blend of three cheese flavors, as the smooth fromage blanc and farmer's cheese gently complement the sharpness of the Roquefort. And, while cheese and pears are always good partners, this particular combination is a marriage made in heaven.

Preheat the oven to 375°F (190°C). First of all make the Crust of the cheesecake by mixing the bread crumbs and Pecorino together, then pour in the butter, adding a good grinding of the pepper. Press the crumb mixture firmly down over the bottom of a springform cake pan 9 inches (23 cm) in diameter, then bake in the preheated oven for 15-20 minutes. Then remove it from the oven and turn the heat down to 350°F (180°C).

Now make the Filling. First beat together the eggs and farmer cheese in a bowl, then stir in the fromage blanc and seasoning. After that stir the Roquefort in, together with the chives. Pour the mixture into the pan and scatter the sliced scallions over the top, then place it on the high rack of the oven and bake for 30-40 minutes or until the center feels springy to the touch. Allow the cheesecake to cool and settle for about 20 minutes before serving cut into slices.

The Pears in Balsamic Vinaigrette can be prepared up to 2 hours before serving.

Thinly pare off the skins of the pears using a potato peeler and being careful to leave the stems intact. Now lay each pear on its side with the stem flat on a board, then take a very sharp knife and make an incision through the tip of the stem. Turn the pear the right way up and gently cut it in half, first sliding the knife through the stem and then through the pear.

Now remove the central core of each half, then, with the pear core-side-down, slice it thinly but leave the slices joined at the top. Press gently and the slices will fan out.

Make up the vinaigrette by crushing the clove of garlic and sea salt together with a mortar and pestle until it becomes a creamy paste. Now add the mustard and several grinds of black pepper. Work these into the garlic, then, using a small whisk, add the balsamic vinegar and then the oil – whisking all the time to amalgamate. Serve 1 pear half with each portion of the cheesecake, with a little of the vinaigrette spooned over.

Libyan Soup *with* Couscous

Serves 6

This recipe first appeared in the Food Aid Cookery Book, published in 1986. Its contributor, Mary El-Rayes, has kindly given me permission to reprint it here. It's the perfect soup to serve on a cold winter's day with pita bread warm from the oven.

Begin by preheating a small frying pan over medium heat. Add the coriander and cumin seeds and dry-roast for about 2-3 minutes, stirring until they change color and begin to dance. This will draw out their full spicy flavor. Transfer them to a mortar and pestle and crush them quite finely.

Heat 1 tablespoon of the oil in a large 3 quart saucepan and gently cook the onion until soft and lightly brown, about 5-6 minutes. Add the crushed garlic and cook for 2 minutes. Add the crushed spices, allspice and chili powder and stir them into the juices in the pan. Now transfer all this to a plate and keep it aside.

Heat the remaining tablespoon of the oil in the same pan until it's very hot. Add the pieces of lamb and brown them, quickly turn them over and keeping them on the move.

Turn the heat down and return the onion-and-spice mixture to the pan. Stir in the tomato paste, chopped chili and sugar. Stir everything together, then add the water and stock. Give it all another good stir. Drain the soaked chick-peas, discarding their soaking liquid. Add the chick-peas to the saucepan, give a final stir and cover with a tight-fitting lid. Simmer as gently as possible for 1 hour or until the chick-peas are tender.

Just before serving, taste the soup and add salt to taste. Add the couscous, parsley and mint and take the pan off the heat. Put the lid back on and let it stand for 3 minutes before serving it in hot soup bowls. Serve with the lemon wedges to squeeze into the soup and some warm pita bread.

1 heaping teaspoon coriander seeds

1 heaping teaspoon cumin seeds

2 tablespoons oil

1 large onion, chopped

2 garlic cloves, crushed with 1 teaspoon sea salt with a mortar and pestle

1 heaping teaspoon ground allspice

2 heaping teaspoons mild chili powder

6 ounces (175 g) finely chopped raw lamb, leg steak or similar

½ cup tomato paste

1 green chili, seeded and chopped

2 teaspoons sugar

3¾ cups water

2½ cups good lamb stock

⅔ cup dried chick-peas, soaked overnight in twice their volume of cold water

Salt to taste

⅓ cup couscous

1 tablespoon chopped fresh parsley

1 tablespoon chopped fresh mint

Lemon wedges, for garnish

Pita bread

BLACK BEAN SOUP *with* BLACK BEAN SALSA

Serves 4 to 6

1½ cups dried black beans

2 tablespoons olive oil

3 ounces (75 g) pancetta
   or smoked bacon,
   finely chopped

1 large onion, finely chopped

1 large garlic clove, crushed

½ cup finely chopped carrot

½ cup finely chopped
   rutabaga

½ cup or ½ bunch fresh
   cilantro stalks, finely
   chopped and leaves
   reserved for the Salsa

1 teaspoon cumin seeds

1 teaspoon Tabasco sauce

1 quart chicken stock

Juice of ½ lime, reserving
   the other ½ for the Salsa

Salt to taste

Freshly ground black pepper
   to taste

1 heaping tablespoon crème
   fraîche

This soup is simply stunning, one you'll want to make over and over again. Black beans don't have a strong flavor of their own but they do carry other flavors superbly, while at the same time yielding a unique velvety texture. If you forget to soak the beans overnight, bring them up to the boil for 10 minutes and then presoak them for three hours. Serving salsa with soup makes a clever contrast of the cold refreshing textures of the vegetables and the hot lusciousness of the soup.

The night before serving, it's best to start the soup by throwing the beans into a pan and covering them with approximately twice their volume of cold water. The day of serving, drain them in a colander, rinse under cold running water and set aside. Now take a large saucepan, about 3 quarts capacity, and heat the 2 tablespoons of olive oil. As soon as it's really hot, add the chopped pancetta and cook for about 5 minutes. Turn the heat down to medium and stir in the onion, garlic, carrot, rutabaga and cilantro stalks. Continue to cook for 10 minutes, covered, stirring everything once to twice.

While that's happening, heat a small frying pan over medium heat. Add the cumin seeds and dry-roast them for 1-3 minutes until they become very aromatic, begin to change color and start to dance in the skillet. At that point remove them from the frying pan and crush them to a coarse powder with a mortar and pestle. Add this to the vegetables along with the drained beans, Tabasco sauce and stock. Bring everything up to a gentle simmer and cook covered for about 1½ hours. It's very important to keep the simmer as gentle as possible, so you might need to use a heat diffuser here.

When the time is up, use a slotted spoon to remove ⅔ cup of the beans; rinse and drain them in a sieve and set aside for the Salsa. Now you need to purée the soup, and the best way to do this is in a blender, although a food processor will do just as fine. When the soup is puréed, return it to the saucepan, add the lime juice, season with the salt and pepper and it's now ready for reheating later when you want to serve it.

For the Salsa, pour boiling water over the tomatoes and leave them for 1 minute. Slip the skins off, cut them in half and gently squeeze each half in your hand to remove the seeds. Chop the tomatoes into a small dice and place them in a bowl along with the reserved beans, red onion, green chili, cilantro leaves and extra virgin olive oil. Add the lime juice, salt and pepper and leave it aside for about 1 hour for the flavors to mingle and be absorbed.

To serve the soup, reheat it very gently, being careful not to allow it to come to the boil, as boiling always spoils the flavor of soup. Serve in warm soup bowls, adding a spoonful of the crème fraîche and an equal portion of the Salsa sprinkled over the surface.

For the Salsa

2 large tomatoes, not too ripe

⅔ cup cooked black beans (see recipe)

1 small red onion, finely chopped

1 green chili, seeded and chopped

Cilantro leaves reserved from the soup

½ tablespoon extra virgin olive oil

Juice of ½ lime reserved from the soup

Salt to taste

Freshly ground black pepper to taste

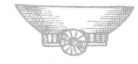

BEEF *in* DESIGNER BEER

Serves 4 to 6

≈

In the "sixties," every other restaurant was a bistro and every other bistro served Carbonnade de Boeuf à la Flamande, a traditional Flemish recipe which translates as Beef in Beer. But like other once-hackneyed "sixties" recipes, I think it's been neglected and there's a whole new generation now who probably haven't yet tasted it. For them, here is the "nineties" version, the only difference being that we now have a vast range of beers with smart labels to choose from. Not sure which one to use? Do what I do and go for the prettiest label!

FOR THE CHEESE CROUTONS

1 tablespoon olive oil

1 garlic clove, crushed

6 slices French baguette, cut slightly diagonally 1 inch (2.5 cm) thick

2 tablespoons whole grain mustard

1 cup grated Gruyère cheese

FOR THE BEEF

1 tablespoon olive oil

2 pounds (900 g) skirt or braising steak, cut into 2 inch (5 cm) squares

12 ounces (350 g) onions, quartered

2 garlic cloves, crushed

1 heaping tablespoon flour

2 cups designer beer (see introduction)

Salt to taste

Freshly ground black pepper to taste

A few fresh thyme sprigs

2 bay leaves

For the Croutons, preheat the oven to 350°F (180°C). Drizzle the olive oil onto a large solid baking sheet, add the crushed garlic, then, using either your hands or a piece of paper towel, spread the oil and garlic all over the baking sheet. Place the bread slices on top of the oil, then turn them over so that both sides have been lightly coated with the oil. Bake for 20-25 minutes until crisp and crunchy. This can be done well ahead of time.

For the Beef, preheat the oven to 300°F (150°C). Place a large, wide ovenproof casserole over high heat and cook the olive oil until sizzling hot. Put only enough meat that can fit in a single layer in the pan and fry on all sides until it turns a dark mahogany color. Continue browning the meat in batches until all is done then set aside. To the same casserole, add the onions and cook over high heat, stirring, until they become darkly tinged at the edges, about 5 minutes. Add the garlic and cook for about 30 seconds. Turn the heat down, return the meat to the casserole and sprinkle in the flour, stirring, until all the flour has been absorbed into the juices. It will look rather stodgy and unpromising at this stage but not to worry. The long slow cooking will transform its appearance.

Gradually stir in the beer then gently let the stew come up to the simmering point. While that's happening, add the salt, black pepper, thyme and bay leaves. Then, just as it begins to bubble, cover, transfer to the center rack of the oven and cook for 2½ hours. Don't be tempted to taste it now or halfway through the cooking, as it does take 2½ hours for the beer to mellow and become a luscious sauce.

Just before serving, preheat the broiler. Spread the Croutons with the mustard and sprinkle with the grated Gruyère. Arrange them on top of the meat and pop the casserole under the broiler until the cheese is bubbling. Serve immediately.

Black Bean Chili *with* Avocado Salsa

Serves 4 to 6

The now-familiar chili con carne has suffered from its fair share of convenience shortcut versions, but when it's made properly with the right ingredients, it is still a wonderful concept. I think this version is even better than the original, using black beans and introducing the subtle flavoring of lime and cilantro – and adding a contrasting garnish at the end.

Either presoak the beans overnight or start this recipe 3 hours ahead of time and begin by placing the beans in a large saucepan, covering them with cold water and bringing them up to boiling point and boiling for 10 minutes. Then turn the heat off and let them soak for 3 hours. Toward the end of the soaking time preheat the oven to 300°F (150°C).

Strip the leaves off the cilantro stalks into a bowl, cover with plastic wrap and place in the refrigerator. Then chop the cilantro stalks very finely. After that take an ovenproof casserole of 2 quarts capacity with a tight-fitting lid, heat half the oil in it and cook the onions, garlic, cilantro stalks and chilies gently for about 5 minutes. Then transfer them to a plate, spoon the rest of the oil into the casserole, turn the heat up high, add about a third of the beef and brown it well. Then remove it and brown the rest in 2 batches. Now return everything to the casserole and stir in the flour. Add the drained beans, followed by the tomatoes. Stir well and bring it up to simmering point. Cover, transfer the casserole to the oven to cook for 1½ hours.

Toward the end of that time, seed and finely chop the bell pepper. Then when the time is up, stir the bell pepper in to join the meat and beans. Cover and give it a further 30 minutes cooking.

While the meat finishes cooking, make up the Salsa. Skin the tomatoes by pouring boiling water over them, then leaving for exactly 1 minute before draining and slipping the skins off when they're cool enough to handle. Then cut each tomato in half and, holding each half over a saucer, squeeze gently to extract the seeds. Now chop the tomato flesh as finely as possible.

Next halve the avocado, remove the stone, cut each half into quarters and peel off the skin. Chop the avocado into minutely small dice, and do the same with the onion. Finally combine the tomato, avocado and onion together in a bowl, add seasoning, the juice of half the lime, half the chopped cilantro leaves and a few drops of the Tabasco.

Before serving, add salt to taste. Then stir in the rest of the cilantro leaves and the juice of half the lime.

1⅓ cups dried black beans

1 bunch fresh cilantro (reserving leaves for the Salsa)

2 tablespoons olive oil

2 onions, chopped

1 garlic clove, crushed

2 fresh green chilies, seeded and chopped small

1 pound (450 g) skirt or braising steak, cut into very small pieces

2 tablespoons flour

2 (14 ounce) (400 g) cans chopped tomatoes

1 large red bell pepper

Salt to taste

½ reserved cilantro leaves, roughly chopped

Juice of ½ lime

1 cup crème fraîche, for garnish

For the Salsa

2 large firm tomatoes

1 ripe firm avocado

½ small red onion, finely chopped

Salt to taste

Freshly ground black pepper to taste

Juice of ½ lime

½ reserved chopped cilantro leaves

A few drops Tabasco sauce

Braised Lamb *with* Flageolet Beans

Serves 4

1⅓ cups dried flageolet beans

2 pounds (900 g) lamb shoulder chops, filleted

2 tablespoons oil

2 large onions, halved and cut into ½ inch (1 cm) rounds

2 garlic cloves, finely chopped

¼ cup flour

½ tablespoon chopped fresh thyme leaves

2½ cups lamb stock or water

Freshly ground black pepper to taste

4 small fresh thyme sprigs

3 small bay leaves

8 ounces (225 g) cherry tomatoes

Salt to taste

Though the lamb shoulder chop is quite an economical cut, it provides very sweet meat that responds perfectly to long slow cooking. The presoaked dried green flageolets absorb the flavors of the lamb, garlic and herbs, making this a comforting winter warmer.

You start this recipe by soaking the beans. To do this, cover the beans with twice their volume of cold water, then soak them overnight. Alternatively, on the same day, boil them for 10 minutes, then leave them to soak for a minimum of 2 hours.

When you're ready to cook the lamb, preheat the oven to 275°F (140°C), trim off any excess fat and then cut the lamb into cubes about ¼ inch (5 mm) thick. Now place an ovenproof casserole dish of approximately 4 pints capacity over direct heat, add 1 tablespoon of oil, then as soon as it's smoking hot, brown the pieces of meat, a few at a time, wiping them first with paper towels so that they're absolutely dry when they hit the oil (don't add more than 6 pieces at a time). Then as soon as each piece is nicely browned on both sides, remove the cubes to a plate and carry on until all the meat is browned.

Next add the other tablespoon of oil and, keeping the heat high, brown the onions around the edges, moving them around until they take on a nice dark caramel color – this will take about 5 minutes – then add the garlic, stir that into the onions and let it

cook for another minute or so. Now sprinkle in the flour and give it all a good stir, allowing the flour to soak into the juices. Add the thyme leaves, then gradually add the stock, stirring all the while as you pour it in. Next return the meat to the casserole and season it well with freshly ground black pepper, but no salt at this stage. After that drain the beans, discarding their soaking water, and add them to the casserole as well.

Finally add the thyme sprigs and bay leaves, and as soon as everything has come up to simmering point, place a tight-fitting lid on and transfer the casserole to the center rack of the oven. Give it 1½ hours, and toward the end of that time, pour boiling water over the tomatoes and then after 30 seconds drain off the water and slip the skins off. Add these to the casserole along with a good seasoning of salt, then replace the lid and carry on cooking for a further hour.

Before serving remove the bay leaves and sprigs of thyme and taste to check the seasoning.

BRAISED STEAK AU POIVRE *in* RED WINE

Serves 4

While the French classic steak au poivre or peppered steak, is a wonderful idea, steak is expensive and in the winter the original recipe can be adapted to braising – which is far easier for entertaining and tastes every bit as good. I like to serve it with some crispy-skinned butter-jacket potatoes.

Preheat the oven to 300°F (150°C). Crush the peppercorns coarsely with a mortar and pestle, then mix them together with the flour on a plate. Now dip the pieces of meat into this mixture, pressing it well in on all sides. Next heat 2 tablespoons of the drippings or oil in an ovenproof casserole with a tight-fitting lid, and when it is really hot and beginning to shimmer quickly brown the pieces of meat, about 4 at a time, on both sides, then transfer them to a plate.

After that add the remaining drippings or oil to the pan and brown the onions for 3-4 minutes, still keeping the heat high. Then add the crushed garlic and cook for another minute. Now add any remaining flour and pepper left on the plate to the pan, stirring well to soak up the juices, then add the wine a little at a time, continuing to stir to prevent any lumps forming, and scraping up any crusty residue from the bottom and edge of the pan. When it's at simmering point, add the meat to the sauce, season it with salt, then pop the bay leaves and thyme sprig in. Bring it back to a simmer then put a lid on the casserole and transfer it to the middle rack of the oven to cook for 2 hours or until the meat is tender.

When you're ready to serve, remove the herbs, add the crème fraîche, stir it well in, then taste to check for seasoning before serving.

½ tablespoon black peppercorns

2 tablespoons flour

2 pounds (900 g) good-quality skirt or braising steak, cut into 2 inch (5 cm) pieces

3 tablespoons beef drippings or olive oil

2 large onions, finely chopped

2 large garlic cloves, crushed with 1 teaspoon sea salt with a mortar and pestle

2 cups red wine

Salt to taste

2 bay leaves

1 large thyme sprig

½ cup crème fraîche

BRAISED STEAK *in* MADEIRA *with* FIVE KINDS *of* MUSHROOMS

Serves 4 to 6

½ ounce (15 g) dried porcini
   mushrooms

2 pounds (900 g) skirt or
   braising steak (1 thick
   slice)

2 medium onions

2 tablespoons olive oil

2 tablespoons flour

3 tablespoons butter

1¼ cups dry Maderia

1 bay leaf

A few fresh thyme sprigs

Salt to taste

Freshly ground black pepper
   to taste

1½ cups button mushrooms

1½ cups portobello
   mushrooms

2 cups oyster mushrooms

2 cups shiitake mushrooms

1 large garlic clove, crushed

This recipe is really a very moveable feast. For an everyday version you could replace the Madeira with cider or beer and use just one variety of mushroom.

First of all soak the dried porcini by placing them in a bowl with 2 cups warm water for at least 30 minutes. Meanwhile, trim the beef of any hard gristle and membrane, and if it's a whole slice divide it into 4 pieces. Cut the onions in half lengthwise and then into ½ inch (1 cm) wedges. Now in a large shallow ovenproof casserole with a tight-fitting lid, heat half the olive oil and sauté the onions until nicely tinged brown at the edges, then remove them to a plate. Heat the remaining oil in the casserole, turning the heat up really high, then brown the pieces of meat, two at a time on both sides, and remove them as they're done to join the onions.

Preheat the oven to 250°F (120°C). Next drain the porcini through a sieve lined with paper towels, reserving the liquid, and chop them roughly. Now stir the flour into the oil left in the casserole along with 1 tablespoon of butter, then slowly add the mushroom water, stirring well after each addition, and follow that with the Maderia, whisking well to blend everything. As soon as the liquid comes up to simmering point, add the onions and the browned beef to the casserole, along with the chopped porcini. Add the bay leaf and thyme, season with the salt and pepper, then put a lid on and place the casserole in the oven for 1½ hours. After that chop the button and portobello mushrooms roughly (not too small). Add these to the casserole, sprinkling them on the steak and spooning the juices over, then replace the lid, return the casserole to the oven and let it cook slowly for another 1½ hours.

When you're ready to serve, slice the oyster and shiitake mushrooms into ½ inch (1 cm) strips, reserving a few small whole ones for garnish, then melt the remaining butter in a skillet, add the garlic and mushrooms and season with the salt and pepper. Toss everything around in the pan for 2-3 minutes.

Now remove the casserole from the oven, taste to check the seasoning, then serve the steaks with the sauce spooned over and garnished with the whole shiitake and oyster mushrooms.

CLASSIC ROAST PORK *with* CRACKLINGS

Serves 8

This recipe is for pork loin roast, which provides maximum cracklings, but the butcher must chine it for you – that is, loosen the bone, yet leave it attached so that it can eventually be cut away to make carving easier.

How to get crisp, crunchy cracklings is not a problem if you follow a few simple guidelines. Buy the pork a couple of days before you need to cook it, remove any plastic wrap, put it on a plate immediately and dry it as thoroughly as possible with absorbent paper towels. After that, leave it uncovered in the lowest part of the refrigerator so that the skin can become as dry as possible before you start cooking.

5 pounds (2.2 kg) pork loin
   roast, chined

1 small onion

1 tablespoon sea salt

Freshly ground black pepper

1 tablespoon flour

1¼ cups dry cider

1¼ cups vegetable stock
   (or potato water)

Preheat the oven to 475°F (250°C). While the oven is preheating, score the skin of the pork. It will be scored already, but it's always best to add a few more lines. To do this you can use the point of a very sharp paring knife, or you can even buy a special scalpel from a kitchenware store! What you need to do is score the skin all over into thin strips, bringing the blade of the knife about halfway through the fat beneath the skin.

Now place the pork in a solid roasting pan, approximately 12 x 10 inches (30 x 25 cm), skin-side-up, half the onion and wedge the 2 pieces in slightly underneath the meat. Now take about 1 tablespoon of crushed salt crystals and sprinkle it evenly over the skin, pressing it in as much as you can. Then place the pork on a high rack in the oven and roast the meat for 25 minutes. After that turn the heat down to 375°F (190°C) and calculate the cooking time, allowing 35 minutes to the pound (450 g). In this case it would be 2½ hours.

There's no need to baste pork as there is enough fat to keep the meat moist. The way to tell if the meat is cooked is to insert a skewer in the thickest part, and the juices that run out should be absolutely clear without any trace of pinkness. When the pork is cooked remove it from the oven and give it at least 30 minutes resting time before carving. While that is happening, tilt the pan and spoon all the fat off, leaving only the juices. The onion will probably be black and charred, which gives the gravy a lovely rich color. Leave the onion in, then place the roasting pan over direct heat, turned to low, sprinkle in the flour and quickly work it into the juices with a wooden spoon.

Now turn the heat up to medium and gradually add the cider and the stock, this time using a balloon whisk until it comes up to simmering point and you have a smooth rich gravy. Taste and season with salt and pepper, then discard the onion and pour the gravy into a warmed gravy boat.

Serve the pork carved in slices, giving everyone some cracklings and one Roasted Stuffed Apple (see page 253).

Broccoli Soufflé *with* Three Cheeses

*Serves 4 as a light lunch together with a green salad,
or 6 to 8 as a starter.*

Melted butter for the dish
and parchment collar

⅓ cup freshly grated
Parmesan cheese,
preferably Parmigiano-
Reggiano

1 pound (450 g) broccoli,
with the very thick stalks
trimmed

Salt to taste

3 large eggs plus 2 egg whites

¼ stick butter

⅓ cup flour

⅔ cup milk

Freshly ground black pepper
to taste

¼ teaspoon cayenne pepper

¼ whole nutmeg, grated

⅓ cup grated sharp Cheddar
cheese

⅓ cup grated Gruyère cheese

The secret of a well-risen soufflé lies precisely in the size of dish you use. If you want it to look amazing use a small dish with a collar tied around – this way you can pile the mixture up high, then when it's cooked remove the collar to reveal a spectacular height! Of course it all tastes the same, but it's good to have some fun when you're cooking, and this is great fun! One thing to remember when making soufflés is that you must have the bowls and whisks spanking clean, then wipe them with a little lemon juice and paper towels to ensure they're absolutely grease-free.

First of all prepare the soufflé dish and its collar. To do this, cut a piece of parchment paper from the roll, 20 x 12 inches (50 x 30 cm) in length. Fold in half along its length so that it now measures 20 x 6 inches (50 x 15 cm) doubled. Now turn up a 2 inch (5 cm) fold all along the length to stabilize the base of the collar.

Next butter a 3 cup capacity soufflé dish measuring 5 inches (13 cm) diameter and 3 inches (7.5 cm) high, such as Apilco (available from kitchenware stores) really well and sprinkle the inside with some of the Parmesan, tipping the dish from side to side to give the base and sides a light coating. Empty out the excess, then tie the paper collar around the dish with the 1 inch (2.5 cm) folded bit at the bottom. The paper will overlap around the circumference by 3 inches (7.5 cm) and stand 2 inches (5 cm) above the rim of the dish. Fix the collar in place with string and tie with a bow so that when it comes out of the oven you can

remove it quickly and easily. Now butter the inside of the paper and that's it – the dish is now ready to receive the soufflé.

To make the soufflé, preheat the oven to 400°F (200°C). Place the oven rack in the lower third of the oven with no rack above. Place the broccoli in a steamer, sprinkle with salt and steam over simmering water until tender – approximately 8-10 minutes. While the broccoli is cooking, prepare the eggs. Have ready a large bowl containing the extra egg whites and two small bowls. Separate the eggs into the small bowls one at a time, transferring the whites from the small bowl into the larger bowl as you go. When the broccoli is tender, remove it and leave to cool until barely warm. Then pop it into the processor and process it almost to a purée.

Next place the butter, flour and milk in a small saucepan and whisk with a balloon whisk over a medium heat until you have a smooth, glossy paste. Season to taste with the salt and pepper, then season with about the same amount again – this extra is really to season the large volume of eggs. Transfer to a mixing bowl and add the cayenne, nutmeg, Cheddar, Gruyère and half of the grated Parmesan. Add the 3 egg yolks plus the broccoli and mix everything together thoroughly.

Now the vital part – the beating of the egg whites. If you're using an electric mixer, switch it on to low and beat the whites for approximately 30 seconds or until they start foaming. Then increase the speed of the mixer to medium and then to high, moving the beaters around and around the bowl while it's beating, until you get a smooth glossy mixture that stands in stiff peaks when the beaters are removed from the bowl. It's better to underbeat than overbeat, so watch carefully.

Next, using a large metal spoon, stir 1 spoonful of the egg whites into the broccoli to lighten the mixture, then empty the broccoli mixture into the egg whites and fold, using cutting and turning movements, until everything is well amalgamated. Don't be tempted to do any mixing – it must be careful folding done as quickly as possible. Now pour the mixture into the prepared dish, sprinkle the top with the remaining Parmesan and place on a rack in the lower third of the oven (with no rack above) for 40-45 minutes. When it's done it should be nicely browned on top, well risen and beginning to crack. It should feel springy in the center but it's important not to over-cook it, as it should be nice and moist, almost runny inside, because as you are taking it from the oven to the table, and even as you're serving it, it will go on cook-ing. Divide among warm serving plates and serve it absolutely immediately.

NOTE: This soufflé can be made with other vegetable purées: parsnips, Jerusalem artichokes or zucchini would make lovely alternatives.

An Authentic Ragù Bolognese

Makes 8 (8 ounce) (225 g) servings, each serving 2 people.

6 tablespoons extra virgin
    olive oil

2 medium onions, finely
    chopped

4 large garlic cloves, chopped

5 ounces (150 g) pancetta
    or bacon, chopped

1 pound (450 g) lean ground
    beef

1 pound (450 g) ground pork

8 ounces (225 g) chicken
    livers

2 (14 ounce) (400 g) cans
    Italian chopped tomatoes

14 ounces (400 g) double
    concentrate tomato paste

1¾ cups red wine

Salt to taste

Freshly ground black pepper
    to taste

½ whole nutmeg, grated

1 bunch (or 1 ounce) (25 g)
    fresh basil leaves

In Britain, it's really sad that so often stewed ground beef with the addition of herbs and tomato purée gets presented as bolognese sauce – even, dare I say it, in lesser Italian restaurants. Yet properly made, an authentic ragù bolognese bears absolutely no resemblance to this travesty. The real thing is a very slowly cooked, thick, concentrated, dark mahogany-colored sauce, and because of this, very little is needed to coat pasta and give it that evocative flavor of Italy. Making ragù is not at all difficult. If you give a little of your time to make it in bulk, and freeze it for the future, you'll always have the basis of a delightful meal when there's not time to cook.

Preheat the oven to 275°F (140°C). Heat 3 tablespoons of the olive oil in a large skillet. Add the onions and garlic and cook over medium heat for about 10 minutes, stirring from time to time. Add the pancetta, and cook for 5 minutes. Now transfer this mixture to a large ovenproof casserole of 3 quarts capacity.

In the same frying pan, add a tablespoon of the oil and turn up the heat to its highest. Add the ground beef and cook until brown, breaking it up and moving it around the pan. Add the browned beef to the casserole. Heat another tablespoon of the oil in the same pan and do exactly the same with the ground pork. Transfer the browned pork to the casserole.

Trim the chicken livers, rinse under cold running water, dry them thoroughly with paper towels and chop them minutely small. In the same pan, heat the remaining tablespoon of the oil and brown the chicken livers. Add these to the casserole. Place the casserole on medium heat and stir in the tomatoes, tomato paste, red wine, a really good seasoning of the salt and pepper and the nutmeg. Allow this to come up to the simmering point. Chop half of the basil leaves very finely and add to the casserole. Place the casserole on the center rack of the oven and leave it to cook slowly, uncovered, for 4 hours. It's a good idea to have a look after 3 hours to make sure all is well. What you should end up with is a thick, concentrated sauce with only a trace of liquid left. Remove it from the oven and taste to check the seasoning. Chop the remaining basil leaves and stir them in.

When the sauce is completely cooled, divide it, using scales, by spooning 8 ounces (225 g) into plastic freezer bags. Seal them, leaving a little bit of air at the top to allow room for expansion. Each 8 ounce (225 g) package, thoroughly defrosted and reheated, will provide enough ragù for 8 ounces (225 g) of pasta, which will serve 2 people.

If you don't have a 3 quart capacity ovenproof casserole you can use a large baking dish preheated in the oven, but make sure everything comes up to the simmering point in a large saucepan first.

CRÊPE CANNELLONI *with* RAGÙ

Serves 4

In Umbria, Italy, they make crêpes for their cannelloni. Stuffed with Ragù Bolognese and topped with Béchamel and mozzarella, it's a truly inspired version.

You may assemble all this well in advance, but make sure everything is cold before you cover and chill it until needed. These can also be cooked, three crêpes per person, in individual ovenproof dishes, in which case the cooking time is reduced to 20 minutes.

You will also need an ovenproof baking dish 10 x 8 inches (25 x 20 cm), 2 inches deep (5 cm) or the equivalent, well buttered. Preheat the oven to 400°F (200°C).

Both the Crêpes and the ragù can be made well ahead and chilled or frozen. Make the béchamel sauce by the all-in-one method, that is by adding everything (except the mozzarella) to a saucepan and whisking over medium heat till smooth and thickened. Then continue to cook gently for 5 minutes, whisking now and then to prevent it sticking. Now lay the crêpes out and place an equal quantity (about a heaping tablespoon) of cold ragù on each one and roll up, folding in the edges. Next lay the crêpes in the ovenproof dish side by side with the ends tucked up underneath, then sprinkle over the grated mozzarella. Pour the sauce over the top to give an even covering. Finally sprinkle over the grated Parmesan and oil and place the dish on a high rack in the oven for 30 minutes or until the surface is golden and the sauce bubbling.

1 recipe Crêpes (see page 259)

2 (8 ounce) (225 g) portions (¼ recipe) Ragù Bolognese (see preceeding recipe)

FOR THE BÉCHAMEL SAUCE

3 tablespoons butter

¼ cup flour

Scant 2 cups cold milk

Freshly grated nutmeg

Salt to taste

Freshly ground black pepper to taste

¾ cup grated mozzarella

FOR THE TOPPING

½ cup freshly grated Parmesan cheese, preferably Parmigiano-Reggiano

½ tablespoon olive oil

1 recipe of Basic Crêpes
    (see page 259)

FOR THE SAUCE
2½ cups milk
½ stick butter
⅓ cup flour
1 bay leaf
Salt to taste
Freshly ground black pepper
    to taste
A good grating of fresh
    nutmeg
⅓ cup heavy cream

FOR THE FILLING
1 pound (450 g) fresh
    spinach leaves
1 tablespoon butter
⅔ cup ricotta cheese
1¼ cups crumbled
    Gorgonzola cheese
⅔ cup grated Parmesan
    cheese, preferably
    Parmigiano-Reggiano
Fresh nutmeg to taste
Freshly ground black pepper
    to taste
1 bunch scallions,
    finely sliced,
    including the green parts

FOR THE TOPPING
1 cup grated mozzarella
    cheese
½ cup grated Parmesan
    cheese, preferably
    Parmigiano-Reggiano

CRÊPE CANNELLONI *with* SPINACH *and* FOUR CHEESES

Serves 4 to 6

Crêpes make brilliant cannelloni – better and lighter, I think, than pasta. Four-star Italian cheese and spinach make this a wonderful vegetarian version. If you're entertaining you may prefer to serve it as a starter in individual ovenproof baking dishes, in which case you should place two crêpes per person in each.

Begin by making the Sauce. Place the milk, butter, flour and bay leaf in a saucepan and bring everything up to the simmering point, whisking all the time, until the sauce has thickened. Season it with the salt, pepper and nutmeg. Turn the heat down to its lowest and let it simmer very gently for 2 minutes. Remove from the heat and stir in the cream. Remove the bay leaf and set aside.

Meanwhile, for the Filling, place the spinach in a large saucepan with the butter and cook it briefly for 1-2 minutes, tossing it around until it wilts and collapses down. Drain it in a colander and squeeze hard to get rid of all the excess juice. Transfer the spinach to a bowl and chop it roughly with a knife. Add the ricotta, Gorgonzola, Parmesan and a grating of the nutmeg and pepper and mix well. Add the scallions and 4-5 tablespoons of the Sauce.

To assemble, preheat the oven to 400°F (200°C). Lay a crêpe out and place 2 tablespoons of the filling onto it. Roll it up, tucking in the edges. Repeat this with the remaining crêpes. Lay the filled crêpes side-by-side in individual gratin dishes or a well-buttered 9 x 9 x 2 inch (23 x 23 x 5 cm) baking dish. Scatter the mozzarella evenly over the top. Next pour over the Sauce. Finally sprinkle the Parmesan all over the surface. Bake the cannelloni on the highest rack of the oven for 25-30 minutes until the top is brown and the Sauce is bubbling. If you make individual cannelloni in separate dishes, the cooking time will be about 20 minutes.

FOIL-BAKED SALMON SERVED *with*
ENGLISH PARSLEY SAUCE

Serves 4

Now that farmed salmon is plentiful and available all year round, we can all enjoy luxury fish at affordable prices. However, this recipe works equally well using cod cutlets, halibut or other firm white fish. Another luxury – perhaps because of its sheer rarity nowadays – is a classic parsley sauce, so simple but so delightfully good.

To make the Sauce, place the milk, bay leaf, onion slice, mace, parsley stalks and peppercorns in a saucepan. Bring everything slowly up to simmering point, then pour the mixture into a bowl and leave it aside to get completely cold.

Meanwhile, to prepare the salmon, take a sheet of foil large enough to wrap all the fish steaks in and lay it over a shallow, solid baking sheet. Wipe the pieces of salmon with paper towels and place on the foil. Then place the parsley stalks, a bay leaf and a slice of lemon over each steak, and season with the salt and pepper. Finally, sprinkle the wine over, bring the foil up either side, then pleat it, fold it over and seal it at the ends.

When you need to cook the salmon, preheat the oven to 350°F (180°C) and bake the salmon on the high oven rack for 20 minutes exactly. Then, before serving, slip off the skin, using a sharp knife to finis a cut and just pulling it off all around.

When you're ready to finish the sauce, strain the milk back into the saucepan, discarding the flavorings, then add the flour and butter and bring everything gradually up to simmering point, whisking continuously until the sauce has thickened. Now turn the heat down to its lowest possible setting and let the sauce cook for 5 minutes, stirring from time to time. When you're ready to serve the sauce, add the parsley, cream and lemon juice. Taste and add seasoning, then transfer to a warm pitcher to pour over the fish at the table.

FOR THE PARSLEY SAUCE
2 cups milk

1 bay leaf

1 slice onion, ¼ inch (6 mm) thick

1 blade mace

A few chopped parsley stalks

10 black peppercorns

3 tablespoons flour

3 tablespoons butter

1 cup finely chopped fresh parsley

1 tablespoon light cream

1 teaspoon lemon juice

Salt to taste

Freshly ground black pepper to taste

4 (6 ounce) (175 g) salmon steaks

A few parsley stalks

4 small bay leaves

4 slices lemon

Salt to taste

Freshly ground black pepper to taste

2 tablespoons dry white wine

LINGUINI *with* MUSSELS *and*
WALNUT PARSLEY PESTO

Serves 2

FOR THE PESTO

2 tablespoons olive oil

⅛ cup walnuts, chopped

1 cup curly parsley leaves

1 garlic clove

Salt to taste

*Freshly ground black pepper
to taste*

FOR THE LINGUINI
WITH MUSSELS

1 tablespoon olive oil

1 shallot, chopped

1 garlic clove, chopped

*2 pounds (900 g) mussels,
cleaned and prepared*

¾ cup dry white wine

Salt to taste

*Freshly ground black pepper
to taste*

*6 ounces (175 g) dried
linguini or other pasta*

*⅓ cup chopped fresh parsley,
for garnish*

For me, mussels are still a luxury food that cost very little money. I don't think anything can match their exquisite, fresh-from-the-sea flavor. In this recipe every precious drop of mussel juice is used, which gives a lovely, concentrated flavor. Now that mussels come ready cleaned and prepared, it makes the whole thing very simple and easy. All you have to do is put them in cold water, then pull off any beardy strands with a sharp knife, use the mussels as soon as possible and discard any that don't close tightly when given a sharp tap.

For the Pesto: Select a large pan that will hold the mussels, then heat 1 tablespoon of olive oil and sauté the walnuts to get them nicely toasted on all sides – this will take 1-2 minutes. Place the walnuts and any oil left in the pan into a blender or food processor and add the parsley, garlic, the remaining table-spoon of oil and seasoning, then purée.

Next heat the olive oil in the same pan, add the shallot and chopped garlic and cook over a medium heat for about 5 minutes. Now turn the heat up high, add the prepared mussels, the wine and some of the salt and pepper. Cover, turn the heat down to me-dium and cook for about 5 minutes, shaking the pan once or twice, or until they have all opened.

During those 5 minutes bring another large pan of salted water up to the boil. When the mussels are cooked, remove them from the heat and transfer to a warm bowl using a slotted spoon and shaking each one well so that no juice is left inside. Keep

8 mussels aside still in their shells, for a garnish. Remove the rest from their shells and keep warm, covered with foil in a low oven.

Place a sieve lined with cheesecloth over a bowl and strain the mussel liquid.

Now pop the pasta into the boiling water and cook for 8 minutes (some pasta might need 10 minutes, so follow the instructions on the package). Then pour the strained mussel liquid back into the original saucepan and fast-boil to reduce it by about one third. After that turn the heat to low and stir in the Pesto.

Now add the shelled mussels to the Pesto sauce and remove from the heat. As soon as the pasta is cooked, quickly strain it into a colander and divide it between two hot pasta bowls. Spoon the mussels and Pesto over each portion, add the mussels in their shells and scatter the chopped parsley over all. Serve absolutely immediately.

Luxury Fish Pie *with* Rösti Caper Topping

Serves 4 to 6

*T*his is a perfect recipe for entertaining and wouldn't need anything to go with it other than a simple green salad. The fish can be varied according to what's available as long as you have 2¼ pounds (1 kg) in total.

Preheat the oven to 425°F (220°C). First of all, prepare the potatoes for the Rösti Caper Topping by scrubbing them, but leaving the skins on. If there are any larger ones, cut them in half. Then place them in a saucepan with enough boiling, salted water to barely cover and cook for 12 minutes after they have come back to the boil, covered. Strain off the water and cover them with a clean dishcloth.

Meanwhile, for the Fish Mixture, heat the wine and stock in a medium saucepan, add the bay leaf and some salt and pepper; then cut the fish in half if it's a large piece, add it to the saucepan and poach the fish gently for 5 minutes. It should be slightly undercooked. Remove the fish to a plate and strain the liquid through a sieve into a bowl.

Now rinse the pan you cooked the fish in, melt the butter in it, whisk in the flour and gently cook for 2 minutes. Gradually add the strained fish stock little by little, whisking all the time. When you have a smooth sauce turn the heat to its lowest setting and let the sauce cook for 5 minutes. Whisk in the crème fraîche, cornichons,

parsley and dill. Give it all a good seasoning and remove it from the heat.

To make the Rösti, use the coarse side of a grater to grate the potatoes into a bowl. Add the capers and the melted butter, lightly toss so that the potatoes get a good coating of butter.

Remove the skin from the halibut and divide it into chunks, quite large if possible, and combine the fish with the sauce. If you're going to cook the fish pie more or less immediately, add the raw scallops and shrimp to the fish mixture, then spoon it into a well buttered baking dish about 2 inches (5 cm) deep of 3 pints capacity. Sprinkle the Rösti evenly on top, not pressing it down too firmly. Finally scatter the cheese over the surface and bake on the high rack of the oven for 35-40 minutes.

If you want to make the fish pie in advance, remember to let the sauce get completely cold before adding the cooled halibut, raw scallops and shrimp. When the topping is on, cover the dish loosely with plastic wrap and refrigerate it until you're ready to cook it. Then give it an extra 5-10 minutes cooking time.

FOR THE FISH MIXTURE

⅔ cup dry white wine

1¼ cups fish stock

1 bay leaf

Salt to taste

Freshly ground black pepper to taste

1½ pounds (675 g) halibut

½ stick butter

⅓ cup plus 1 tablespoon flour

2 tablespoons crème fraîche

6 cornichons (continental gherkins), drained, rinsed and chopped

⅓ cup chopped fresh parsley

½ tablespoon chopped fresh dill

8 ounces (225 g) sea scallops, including the coral, cut in half

4 ounces (100 g) uncooked shrimp, thoroughly defrosted if frozen, shelled

FOR THE RÖSTI CAPER TOPPING

2 pounds (900 g) round white or red potatoes, even-sized if possible, peeled

1 tablespoon salted capers or capers in brine, drained, rinsed and dried

½ stick butter, melted

½ cup finely grated sharp Cheddar cheese

GORGONZOLA CHEESE *and* APPLE STRUDEL *with* SPICED PICKLED PEARS

Serves 6

---

12 ounces (350 g) young leeks
    weighed after trimming
    (this will be about
    1½ pounds (675 g)
    bought weight)

8 ounces (225 g) prepared
    weight of celery
    (reserve the leaves)

1 stick butter

1 small Rome apple

1 small dessert apple,
    such as Granny Smith

8 ounces (225 g) mozzarella,
    cut in ½ inch (1 cm) cubes

12 scallions, white parts only,
    chopped

1 cup chopped walnuts

3 tablespoons chopped
    parsley, flat-leaf or curly

Salt to taste

Freshly ground black pepper
    to taste

1 slice white bread,
    crust removed

2 garlic cloves

10 sheets frozen phyllo
    pastry, 18 x 10 inches
    (45 x 25 cm), thawed

6 ounces (175 g) Gorgonzola
    cheese, cut in ½ inch
    (1 cm) cubes

Here is a recipe that provides something really stylish for vegetarian entertaining. Serve the strudel with the pickled pears (see following recipe). It's a brilliant combination of crisp pastry, melting cheese and the sharpness of the pears.

Preheat oven to 375°F (190°C). First of all prepare the leeks by trimming and discarding the outer layers, then slice each one vertically almost in half and rinse them under cold running water, fanning them out to get rid of any grit and dust. Then dry them in a cloth and cut them into ½ inch (1 cm) pieces. Now rinse and chop the celery into slightly smaller pieces.

Then melt 3 tablespoons of the butter in a skillet 9 inches (23 cm) in diameter. Keeping the heat at medium, sauté the leeks and celery for about 7-8 minutes until just tinged brown; stir them and keep them on the move to stop them sticking at the edges. Then transfer them to a large bowl and while they are cooling you can deal with the other ingredients.

The apples need to be cored and chopped into ½ inch (1 cm) pieces, leaving the skins on, then as soon as the leeks and celery have cooled, add the apples, cubed mozzarella, scallions, walnuts and 1 tablespoon of the chopped parsley. Season everything well and stir to mix it all together.

Now you need to make a bread crumb mixture, and to do this, place the bread, garlic, the rest of the parsley and the reserved celery leaves in a food processor. Switch it on and blend until everything is smooth. If you don't have a food processor, grate the bread, and chop everything else finely and mix together.

Next take a large clean cloth and dampen it under cold water, lay it out on a work surface, then carefully unwrap the phyllo pastry sheets and lay them on the damp cloth, folding it over. It is important to keep the pastry sheets in the cloth to prevent them drying out.

It is quite complicated to explain how to assemble a strudel, but to actually do it is very easy and only takes a few minutes.

Place a buttered 16 x 12 inch (40 x 30 cm) baking sheet on a work surface. Because the phyllo sheets are too small to make a strudel for 6 people, we're going to have to "weld" them together. To do this, first of all melt the remaining butter in a small saucepan, then take 1 sheet of phyllo pastry (remembering to keep the rest covered), lay it on one end of the baking sheet and brush it with melted butter. Then place another sheet beside it overlapping it by about 2 inches (5 cm), then brush that with melted butter. Place a third sheet next to the second overlapping it again by 2 inches (5 cm).

Now sprinkle a quarter of the bread crumb mixture all over the sheets and then place 2 more sheets of phyllo, this time horizontally, buttering the first one with melted butter and welding the other one with a 2 inch (5 cm) join. Brush that layer as before with melted butter and repeat the sprinkling of bread crumbs.

Then place the next 3 sheets as you did the first 3, again brushing with butter and sprinkling with crumbs. Then place the final 2 sheets horizontally and brush with butter.

After that place half the cheese and vegetable mixture all the way along the phyllo, sprinkle the cubes of Gorgonzola on top of that, then finish off with the rest of the mixture on top. Now just pat it together firmly with your hands. Take the edge of the pastry that is nearest to you, bring it up over the filling, then flip the whole thing over as if you were making a giant sausage roll. Neatly push in the vegetables before tucking the pastry ends underneath. Now brush the entire surface with the remaining butter, scatter the rest of the crumb mixture over the top and bake in the oven for 25-30 minutes or until it has turned a nice golden brown color.

To serve the strudel, cut off the ends (they are great for the bird feeder but not for your guests) and cut the strudel into slices, giving each person 1 pickled pear.

SPICED PICKLED PEARS

6 hard pears (Bosc or similar
    variety)

½ cup brown sugar

1½ cups cider vinegar

1 tablespoon balsamic
    vinegar

1 tablespoon mixed
    peppercorns

4 whole cloves

6 crushed juniper berries

Preheat the oven to 375°F (190°C). To pickle the pears, first peel them using a potato peeler, but be very careful to leave the stems intact as they look much prettier. Place all the rest of the ingredients in an ovenproof casserole, then bring everything up to simmering point, stirring all the time to dissolve the sugar. Now carefully lower the pears into the hot liquid, laying them on their sides, cover with a lid and transfer the pears to the oven for 30 minutes.

After that remove the lid and carefully turn the pears over. Test with a skewer to see how they are cooking – they'll probably need another 30 minutes altogether, so cover with the lid and leave them in the oven till they feel tender when pierced with a skewer. Then remove them and allow them to cool in their liquid until needed. When serving, there's no need to reheat the pears as they taste much better cold.

MEATBALLS *in* GOULASH SAUCE

Serves 4 to 6

This recipe never fails to please – ground beef and pork together with bell pepper and onion is a wonderful combination of flavors. The meatballs are very light and the sauce rich and creamy. A classic Hungarian accompaniment would be buttered noodles tossed with poppy seeds (see Note below).

Preheat the oven to 275°F (140°C). First make the meatballs. In a large bowl place the ground meats, chopped bell pepper, onion, garlic, parsley and bread crumbs. Mix well, then add the egg and a good seasoning of the salt and freshly ground black pepper. Now combine everything as thoroughly as possible, using either your hands to a large fork. Then take pieces of the mixture, about a tablespoon at a time, squeeze and roll each one into a small round – you should get 24 altogether – then coat each one lightly with the seasoned flour.

Heat up the oil in a large ovenproof casserole of 2 quarts capacity with a tight-fitting lid, and when it's smoking hot, brown the meatballs a few at a time. Then transfer them to a plate.

Next make the Sauce in the same pan. Heat the oil, add the onion and red bell pepper and cook for about 5 minutes, then add the garlic, cook for another minute, and stir in the paprika and any remaining bits of seasoned flour. Stir to soak up the juices, then add the tomatoes, season with salt and pepper, then bring it all up to simmering point, stirring all the time.

Now add the meatballs to the Sauce, bring back to simmering point, cover with a tight-fitting lid and transfer it to the middle rack of the oven for 1½ hours. Just before serving, lightly stir in the crème fraîche to give a marbled effect. Spoon the meatballs onto freshly cooked noodles and sprinkle a little of the extra paprika on as a garnish as they go to the table.

NOTE: For the noodles, use 3 ounces (85 g) green tagliatelle per person, drained then tossed in 1 tablespoon butter and 1 teaspoon poppy seeds.

12 ounces (350 g) lean
ground beef
12 ounces (350 g) ground
pork
½ medium red bell pepper,
seeded and finely chopped
1 small onion,
very finely chopped
1 large garlic clove, crushed
⅓ cup fresh chopped parsley
1 cup bread crumbs
1 large egg, beaten
Salt to taste
Freshly ground black pepper
to taste
2 tablespoons flour, seasoned
2 tablespoons olive oil

FOR THE SAUCE

1 tablespoon olive oil
1 medium onion, chopped
½ medium red bell pepper,
seeded and finely chopped
1 large garlic clove, crushed
2 tablespoons hot Hungarian
paprika
1 pound (450 g) ripe tomatoes, peeled and chopped,
or 1 (14 ounce) (400 g)
can Italian chopped
tomatoes
Salt to taste
Freshly ground black pepper
to taste
Approximately ½ cup crème
fraîche
A little extra paprika,
for garnish

Mashed Black-Eyed Beancakes *with* Ginger Onion Marmalade

Serves 4

¾ cup dried black-eyed peas

⅔ cup green lentils

2½ cups water

1 bay leaf

2 fresh thyme sprigs

Salt to taste

Freshly ground black pepper
 to taste

1 tablespoon olive oil

1 medium red onion,
 finely chopped

1 medium carrot,
 finely chopped

1 small red bell pepper,
 seeded and finely
 chopped

1 green chili, seeded and
 finely chopped

1 garlic clove, chopped

¼ teaspoon ground mace

1 teaspoon chopped fresh
 thyme

1 tablespoon sun-dried
 tomato paste

⅓ cup whole-wheat flour

4-5 tablespoons olive oil
 for frying

Watercress sprigs, for garnish

Black-eyed peas are the lovely nutty beans that are popular in recipes from the deep south of America, and with the addition of other vegetables they make very good Beancakes. Fried crisp and crunchy on the outside and served with this delectable Ginger Onion Marmalade (see following recipe), this makes a splendid vegetarian main course.

First of all the black-eyed peas need soaking. This can be done by covering them with twice their volume of cold water and leaving them overnight or alternatively bringing them up to the boil, boiling for 10 minutes and then leaving to soak for 2 hours. The green lentils won't need soaking.

Once this is done, take a medium-sized saucepan, add the drained peas and the lentils, then pour in the water, add the bay leaf and sprigs of thyme, then bring everything up to a gentle simmer and let it cook for about 40-45 minutes, by which time all the water should have been absorbed and the peas and lentils will be completely soft. If there's any liquid still left, drain them in a colander.

Remove the bay leaf and thyme sprigs. Now you need to mash the legumes to a pulp, and you can do this using a fork, potato masher or electric mixer. After that give them a really good seasoning with the salt and freshly ground black pepper and put a clean towel over them to stop them becoming dry.

Now take a really large skillet, add the tablespoon of olive oil, then heat it over

medium heat and add the onion, carrot, bell pepper, chili and garlic. Sauté them all together for about 6 minutes, moving them around the skillet to soften and turn golden brown at the edges.

After that, mix all the vegetables into the mashed pea-and-lentil mixture, add the mace, chopped thyme and tomato paste, then dampen your hands and form the mixture into 12 round cakes measuring approximately 2½-3 inches (6-7.5 cm) in diameter. Then place them on a plate or a lightly oiled tray, cover with plastic wrap and keep them in the refrigerator until needed, but for 1 hour minimum.

When you're ready to serve the beancakes, coat them lightly with the wholewheat flour seasoned with salt and freshly ground black pepper, then heat 2 tablespoons of the olive oil. When it is really hot reduce the heat to medium and fry the beancakes in two batches for 3 minutes on each side until they're crisp and golden, adding more oil if needed.

Drain them on paper towels and serve garnished with sprigs of watercress and the Ginger Onion Marmalade.

Ginger Onion Marmalade

This is not only a wonderful accompaniment to the beancakes but is great as a relish for all kinds of other dishes – meat, fish or vegetarian.

First of all, peel and slice the onions into ¼ inch (5 mm) rings (slice any really large outside rings in half). Then take a solid medium-sized saucepan and heat the olive oil. When the oil is hot, add the onions and the rosemary, stir well, and toss the onions around till they're golden and tinged brown at the edges (about 10 minutes).

After that pour in the white wine and white wine vinegar, followed by the brown sugar and the ginger, then stir and bring everything up to simmering point. Add the salt and pepper, then turn the heat down to low again and let everything simmer very gently for 1¼ hours or until all the liquid has almost disappeared. Then remove the rosemary, pour everything into a serving bowl and you can serve it warm – or I think it's quite nice cold with the hot beancakes.

12 ounces (350 g) onion

2 tablespoons olive oil

3 rosemary sprigs

1 cup dry white wine

¼ cup white wine vinegar

¼ cup dark brown sugar

1 tablespoon grated fresh ginger root

Salt to taste

Freshly ground black pepper to taste

Oven-Baked Mackerel
Stuffed *with* Pesto Mash

Serves 4

12 ounces (350 g) red
  potatoes, peeled and cut
  into evenly sized pieces

½ cup fresh pesto

6 scallions, finely chopped,
  including the green parts

Salt to taste

Freshly ground black pepper
  to taste

About 1½ slices whole-wheat
  bread, cubed

1 tablespoon rolled oats

4 (10 ounce) (280 g) very
  fresh mackerel,
  heads removed

A little olive oil

Lemon quarters, for garnish

A few flat-leaf parsley sprigs,
  for garnish

It takes only one word to describe this recipe – wow! It's simply one of the best fish recipes ever. Easy to make and such a divine combination of flavors, it can also be prepared in advance, so all you have to do is just pop it in the oven, then make a salad and a nice lemony dressing. One important point, though: buy fresh pesto, available from most supermarkets (it's not quite the same with bottled pesto).

Preheat the oven to 400°F (200°C). First cook the potatoes in boiling salted water for 20 minutes. Test them with a skewer and, when they're absolutely tender, drain them well. Leave them in the saucepan and cover with a dishcloth to absorb some of the steam.

Next add all but 1 tablespoon of the pesto to the potatoes, then use an electric mixer to mash them – start with a slow speed to break them up, then go on to high until you have a smooth, lump-free purée. Now fold in the scallions and taste to check the seasoning. Add the salt and pepper if needed.

Next make the topping for the fish by dropping the cubes of bread into a processor or blender with the motor switched on, them follow with the rolled oats until everything is uniformly crumbled.

To prepare the fish, wipe them inside and out with paper towels, lay them on a solid baking sheet, approximately 16 x 12 inches (40 x 30 cm), lined with foil and brushed with a little of the olive oil. Make 3 diagonal cuts about 1 inch (2.5 cm) in depth all along the top side of the mackerel.

Spoon the pesto mash into the body cavities, pack it in neatly, then fork the edges to give some texture. Now brush the surface of the fish with the olive oil, scatter it with the crumbs and finally add ½ tablespoon of the olive oil to the remaining pesto and drizzle it over the crumbs using a teaspoon.

Now it's ready for the oven. Bake for 25 minutes on the high rack, then serve with the lemon quarters and sprigs of the flat-leaf parsley.

OXTAIL BRAISED *in* GUINNESS *with* CANNELLINI BEANS

Serves 6

I am not surprised that oxtail has become rather fashionable in restaurants now, because any meat that is cooked near the bone has a special sweetness and succulence. But it's still a very economical dish to prepare at home, and the addition of cannellini beans in this recipe means that they too absorb all that lovely flavor. This version is a winner.

First the beans need to soak, and to do this either soak them in cold water overnight or put them in a large saucepan with 2 quarts of cold water and bring them up to the boil for 10 minutes, then turn the heat off and leave them to soak for a minimum of 2 hours.

Preheat the oven to 300°F (150°C). To make the casserole, heat 2 tablespoons of the oil in a large skillet, then wipe the pieces of oxtail with paper towels and coat them lightly in the seasoned flour and fry in hot oil on all sides until they are a nutty brown color. Then, using a slotted spoon, transfer the pieces of oxtail to an ovenproof casserole of 4 quarts capacity.

Now add the rest of the oil and as soon as that's hot, add the onions and fry these for about 5 minutes until brown at the edges before transferring them to join the oxtail in the casserole. Remove the skillet from the heat, then drain the beans in a colander. Add them to the casserole along with the garlic, thyme and bay leaves, and add a good seasoning of black pepper.

Next wipe the portobello mushrooms with some damp paper towels, halve them (or quarter them if they are very large), then add these to the casserole as well, tucking them in among the beans and oxtail. Now return the skillet to the heat. Add any remaining seasoned flour, stir it in to soak up the juices and gradually add the stock and the Guinness, whisking all the time until it reaches simmering point. Pour it over the oxtail and the rest of the ingredients, cover with a tight-fitting lid and place in the preheated oven for 2½ hours.

Then add the button mushrooms, halved and wiped as above, put the lid back on and give the casserole a further hour in the oven. When you next remove it, you will see that some of the fat from the oxtail has bubbled up to the top – spoon this off by skimming a tablespoon across the surface. Then season everything well with salt before serving with a lightly cooked green vegetable.

1⅓ cups dried cannellini beans

4 tablespoons olive oil

3-3½ pounds (1.3-1.5 kg) oxtail

2 tablespoons flour, seasoned

2 large onions, halved and thickly sliced

4 garlic cloves

2 good thyme sprigs

2 bay leaves

Freshly ground black pepper to taste

12 ounces (250 g) portobello mushrooms

2½ cups beef stock

2 cups Guinness stout beer

12 ounces (350 g) button mushrooms

Salt to taste

FOR THE SAUCE

¾ cup extra virgin olive oil

3 large garlic cloves

2 fresh green chilies, halved and seeded

⅓ cup chopped walnuts

3 ripe plum tomatoes, skins removed

Salt to taste

Freshly ground black pepper to taste

2 tablespoons balsamic vinegar

2 tablespoons flour

Salt to taste

Freshly ground black pepper to taste

½ tablespoon finely grated Parmesan cheese, preferably Parmigiano-Reggiano

¼ cup milk

4 (6 ounce) (175 g) thick fish fillets (cod, haddock, monkfish or halibut), skins removed

¼ stick butter

1 tablespoon oil

A few flat-leaf parsley sprigs, for garnish

*T*his method of cooking fish with a light dusting of flour and grated Parmesan is excellent, but to make it even more special serve it with a Romesco sauce made with walnuts. The advantage of Romesco is that you can make it well ahead; it's always served at room temperature, so keep it in the refrigerator and remove it about one hour before serving.

To make the Sauce, take a good solid skillet and heat 1 tablespoon of the oil over medium heat, then lightly sauté the whole garlic cloves for about 3 minutes or until they feel softened and have turned golden. Then add the chilies and walnuts and continue to cook for another 2 minutes.

Now put them into a processor, then return the skillet to a high heat and when the oil begins to smoke put the tomatoes in half lengthwise and place them in the hot pan cut-side-down. Keep the heat high and cook the tomatoes until they are charred and blackened all over – this will take about 1½-2 minutes on each side.

Next add the tomatoes to the processor blender, turn it on to a low speed and add the rest of the oil in a slow, steady stream. The sauce will then begin to thicken and assume the consistency of mayonnaise. After that add some salt and pepper, then transfer the sauce to a bowl and stir in the balsamic vinegar. Cool, cover with plastic wrap and chill until needed. But let it come back to room temperature before serving.

When you're ready to cook the fish, mix the flour, seasoning and cheese together on a plate and pour the milk into a shallow dish. Now wipe and dry the fish with paper towels. Then dip each piece first into the milk and then into the flour mixture, making sure it's well coated and that you shake off any surplus.

Next heat the butter and oil in a large skillet and as soon as it's really hot cook the fish for 2-3 minutes on each side, depending on its thickness. The coating should be golden brown, and as soon as it's cooked remove the fillets carefully with a spatula to warm serving plates.

Serve with a little of the Sauce spooned over, and garnish with the parsley.

PEPPER-CRUSTED MONKFISH *with* RED BELL PEPPER RELISH

Serves 4

*F*illeted monkfish can be quite pricey, but there is no waste with head or bones. It has a lovely firm, meaty texture, and I think this particular recipe would be a superb choice for someone who wants to cook something quite special but has very little time. The pieces of fish are coated with crushed mixed peppercorns and this simplest of sauces not only tastes divine but looks amazingly colorful in contrast to the fish.

Begin the Relish by heating the oil in a medium-sized saucepan. When it's really hot add the strips of pepper and toss them around, keeping them on the move so they get nicely toasted and browned at the edges. Then add the tomatoes, the whole garlic clove and the chopped anchovies. Give it all a good stir, put a lid on and, keeping the heat at its lowest possible setting, let the whole thing stew gently, stirring once or twice, for 25 minutes or until the peppers are soft.

Then whirl everything to a coarse purée in a blender or food processor. Taste and season with the salt and freshly ground pepper, then empty into a serving bowl and stir in the balsamic vinegar. It is now ready for serving and can be made in advance.

To cook the fish first cut it into small rounds about ¾ inch (2 cm) thick. Crush the peppercorns with a mortar and pestle – or using the end of a rolling pin in a small bowl – to a fairly coarse texture, then combine them with the flour.

Next heat the oil until very hot in a good solid skillet. Dip each piece of fish in the flour-and-peppercorn mixture, pressing them gently on all sides to get an even coating. Now fry the fish in 2 batches, for about 2-3 minutes on each side, until they're tinged nicely brown. Keep the first batch warm while you cook the second.

Serve garnished with the watercress or fresh cilantro sprigs, and the sauce passed around separately.

FOR THE RED BELL PEPPER RELISH

1 tablespoon olive oil

2 medium red bell peppers, seeded and cut into strips

2 medium tomatoes, skins removed (canned Italian tomatoes would be fine)

1 large garlic clove

3 anchovy fillets, chopped

Salt to taste

Freshly ground black pepper to taste

1 tablespoon balsamic vinegar

2 pounds (900 g) monkfish (off-the-bone weight)

3 tablespoons mixed peppercorns

4 tablespoons flour, seasoned with 1 teaspoon salt

⅓ cup olive oil

Watercress or fresh cilantro sprigs, for garnish

PORK BRAISED *in* CIDER VINEGAR SAUCE

Serves 4

1 tablespoon butter

2 tablespoons peanut oil

2 pounds (450 g) pork shoulder, trimmed and cut into 1 inch (2.5 cm) cubes

12 shallots

2½ cups medium-sweet cider

⅔ cup cider vinegar

4 fresh thyme sprigs

2 bay leaves

Salt to taste

Freshly ground black pepper to taste

⅓ cup crème fraîche

This recipe has an autumnal ring to it and is for me the first casserole of the winter months. Pork shoulder is an excellent cut for braising and this recipe is superb for serving to friends and family, because it just cooks away all by itself until you're ready to serve it. I also think it tastes even better the next day, so if you make it that far ahead, don't add the crème fraîche until it's reheated. The reheating will take about 25 minutes in a casserole over gentle direct heat. Note here, though, that it's important to use a good quality cider vinegar.

Preheat the oven to 325°F (160°C). First place a wide, shallow ovenproof casserole of 5 pints capacity over fairly high heat. Add half the butter and 1 tablespoon of the oil. Dry the pieces of pork with paper towels, then brown them a few at a time in the hot butter and oil. Transfer to a plate and set aside.

Add the rest of the butter and the oil and, when that's very hot, add the shallots and carefully brown these on all side to a nice glossy caramel color. Pour in the cider and cider vinegar and stir well, scraping the bottom and sides of the casserole. Return the meat, add the thyme and the bay leaves and season to taste with the salt and pepper. Bring just to the simmering point, then transfer the casserole uncovered to the oven to bake for approximately 1 hour and

15 minutes or until the liquid is reduced and the meat is tender.

Using a slotted spoon, transfer the meat and shallots to a warm serving dish, discarding the herbs. Place the casserole back over direct heat. Bring it up to the boil and reduce the liquid to about half of its original volume. Finally, whisk in the crème fraîche and taste to check the seasoning. Pour the sauce over the meat and serve. This is great served with Potato and Apple Rösti (see page 251) and Spiced Sautéed Red Cabbage with Cranberries (see page 254).

If you don't have a wide shallow casserole, use an ovenproof dish of the same size, but preheat it first in the oven. Bring everything to a simmering point in a frying pan before you pour it into the dish, then finish the sauce in a saucepan.

POT-ROASTED BEEF *in* RED WINE *with* RED ONION MARMALADE

Serves 4 to 6

It has to be said that roasting meat does require a little attention, with basting and so on. But the great thing about a pot roast is that it feeds the same number of people, but leaves you in peace until you're ready to serve. Its other great virtue is that it enables you to use some of those very lean, delicious cuts of meat that are not suitable for roasting, such as brisket or round.

Preheat the oven to 275°F (140°C). Take a medium-sized ovenproof casserole with a tight-fitting lid, melt half of the butter in it and when it begins to foam turn the heat up high. Dry the meat thoroughly with paper towels and then brown it on all sides in the hot butter, browning one flat side first, then turning it over on the other side, and moving it around to get the round edges browned as well.

Then remove the meat, wipe the casserole with some paper towels and return the meat to it, adding the bay leaves, thyme, the wine and some salt and pepper. Bring it all up to simmering point, put on a tight-fitting lid, using foil if necessary to seal it, then transfer it to the oven and leave it to cook without looking at it for 3 hours.

When the cooking time is up, remove the meat from the casserole, cover it with foil and leave it to relax for 10 minutes. Meanwhile remove the herbs, place the casserole over direct heat and boil briskly to reduce the liquid slightly. Mix the flour and remaining butter to a smooth paste, then add this mixture in small pieces to the hot liquid and whisk with a balloon whisk until it comes back to the boil and you have a smooth, slightly thickened sauce.

While the beef is cooking, make the Red Onion Marmalade. Melt the butter in a medium-sized saucepan, stir in the chopped onions and the thyme and let them soften for about 10 minutes. Then add the wine and wine vinegar, bring it all up to a gentle simmer and add a seasoning of the salt and freshly ground black pepper. Turn the heat to its lowest setting and let the whole thing cook really slowly with the lid off for about 50 minutes to 1 hour or until all the liquid has evaporated. Remove it from the heat, but reheat gently before serving.

¼ stick butter

2½ pounds (1.1 kg) rolled brisket or round rump roast

2 bay leaves

1 small bunch thyme

2 cups red wine

Salt to taste

Freshly ground black pepper to taste

1½ tablespoons flour

FOR THE RED ONION MARMALADE

¼ stick butter

1 large red onion, very finely chopped

1 teaspoon chopped fresh thyme

1 cup red wine

¼ cup red wine vinegar

Salt to taste

Freshly ground black pepper to taste

Red Onion Tarte Tatin

Serves 6 as a starter or 4 as a main course.

2½ pounds (1.1 kg) red
onions

¼ stick butter

1 teaspoon superfine sugar

6 small thyme sprigs

Salt to taste

Freshly ground black pepper
to taste

1½ tablespoons chopped
fresh thyme

1 tablespoon balsamic
vinegar

For the Pastry

⅔ cup flour

⅓ cup plus 1 tablespoon
whole-wheat flour

½ stick butter, softened

⅓ cup grated Cheddar cheese

1 teaspoon chopped fresh
thyme leaves

About 2-3 tablespoons cold
water

A few shavings of Parmesan
cheese, preferably
Parmigiano-Reggiano,
for garnish

This is simply the old favorite apple tarte tatin turned into a savory version. The red onions are mellowed and caramelized with balsamic vinegar, and look spectacularly good. And the cheese and thyme pastry provides the perfect background. Everyone in my family says this is ace.

Preheat the oven to 350°F (180°C) and preheat a solid baking sheet as well. Begin by preparing the onions, which should have their outer papery skins removed and then be cut in half lengthwise from stem to root. After that, place over medium heat and as soon as it's hot, add the butter and the sugar, then as soon as the butter begins to sizzle, quickly scatter the sprigs of thyme in, then arrange the onions on the bottom of the skillet, cut-side-down. As you do this you need to think "jigsaw puzzle," so that after the onion halves have been placed in the skillet to cover the surface, all of those left over need to be cut into wedges and fitted in between to fill the gaps. Bear in mind that what you see when you turn the tart out is the cut side of the onions.

When the onions have all been fitted in, give them a good seasoning of the salt and freshly ground black pepper, then scatter over the chopped thyme and sprinkle in the vinegar.

Now turn the heat down under the skillet and let the onions cook very gently for about 10 minutes. After that cover the skillet with foil and place it on the baking sheet on the rack just above the center of the oven and leave it there for the onions to cook for 50-60 minutes.

While the onions are cooking, make the Pastry. This, if you like, can be done by mixing all the ingredients except the water in a processor. When the mixture resembles fine crumbs, gradually add enough cold water to make a soft dough. Then pop the dough into the refrigerator in a plastic bag for 30 minutes to rest.

As soon as the onions have had their cooking time, test them with a skewer: They should be cooked through but still retain some texture. Then, protecting your hands well, remove the skillet from the oven back onto direct heat and increase the oven temperature to 400°F (200°C). Then turn on the heat under the skillet containing the onions to medium, as what you need to do is reduce all the lovely buttery oniony juices – this will probably take about 10 minutes, but do watch them carefully so that they do not burn. By this time you'll be left with very little syrupy liquid in the bottom of the skillet.

While that's all happening, roll out the Pastry to a circle about 10 inches (25 cm) in diameter, then – again being careful to protect your hands – turn the heat off under the skillet and fit the pastry over the onions, pushing down and tucking in the edges all around the inside of the skillet. Then return the tart to the oven on the same baking sheet but this time on the higher rack and give it another 25-30 minutes until the pastry is crisp and golden.

When the tart is cooked, remove it from the oven and allow it to cool for 20 minutes before turning it out. When turning it out it's important to have a completely flat plate or board. Then protecting your hands with a dishcloth, place the plate on top of the pan, then turn it upside down, give it a good shake, and presto – Red Onion Tarte Tatin!

If for any reason some of the onions are still in the pan, fear not: All you need to do is lift them out with a spatula and replace them into their own space in the tart. I think it's nice to serve this tart just warm with a few shavings of Parmesan sprinkled over.

Roast Ribs *of* Traditional Beef *with* Yorkshire Pudding *and* Horseradish, Crème Fraîche *and* Mustard Sauce

Serves 6 to 8

I still think the roast beef of old England served with meaty gravy, crisp Yorkshire Pudding (see page 255) and crunchy roast potatoes is not only one of the world's greatest meals, it is something the British do better than anyone else.

3 rib roast, wing end or sirloin of beef on the bone (approximately 6 pounds) (2.8 kg)

½ tablespoon ground mustard

½ tablespoon flour

Salt to taste

Freshly ground black pepper to taste

1 small onion, halved

FOR THE GRAVY

¼ cup flour

Approximately 4 cups hot vegetable stock or water from the potatoes

Salt to taste

Freshly ground black pepper to taste

FOR THE HORSERADISH CRÈME FRAÎCHE AND MUSTARD SAUCE

4 tablespoons hot horseradish

1 heaping tablespoon crème fraîche

2 teaspoons whole grain mustard

Salt to taste

Freshly ground black pepper to taste

Preheat the oven to 475°F (250°C). If you dust the fat surface of the beef with the mustard and flour – just rub them in gently – then season with salt and pepper, it becomes extra crusty during cooking. So do that first, then place the meat in a solid roasting pan and tuck the 2 pieces of onion in close to the meat.

Now place the meat just above the center in the oven and cook for 20 minutes. Turn the heat down to 375°F (190°C) and cook for 15 minutes to the pound (450 g) for rare, adding another 15 minutes for medium-rare and another 30 minutes for well done.

While the beef is cooking lift it out of the oven from time to time, tilt the pan and baste the meat really well with its own juices. While you're basting close the oven door in order not to lose heat.

When the beef is cooked, remove it from the oven, transfer it to a board and allow it to stand in a warm place for up to an hour, loosely covered with foil, before carving. As the meat relaxes it will be easier to carve. Meanwhile, make the Gravy.

After removing the meat from the roasting pan, tilt to see how much fat remains – you need about 2 tablespoons for this amount of gravy (the rest should be spooned into a dish and used for the Yorkshire Pudding, see page 255). Place the roasting pan over medium heat and sprinkle the flour into the fatty juices. Then, using a wire whisk, blend in the flour using a circular movement.

When you have a smooth paste, slowly add the hot vegetable stock, whisking all the time, and scraping the bottom of the pan to incorporate all the residue from the roast. When the gravy is bubbling, taste to see if it needs a little more seasoning, then let it carry on bubbling. Reduce it slightly to concentrate the flavor.

You can now pour the gravy into the gravy boat and keep it warm if lunch is imminent or, if not, leave it in the roasting pan and reheat gently just before serving.

To make the Horseradish Sauce, simply mix all the ingredients together in the bowl you're going to serve it in.

ROASTED FISH TOPPED *with* SUN-DRIED TOMATO TAPENADE

Serves 6

This is quite simply a fantastic recipe – it takes no time at all but has the kind of taste that makes people think you have spent hours in the kitchen. And another of its great virtues is that, apart from the fish itself and fresh basil leaves, the whole thing is made from pantry ingredients.

Preheat the oven to 400°F (200°C). Begin the Tapenade by reserving 6 whole olives and 6 medium basil leaves from the above ingredients, then all you do to make the Tapenade – which can be made 2 or 3 days in advance – is place all the ingredients in a food processor and blend them together to a coarse paste. It's important not to over process; the ingredients should retain some of their identity, as shown in the photograph.

When you're ready to cook the fish, wipe the fillets with paper towels, season with the salt and pepper, then fold them by tucking the thin end into the center and the thick end on top of that so you have a neat, slightly rounded shape. Place the fish on an oiled baking sheet, then divide the Tapenade mixture equally among them, using it as a topping. Press it on quite firmly with your hands, then lightly roughen the surface with a fork. Dip the reserved basil leaves in olive oil and place one on the top of each piece of fish, following that with an olive. Now place the baking sheet on the high rack in the oven, bake the fish for 20-25 minutes, and serve immediately.

FOR THE TAPENADE

1½ cups pitted black olives in brine, drained and rinsed, or 6 ounces (175 g) bought loose

1 bunch basil leaves

1 cup sun-dried tomatoes, drained, but reserve the oil

1 heaping teaspoon (about 36) green pepper-corns in brine, rinsed and drained

2 large garlic cloves

1 (2 ounce) (50 g) tin anchovies including the oil

⅔ cup capers, drained and pressed between double layers of paper towels

3 tablespoons oil from the tomatoes

Freshly ground black pepper to taste

6 tail-end pieces of cod or haddock weighing 6-7 ounces (175-200 g) each, skin removed

Salt to taste

Freshly ground black pepper to taste

SMOKED HADDOCK *with* SPINACH *and* CHIVE-BUTTER SAUCE

Serves 4

FOR THE SAUCE

1½ sticks butter, melted

3 large egg yolks

Salt to taste

Freshly ground black pepper
   to taste

1 tablespoon lemon juice

¼ cup chopped fresh chives

FOR THE HADDOCK

4 pieces smoked haddock,
   approximately 6 ounces
   (175 g) each, skinned and
   boned

1¼ cups milk

Freshly ground black pepper
   to taste

FOR THE SPINACH

¼ stick butter

2 pounds (900 g) fresh
   spinach, picked over,
   trimmed and thoroughly
   rinsed

1 teaspoon salt

Freshly ground black pepper
   to taste

My thanks to top chef and dear friend Simon Hopkinson for this superb recipe, which he cooked for me at his restaurant Bibendum one day for lunch – and had invented that day! Now, thanks to his generosity, all of us can make and savor what has become one of my very favorite fish recipes.

First you need to make the Sauce: Place the butter in a small saucepan and let it melt slowly. Meanwhile blend the egg yolks and seasoning in a blender or food processor.

Then turn the heat up and when the butter reaches the boil, pour it into a measuring cup and start to pour this very slowly into the blender in a thick trickle, with the motor running, until all the butter is added and the sauce is thickened. Then, with the motor still switched on, slowly add the lemon juice. Then keep the sauce warm by placing it in a bowl over some hot water.

To cook the Haddock, place it in a skillet, pour in the milk, add some freshly ground black pepper, then bring it all up to a gentle simmer. Cover and poach for 6-7 minutes.

While that is happening, cook the Spinach: Melt the butter in a large saucepan and pile the spinach in with the salt and some freshly ground black pepper. Put the lid on and cook it over medium heat for 2-3 minutes, turning it all over halfway through. Quite a bit of water will come out, so what you need to do then is drain the spinach in a colander and press down a small plate on top to squeeze out every last bit of juice. Cover with a cloth and keep warm.

When the Haddock is ready divide the Spinach among 4 warm serving plates and place the haddock pieces on top. Now just add a little of the poaching liquid (about 2 tablespoons) to the sauce and whisk it along with the chives, then pour the sauce over the haddock and spinach and serve immediately.

STEAK *and* KIDNEY PUDDING

Serves 6

I've subtitled this recipe "Kate and Sidney make a comeback," after the Cockney slang version of this world-famous recipe. It's certainly time for a revival because it has been shamefully neglected and because it really is the ultimate in comfort food. Homemade is a far superior thing to any factory version and, believe it or not, it's dead simple to make. Once it's on the heat you can forget all about it till supper time – except for the amazingly appetizing wafts coming out of the kitchen.

To make the Pastry, first sift the flour and salt into a large mixing bowl. Add some freshly ground black pepper, then add the suet and mix it into the flour using the blade of a knife. When it's evenly blended, add a few drops of cold water and start to mix with the knife, using curving movements and turning the mixture around. The aim is to bring it together as a dough, so keep adding drops of water until it begins to get really sticky.

Now abandon the knife, go in with your hands and bring it all together until you have a nice smooth elastic dough that leaves the bowl clean. It's worth noting that suet pastry always needs more water than other types, so if it is still a bit dry just go on adding a few drops at a time.

After that, take a quarter of the dough for the top, then roll the rest out fairly thickly. What you need is a round approximately 13 inches (33 cm) in diameter. Now line a well-buttered pudding basin of 3 pints capacity with the pastry, pressing it well around.

To make the Filling, chop the steak and kidney into fairly small cubes, toss them in the seasoned flour, then add them to the pastry-lined basin with the slices of onion. Add enough cold water to reach almost the top of the meat and sprinkle in the Worcestershire sauce and a seasoning of the salt and pepper.

Roll out the pastry top, dampen its edges and put it in position on the pudding. Seal well and cover with a double sheet of aluminum foil, pleated in the center to allow room for expansion while cooking. Now secure it with string, making a little handle so that you can lift it out of a hot steamer. Then place it in a steamer over boiling water. Steam for 5 hours, topping off the boiling water halfway through. You can either serve the pudding by spooning portions straight out of the bowl, or slide a palette knife around the edge and turn the whole thing out onto a serving plate (which is more fun!) and pass around the Steak and Kidney Gravy (see following recipe).

FOR THE SUET CRUST PASTRY

2½ cups self-rising flour

Salt to taste

Freshly ground black pepper to taste

6 ounces (175 g) (1½ cups) shredded beef suet or grated chilled butter

FOR THE FILLING

1¼ pounds (575 g) chuck steak

8 ounces (225 g) ox kidney after trimming, so buy 10 ounces (280 g)

2 tablespoons flour, well-seasoned

1 medium onion, sliced

Cold water

1 teaspoon Worcestershire sauce

Salt to taste

Freshly ground black pepper to taste

STEAK *and* KIDNEY GRAVY

*Meat trimmings from the
steak and kidney
(see preceding recipe)*

1 medium onion, halved

2½ cups water

Salt to taste

*Freshly ground black pepper
to taste*

1 teaspoon beef drippings

1 tablespoon flour

*A few drops Worcestershire
sauce*

Although steak and kidney pudding has a lovely juicy filling, it's always nice to have a little extra gravy spooned around – and because there are always some meat trimmings left over, this is a good way to use them.

Simply place the meat trimmings in a saucepan with half the onion, cover with the water, add some seasoning and simmer for approximately 1 hour. Then strain the stock and in the same pan fry the remaining onion, chopped small, in the beef drippings until soft and blackened at the edges. Then stir in the flour and gradually add the stock little by little to make a smooth gravy. Taste to check the seasoning and add a few drops of the Worcestershire sauce.

Vegetarian Moussaka *with* Ricotta Topping

Serves 4 to 6

Yes, it is possible to make an extremely good Greek-style moussaka without meat, and even non-vegetarians will admit it tastes every bit as good. Serve it with a large bowl of crunchy salad along with some warm pita bread.

Preheat the oven to 350°F (180°C). Begin by preparing the eggplants: To do this cut them into ½ inch (1 cm) dice, leaving the skins on. Place them by small handfuls in a colander, sprinkling with a little salt as you go, then put a small plate with a heavy weight on top – this will draw out any excess juices.

Meanwhile pour the stock into a saucepan together with the Puy lentils (but no salt), cover and simmer for 15 minutes before adding the green lentils. Cover again and cook for a further 15 minutes, by which time most of the liquid will have been absorbed and the lentils will be soft.

While they're cooking heat half of the oil in a large solid skillet and fry the onions until they're soft and tinged brown at the edges (about 5 minutes), then add the chopped bell pepper and soften and brown that too for about another 4 minutes. Next add the garlic, cook for 1 minute more, then transfer everything to a plate.

Now transfer the eggplants to a clean towel to squeeze them dry, then add the remaining oil to the skillet, turn the heat up to high and toss the eggplants in it so they get evenly cooked. When they're starting to brown a little, add the tomatoes and the onion-and-bell pepper mixture to the pan. In a bowl mix the wine, tomato paste and cinnamon together, then pour it over the vegetables. Add the lentils and the chopped parsley, season well and let everything simmer gently while you make the Topping.

All you do is place the milk, flour, butter and nutmeg in a saucepan and, using a balloon whisk, whisk until it comes to simmering point and becomes a smooth glossy sauce. Season with the salt and pepper, remove it from the heat and let it cool a little before whisking in the ricotta cheese followed by the egg.

Finally transfer the vegetable-and-lentil mixture to a shallow dish approximately 9 x 9 x 2½ inches (23 x 23 x 6 cm) deep and spoon the cheese sauce over the top, using the back of a spoon to take it right up to the edges. Sprinkle with the Parmesan and transfer the dish to the preheated oven and bake on the middle rack for 1 hour. Then allow the moussaka to rest for 15 minutes before serving.

2 (8 ounce) (225 g) eggplants
Salt to taste
1¼ cups vegetable stock
⅓ cup Puy or other lentils
⅓ cup green lentils
⅓ cup olive oil
2 medium onions, finely chopped
1 large red bell pepper, seeded and chopped into ¼ inch (5 mm) dice
2 garlic cloves, crushed
1 (14 ounce) (400 g) can chopped tomatoes, drained
1 cup red wine
¼ cup tomato paste or sun-dried tomato paste
1 teaspoon ground cinnamon
⅓ cup chopped fresh parsley
Freshly ground black pepper to taste

For the Topping

1¼ cups whole milk
¼ cup flour
¼ stick butter
¼ whole nutmeg, grated
Salt to taste
Freshly ground black pepper to taste
1 cup ricotta cheese
1 large egg, beaten
⅓ cup freshly grated Parmesan cheese, preferably Parmigiano-Reggiano

Spaghetti alla Carbonara

Serves 2 as a supper dish.

8 ounces (225 g) spaghetti

1½ tablespoons extra virgin olive oil

5 ounces (150 g) pancetta or bacon, sliced or cubed

2 large eggs plus 2 extra yolks

½ cup finely grated Pecorino Romano cheese

¾ cup crème fraîche

Freshly ground black pepper to taste

Extra grated Pecorino Romano cheese, for garnish

This is my favorite, and the very best version I know of the great classic Italian recipe for pasta with bacon and egg sauce. This is one that is made using authentic ingredients: pancetta (Italian cured bacon, which has a wonderful flavor) and Pecorino Romano (a sheep's cheese), which is sharper than Parmesan. However, if you can't get either of these ingredients it's still marvelous made with your local sliced bacon and Parmigiano-Reggiano cheese.

First of all, fill your largest saucepan with at least 2 quarts of hot water and then put it on high heat to come up to the simmering point, adding a pinch of the salt and a few drops of the olive oil. As soon as it reaches the simmering point, add the spaghetti, stir it once, then cook for 8 minutes exactly, or the time indicated on the package.

While the pasta is cooking, heat the olive oil in a frying pan and fry the pancetta until it's crisp and golden, about 5 minutes. In a medium bowl, whisk together the eggs, yolks, cheese and crème fraîche and season generously with the black pepper.

Drain the pasta in a colander, leaving a little of the moisture still clinging. Quickly return it to the saucepan and add the cooked pancetta and any oil in the pan, along with the egg-and-cream mixture. Stir very thoroughly so that everything gets a good coating. The liquid egg cooks briefly as it comes into contact with the hot pasta.

Serve on really hot deep plates with some of the extra grated Pecorino Romano sprinkled on top.

COLCANNON POTATOES

Serves 4

Another supremely good version of mashed potatoes, this is based on the Irish recipe for Colcannon potatoes, which were originally served in a fluffy pile with a sort of well in the center that was filled with melted butter. The idea was to dip each forkful into the butter before eating it! Perhaps our health consciousness would prohibit this today, but even without the butter it's extremely good.

Prepare and cook the potatoes as in the basic recipe (page 247). Meanwhile melt ¼ stick of the butter in a large skillet and sauté the cabbage for about 3 minutes, keeping it on the move until it's tender and slightly golden at the edges. Then add the sliced scallion and continue to cook for another minute.

Next drain the potatoes, return them to the pan, cover with a clean cloth and leave them aside for 2 minutes to allow the cloth to absorb the excess steam. Now, using an electric mixer, add the nutmeg, half-and-half and remaining butter. Whisk the potatoes to a light fluffy mass before tasting and seasoning. Then stir in the contents of the skillet and serve with or without extra melted butter.

1½ pounds (675 g) potatoes, preferably Idaho, Russet or Burbank

¾ stick butter

½ pound (225 g) firm green cabbage, very finely sliced or shredded

12 scallions, trimmed and very finely sliced, including the green parts

A good grinding or two of nutmeg

⅓ cup half-and-half

Salt to taste

Freshly ground black pepper to taste

Feta, Olive *and* Sun-Dried Tomato Scones

Makes 12 Scones

1⅓ cups self-rising flour

½ cup whole-wheat flour

¼ teaspoon baking powder

¼ teaspoon cayenne pepper

¼ teaspoon ground mustard

2 tablespoons extra virgin olive oil

⅓ cup oil-packed sun-dried tomatoes, chopped and drained of oil; discard all but 1 tablespoon

1½ teaspoons chopped fresh thyme

¾ cup feta cheese, cubed small

10 black olives, pitted and roughly chopped

1 large egg

2 tablespoons milk

FOR THE TOPPING
Milk for brushing

½ cup crumbled feta cheese

These are lovely served as a snack or savory at tea time. They also go very well as a companion to soups.

Lightly grease a baking sheet. Preheat the oven to 425°F (220°C). Sift the flours and baking powder into a large bowl, adding any bran left in the sieve. Add the cayenne, mustard, olive oil and reserved sun-dried tomato oil and use a knife to work the mixture until it looks like lump bread crumbs. Stir in the chopped thyme, cubed feta, sun-dried tomatoes and olives.

In a separate bowl, beat the egg with the milk. Add half this mixture to the other ingredients. Using your hands, bring the mixture together to form a dough, adding more of the egg and milk as needed. You should end up with a dough that is soft but not sticky.

Lightly flour a work surface and roll the dough out to a depth of 1 inch (2.5 cm). Stamp out the scones using a 2 inch (5 cm) pastry cutter, either plain or fluted. Put the scones on the prepared baking sheet and brush them with the milk. Finally top each scone with the crumbled feta. Put the sheet on the highest rack of the preheated oven and bake for 12-15 minutes or until they've turned a golden color. Remove to a wire rack until they are cool enough to eat.

FLUFFY MASHED POTATOES

Serves 4

Is there anyone anywhere who does not love a fluffy cloud of creamy mashed potatoes – especially if they are carefully and properly made? Grand chefs sometimes make a great deal of complicated techniques, but if you have an electric mixer, it really couldn't be easier.

Use a potato peeler to peel off the skins as thinly as possible then cut the potatoes into even-sized chunks, not too small. If they are large, quarter them; if they are small, halve them. Put the potato chunks in a large saucepan. Pour boiling water over them until they are completely submerged. Add the salt, cover and simmer gently until they are absolutely tender, about 25 minutes. The way to tell whether they are ready is to pierce them with a skewer in the thickest part; the potato should not be hard in the center. And you need to be careful here, because if they are slightly underdone you do get lumps!

When the potatoes are cooked, drain well. Return to the saucepan and cover with a clean cloth to absorb some of the steam for about 5 minutes. Add the butter, milk and crème fraîche. Start beating with an electric mixer at slow speed to break the potatoes up, then increase the speed to high and whip the potatoes to a smooth, creamy, fluffy mass. Taste and season with the pepper and some more salt if needed.

2 pounds (900 g) potatoes, preferably Idaho, Russet or Burbank

Salt to taste

Freshly ground black pepper to taste

½ stick butter

⅓ cup milk

½ cup crème fraîche

PERFECT ROAST POTATOES

Serves 8

*4 ounces (100 g) drippings
or lard*

4 pounds (1.8 kg) potatoes

Salt to taste

The amounts here are not vital because it depends on who's greedy and who's on a diet and so on, but I find that 8 ounces (225 g) per person is enough – yielding 3 each and a few extras for inevitable second helpings! I like Désirée best of all, but in the U.S., Russet, Burbank or Idaho would be a good choice.

Preheat the oven to 425°F (220°C). First place a shallow solid roasting pan 16 x 12 inches (41 x 30 cm) with the drippings in it on the highest rack of the oven while it preheats. Thinly peel the potatoes using a potato peeler, then cut them into fairly even-sized pieces, leaving the small ones whole. Then place them in a saucepan, pour over boiling water from a kettle, just to cover, then add salt and simmer for about 10 minutes. After that lift on out with a skewer and see if the outer edge is fluffy. You can test this by running the point of the skewer along the surface – if it stays smooth, give it a few more minutes.

Then drain off the water, reserving some for the gravy. Place the lid back on the saucepan and, holding the lid on firmly with your hand protected by a cloth or oven mitt, shake the saucepan vigorously up and down. This shaking roughens up the cooked edges of the potatoes and makes them floury and fluffy – this is the secret of the crunchy edges.

Now, still using the oven mitt to protect your hand, remove the hot roasting pan containing its sizzling drippings and transfer to direct heat (medium). Then use a long-handled spoon and quickly lower the potatoes into the hot drippings. When they are all in, tilt the pan and baste each one so it's completely coated with drippings.

Now place them back on the highest rack of the oven and leave them unattended for 40-50 minutes or until they are golden brown. There's no need to turn them over at half-time – they will brown evenly by themselves.

Sprinkle them with a little salt before serving immediately; they lose their crunch if you keep them waiting. If they're ready before you are, turn the oven off and leave them inside.

POTATO *and* APPLE RÖSTI

Serves 4

This is extremely good served with pork dishes and really meaty pork sausages. I think it goes particularly well with the Pork Braised in Cider Vinegar Sauce (see page 232). If you're cooking it for friends, it can all be made in advance and kept in the refrigerator until needed. And the best news of all is it gets cooked in the oven so there's no last-minute fuss and bother with frying.

2 round white potatoes

2 tablespoons fresh lemon juice

2 Granny Smith apples

Salt to taste

Freshly ground black pepper to taste

Freshly grated nutmeg

1 tablespoon flour

½ stick butter, melted

Scrub the potatoes well then place in a saucepan. Add enough water to just cover and a pinch of salt then boil for 8 minutes (it's important not to over boil them). Drain off the water and let cool.

Sprinkle the lemon juice in a shallow dish. Peel, core, quarter and grate the apples using the coarse side of a grater placed directly over the dish. When all the apple is grated, quickly toss it well in the lemon juice to prevent it turning brown.

Peel the cooked potatoes and grate them in the same way, but this time let the shreds fall into a large bowl. Add the grated apple to the potato, squeezing it in your hand to leave any surplus juice behind. Give everything a good seasoning of the salt, pepper and nutmeg. Stir well to combine as evenly as possible.

Now using your hands, shape the mixture into 8 small flat rounds about 2½ inches (6 cm) in diameter, squeezing firmly to form little cakes that have nice raggedy edges. Place each rösti cake on a plate. Sprinkle the flour on another small plate. Dust each cake lightly with the flour, return it to the first plate, then cover with plastic wrap. They can now sit happily in the refrigerator for up to 6 hours.

Just before serving, preheat the oven to 425°F (220°C). Brush a large baking sheet with the melted butter. Place the little rösti cakes on the sheet and brush their tops with the melted butter. When the oven is up to heat, pop them on the high rack, and cook for 10 minutes using a timer. Use a spatula to turn them over and cook for another 10-15 minutes. They should be crisp and golden on the outside, cooked through and ready to serve.

ROASTED ROOTS *with* HERBS

Serves 4

4 small carrots

4 small parsnips

½ rutabaga, cut into 1 inch (2.5 cm) wedges

1 small turnip, halved and cut into ¾ inch (2 cm) slices

2 medium red onions, cut through the root into quarters

2 red potatoes (5 ounces [140 g] each), cut into 6 wedges

1 large garlic clove, crushed

¼ cup olive oil

1 tablespoon chopped mixed fresh herbs, such as thyme, rosemary and sage

Salt to taste

Freshly ground black pepper to taste

Because oven-roasted vegetables in the Summer Collection were so very popular, I simply had to do a winter version. Here it is and once again it's a winner for entertaining, not least because all the vegetables get cooked together with little or no attention.

Preheat the oven to its highest setting. First scrub the carrots and parsnips, dry them well and place in a large bowl with all the other prepared vegetables. Now add the crushed garlic, olive oil and mixed herbs. Using your hands, mix well to make sure they all have a good coating of the oil. You can leave them like this covered with plastic wrap for up to 2 hours until you are ready to cook them – in which case the oil will have nicely absorbed the flavor of the garlic and herbs.

Arrange the vegetables on a large baking sheet. Sprinkle with the salt and a good grinding of the pepper and cook in the preheated oven on the high rack for 35-40 minutes or until they are cooked through.

ROASTED STUFFED APPLES *with* THYME *and* PARSLEY

Serves 8

This is the perfect accompaniment for Classic Roast Pork with Cracklings (see page 213).

First of all in a small bowl mix the sausage meat, chopped parsley and thyme, and add a good seasoning of salt and pepper. Using a potato peeler or an apple corer, remove the core from the apples, then cut out a little more apple with a sharp knife to make the cavity slightly larger. Now divide the sausage meat mixture into eighths. Then roll each portion into a sausage shape and fit that into the cavity of each apple. There will be some at the top that won't go in, so just pat that into a neat round shape. Now make a small incision around the central circumference of the apple. Brush each one with melted butter and insert a little sprig of thyme on top. Place the apples on a shallow baking sheet. Pop the apples into the oven to roast for about 25 minutes.

1 pound (450 g) good-quality pork sausage meat

1 tablespoon chopped fresh parsley

2 teaspoons chopped fresh thyme

Salt to taste

Freshly ground black pepper

8 small dessert apples, such as Granny Smith

A little melted butter

8 small thyme sprigs

SPICED SAUTÉED RED CABBAGE
with CRANBERRIES

Serves 4 to 6

1 pound (450 g) red cabbage,
  cut into 4 sections and
  cored

½ tablespoon peanut oil

1 medium onion, chopped

1 large garlic clove,
  finely chopped

⅓ teaspoon ground cloves

¾ teaspoon ground cinnamon

⅓ whole nutmeg, freshly
  grated

Salt to taste

Freshly ground black pepper
  to taste

1 cup fresh cranberries

½ heaping tablespoon
  light brown sugar

1½ tablespoons red wine
  vinegar

I have always adored red cabbage cooked long and slow, but it's also extremely good cooked fast so that it retains some bite and crunchiness. Using cranberries rather than the usual apples gives this dish a jewel-like appearance, and their sharp flavor gives an edge to the spiciness.

Shred the cabbage quite finely into ¼ inch (5 mm) shreds, discarding any tough stalky bits. Now heat the oil in a very large frying pan or wok over a medium heat. Stir in the onion and cook for 2-3 minutes. Add the garlic and cook for 2-3 minutes. Turn the heat up to its highest setting and add the cabbage. Using a wooden spoon, stir constantly so that the cabbage comes into contact with the hot pan on all sides.

After about 3-4 minutes of cooking, still stirring, sprinkle in the spices and a seasoning of the salt and pepper followed by the cranberries. Turn the heat down and cook for 5-10 minutes, stirring once or twice during that time. Bite a piece of cabbage to see if it's tender. When it's ready, turn the heat up again, sprinkle in the brown sugar and vinegar, give it all a few more good stirs and then it's ready to serve.

If you're careful not to overcook this in the beginning, you can prepare this in advance and just quickly heat it up for serving.

Traditional Yorkshire Pudding

Serves 6 to 8

I remember when I was about five years old my Yorkshire grandmother giving me slices of hot Yorkshire pudding with light molasses spooned over as a dessert – try it sometime, it's really good.

Preheat the oven to 425°F (220°C). Begin by placing a sieve over a large mixing bowl, then sift the flour in, holding the sieve up high to give the flour a good airing as it goes down into the bowl. Now, with the back of a tablespoon, make a well in the center of the flour and break the eggs into it. Add the salt and pepper.

Now measure the milk and water into a measuring cup. Then begin to beat the eggs with an electric mixer, and as you beat them the flour around the edges will be slowly incorporated. When the mixture becomes stiff, simply add the milk-and-water mixture gradually, keeping the mixer going. Stop and scrape the sides of the bowl with a spatula so that any lumps can be pushed down into the batter, then beat again till all is smooth. Now the batter is ready for use and although it's been rumored that batter left to stand is better, I have found no foundation for this – so just make it whenever is convenient.

To cook the Yorkshire Pudding, remove the meat from the oven (or if it's not ready place it on a lower rack) and turn the oven up to the above temperature. Spoon 2 tablespoons of beef drippings into the roasting pan and allow it to preheat in the oven. When the oven is up to temperature remove the pan using an oven mitt, and place it over direct heat (turned to medium). Then, when the drippings begin to shimmer and smoke a little, pour in the batter. Tip it evenly all around and then place the pan on a high rack in the oven and cook the Yorkshire Pudding for 40 minutes or until golden brown and crisp. Serve it cut into squares presto pronto.

1⅓ cups flour

2 large eggs

Salt to taste

Freshly ground black pepper
  to taste

¾ cup milk

½ cup water

2 tablespoons beef drippings

A Return *to the* Black Forest

Serves 10 to 12

For the Filling

8 ounces (225 g) good-quality
   dark unsweetened
   chocolate (see note)

2 tablespoons water

2 large eggs separated

1 (1½ pound) (750 g) jar
   pitted sour cherries

2 tablespoons cherry brandy

1 cup heavy cream

For the Cake

6 large eggs, separated

⅔ cup superfine sugar

¾ cup cocoa powder, sifted

For the Topping

3½ ounces (100 g) good-
   quality dark unsweetened
   chocolate

1 tablespoon sour-cherry jam

A little cocoa powder,
   for garnish

Though much debased by many frozen versions, the original Black Forest cake, way back in the "sixties," was a delight: a soft, light concoction made with seriously dark chocolate and sour cherries. So here it is – still using the lightest batter (no flour), baked flat, then rolled around a luscious filling and decorated with chocolate curls. (Illustrated on page 192.)

You can make the chocolate Filling well ahead of time. To do this, break the pieces of chocolate into a bowl and add the water. Place the bowl over a saucepan of barely simmering water, making sure the bowl isn't actually touching the water. Then remove the pan from the heat and wait for the chocolate to melt. Beat with a wooden spoon until smooth.

In a small bowl, lightly beat the egg yolks. Beat into the warm chocolate mixture. As soon as the mixture has cooled, whisk the egg whites to soft peaks, then cut and fold them into the chocolate mixture. Cover the bowl with plastic wrap and leave in the refrigerator for a minimum of 1 hour.

Drain the cherries in a sieve, discarding the syrup. Transfer to a shallow dish, spoon over the cherry brandy and leave aside.

To make the Cake, preheat the oven to 350°F (180°C). Line a jelly roll pan 13 x 9 x ½ inch (23 x 30 x 1 cm) with parchment paper, cut and folded to give a depth of at least 1½ inches (4 cm). Beat the egg yolks in a bowl with an electric mixer until they begin to thicken. Beat in the sugar, carefully watching to stop when it falls off the beaters in ribbons. Be careful not to over do this, as it can eventually become too thick. Fold in the sifted cocoa powder. Carefully wash and dry the electric beaters. In a clean bowl, beat the egg whites until they form soft peaks. Take 1 large spoonful, fold it into the chocolatey mixture to slacken it, then gently cut and fold in the rest of the egg whites.

Pour the mixture into the prepared pan and bake on the middle rack of the oven for about 20 minutes or until springy in the

If you want to make the best chocolate dessert in the world, I've got the recipes, but you need to get the best chocolate. Look for continental deluxe unsweetened dark chocolate, such as Ghirardelli or Lindt. I check the amount of cocoa solids – 75% is the best, as this gives all the concentrated flavor of chocolate. Once you've used it, you'll never go back to the normal chocolate with only 51%. Unfortunately, brands found in the United States do not typically list the amount of cocoa solids.

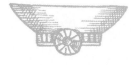

center. It will look very puffy, but a little finger gently pressed into the center should reveal that it is cooked. It's important not to overcook it; otherwise it will be difficult to roll.

Remove from the oven and don't panic as it sinks down, because this is quite normal. Leave it until it's absolutely cool, then turn it out onto a sheet of parchment paper that has been lightly dusted with sifted cocoa powder. Carefully peel away the baking parchment.

Drain the marinated cherries again in a sieve placed over a bowl to catch the excess liqueur. Sprinkle all but 1 tablespoon of the reserved liqueur all over the cake. Remove the chocolate Filling from the refrigerator. Using a small metal spatula, spread it carefully and evenly all over the surface of the cake. Whip the cream softly and spread it all over the chocolate Filling, leaving a good 1 inch (2.5 cm) border all around to allow for it spreading when you roll the cake. Lightly press the cherries into the cream.

Rolling this cake up is going to be a lot easier than you think. All you do is take hold of one edge of the parchment paper beneath it. Lift it and, as you lift, the cake will begin to come up. Just gently roll it over, pulling the paper away as it rolls. If the cake itself cracks as you roll it, this is not a problem – it's all going to get covered in chocolate anyway!

Now to make the chocolate curls for the Topping – don't worry, it's much easier than it sounds. All you do is melt the chocolate using the same method as before, taking great care not to overheat it. Pour it onto an upturned plate 6 inches (15 cm) in diameter. Place in the refrigerator for about 45 minutes until it's set. The chocolate should be firm when to your touch. If it's too soft it won't make nice curls.

To make the curls, use a cheese slicer or a very sharp knife. If you use the knife, hold the blade with both hands. Start at one end and just pull the slicer or knife along the surface of the chocolate toward you until curls form. As you make the curls, place them in a plastic container then put them all in the refrigerator. They're much easier to handle later on if they're well chilled.

Now you can decorate the cake! Spoon the cherry jam into a small saucepan, add the reserved tablespoon of liqueur from the cherries and warm it gently. Brush it all over the surface. Place the chocolate curls all over that. Finally, sift over a little cocoa powder to dust the surface lightly.

Apple Crêpes *with* Calvados

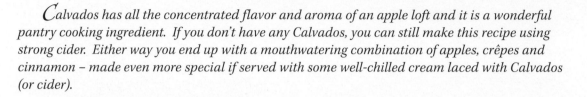

1 large Granny Smith apple

2 tablespoons Calvados

⅓ cup plus 1 tablespoon flour

¼ cup buckwheat flour

1 teaspoon ground
   cinnamon

2 large eggs

1 cup crème fraîche

½ stick butter

Superfine sugar, for garnish

Heavy whipping cream,
   well chilled, for garnish

Calvados has all the concentrated flavor and aroma of an apple loft and it is a wonderful pantry cooking ingredient. If you don't have any Calvados, you can still make this recipe using strong cider. Either way you end up with a mouthwatering combination of apples, crêpes and cinnamon – made even more special if served with some well-chilled cream laced with Calvados (or cider).

Peel, core and quarter the Granny Smith apple. Grate it on the coarse side of the grater into a bowl. Toss the grated apple in the Calvados and side aside for 10 minutes.

Meanwhile, sift the flour, buckwheat flour and cinnamon into a bowl. Then in a separate bowl, whisk the eggs and crème fraîche together. Gradually blend the egg mixture into the flour mixture using an electric mixer until you have a smooth, lump-free batter. Then stir in the apple and Calvados.

Before you make the crêpes, put a large plate in a warm oven so that as you make them they can be kept warm, covered with some foil.

To make the crêpes, melt the butter in a small, solid skillet, then pour it into a cup. To make your first crêpe, heat the skillet over medium heat until it is really hot. Scoop up 1 tablespoon of the batter and pour in an even thin layer over the bottom of the skillet. Cook until it becomes crisp at the edges and is a lovely golden color underneath. Using a metal spatula, turn the crêpe over and cook the other side until crisp and golden (this should take about 45 seconds on each side). Transfer the crêpe to the warm plate in the oven. Use a wedge of paper towel to lubricate the pan again with the melted butter, then continue cooking the crêpes until the batter is all used up.

When you are ready to serve the crêpes, transfer them to warmed serving plates, giving 3 or 4 to each person. Dust them lightly with the superfine sugar. Combine the cream and Calvados for garnish. Pour a little on each serving and pass the rest around separately.

FOR A SPECIAL OCCASION you could flame the crêpes. Pile them on a large plate and dust with the superfine sugar. Warm 3 tablespoons of Calvados in a small pan, light it with a match and pour the flaming Calvados over the pancakes. When the flame has died down, serve each person 3 or 4 crêpes, with the cream served separately.

Basic Crêpes *with* Sugar *and* Lemon

Makes 12 to 14 in a 7 inch (18 cm) pan.

Every year there are people making crêpes for the first time, and I admit it can be a hazardous affair if you don't know the ropes. So here is my tried and trusted crêpe recipe. I want you to know ahead of time that you also need a good solid 7 inch (18 cm) crêpe pan or skillet, some paper towels, parchment paper, a flexible metal spatula or palette knife, and a ladle. Once you get into the swing, you can make loads extra for the freezer and try the recipes on pages 258 and 261.

⅔ cup plus 2 tablespoons flour, sifted

A pinch of salt

2 large eggs

1 cup milk mixed with ⅓ cup water

½ stick butter

Superfine sugar, for garnish

Freshly squeezed lemon juice, for garnish

Lemon wedges, for garnish

First of all, sift the flour and salt into a large mixing bowl with the sieve held high above the bowl so the flour gets an airing. Make a well in the center of the flour and break the eggs into it. Begin whisking the eggs – any sort of whisk or even a fork will do – incorporating any bits of flour from around the edge of the bowl as you do so. Gradually whisk in small quantities of the milk-and-water mixture. (Don't worry about any lumps as they will eventually disappear as you whisk.) When all the liquid has been added, use a rubber spatula to scrape any elusive bits of flour from around the edge into the center, then whisk once more until the batter is smooth, with the consistency of light cream.

Now melt the butter in the pan. Spoon 2 tablespoons of the melted butter into the batter and whisk it in, then pour the rest into a bowl and use it to lubricate the pan, using a wedge of paper towel to smear it around, before you make each crêpe.

Now get the pan really hot, then reduce the heat to medium. Start with a test crêpe to see if you're using the correct amount of batter. I find 2 tablespoons about right for a 7 inch (18 cm) pan. It's also helpful if you spoon the batter into a ladle so it can be poured into the hot pan in one go. As soon as the batter hits the hot pan, tip it around from side to side to get the bottom evenly coated with batter. It should take only half a minute or so to cook; you can lift the edge with a spatula to see if it's tinged gold as it should be. Flip the pancake over with a spatula – the other side will need only a few seconds – then simply slide it out of the pan onto a plate.

Stack the crêpes as you make them between sheets of parchment paper on a plate fitted over simmering water, to keep them warm while you make the rest.

To serve, sprinkle each crêpe with the freshly squeezed lemon juice and superfine sugar. Fold in half, then in half again to form a triangle, or else simply roll it up. Serve sprinkled with a little more sugar, lemon juice and the lemon wedges.

CHOCOLATE BREAD *and* BUTTER PUDDING

9 slices, good-quality day-old
  white bread, each ¼ inch
  (6 mm) thick

5 ounces (150 g) good-quality
  dark unsweetened
  chocolate (see note on
  page 256)

2 cups heavy cream

¼ cup dark rum

½ cup superfine sugar

¾ stick butter

A good pinch of ground
  cinnamon

3 large eggs

Heavy cream, well chilled,
  for garnish

You will also need a shallow
  ovenproof dish
  7 x 9 x 2 inches
  (18 x 23 x 5 cm),
  lightly buttered

I have to thank Larkin Warren for her original recipe from her restaurant, Martha's Vineyard, which I have adapted. It is quite simply one of the most brilliant hot puddings ever invented. It's so simple but so good – and even better prepared two days in advance. Serve in small portions because it is very rich. Though I doubt if there will be any left over, it's also wonderful cold.

The day before serving, begin by removing the crusts from the slices of bread, which should leave you with approximately 9 (4 inch) (10 cm) squares. So now cut each slice into 4 triangles. Next place the chocolate, heavy cream, rum sugar, butter and cinnamon in a bowl set over a saucepan of barely simmering water, being careful not to let the bowl touch the water, then wait until the butter and chocolate have melted and the sugar has completely dissolved. Next remove the bowl from the heat and give it a really good stir to amalgamate all the ingredients.

Now in a separate bowl, whisk the eggs and then pour the chocolate mixture over them and whisk again very thoroughly to blend them together.

Then spoon about a ½ inch (1.5 cm) layer of the chocolate mixture into the base of the dish and arrange half the bread triangles over the chocolate in overlapping rows. Now pour half the remaining chocolate mixture all over the bread as evenly as possible, then arrange the rest of the triangles over that, finishing off with a layer of chocolate. Using a fork to press the bread gently down so that it gets covered very evenly with the liquid as it cools.

Cover the dish with plastic wrap and allow to stand at room temperature for 2 hours before transferring it to the refrigerator for a minimum of 24 (but preferably 48) hours before cooking. When you're ready to cook the pudding, preheat the oven to 350°F (180°C). Remove the plastic wrap and bake in the oven on a high rack for 30-35 minutes, by which time the top will be crunchy and the inside soft and squidgey. Leave it to stand for 10 minutes before serving with the well-chilled cream poured over.

CLASSIC CRÊPES SUZETTE

Serves 6

This is another qualifier for my "sixties" recipe revival. There was a time when this recipe was certainly overexposed, but now that it has become a forgotten rarity, we can all reappreciate its undoubted charm, which remains in spite of changes in fashion.

These little crêpes should be thinner than the Basic Crêpes, so when you're making them as described in the basic recipe on page 259, with the above additions to the batter, use only 1½ tablespoons of the batter at a time in the crêpe pan. If they look a bit ragged in the pan, no matter because they are going to be folded anyway. You should end up with 15 or 16 crêpes.

For the Sauce, mix all the ingredients except the butter in a bowl. At the same time, warm the plates on which the crêpes are going to be served. Now melt the butter in a heavy-bottomed 10 inch (25 cm) skillet. Pour in the Sauce and allow it to heat very gently. Place the first crêpe in the skillet and give it time to warm through before folding it in half and then half again to make a triangular shape. Slide it onto the very edge of the skillet, tilt the skillet slightly so the sauce runs back into the center, then add the next crêpe. Continue like this until they're all reheated, folded and well soaked with the Sauce.

You can flame them at this point if you like. Heat a ladle by holding it over a flame or by resting it on the edge of a hot plate. Away from the heat, pour a little Grand Marnier into the ladle. Return it to the heat to warm the liquor, then light it. Carry the flaming ladle to the table over the pan and pour the flames over the crêpes before serving on the warmed plates.

FOR THE CRÊPES

1 recipe Basic Crêpes (see page 259), with the addition of the grated zest of 1 orange and 1 tablespoon superfine sugar mixed into the batter

FOR THE SAUCE

⅔ cup orange juice (from 3-4 oranges)

Grated zest of 1 orange

Grated zest and juice of 1 small lemon

1 tablespoon superfine sugar

3 tablespoons Grand Marnier, Cointreau or brandy

½ stick unsalted butter

A little extra Grand Marnier for flaming

Dark Chunky Marmalade

Makes 7½ Pints - 3 Quarts

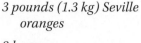

3 pounds (1.3 kg) Seville
oranges

2 lemons

2½ quarts water

6 pounds (2.7 kg) sugar

The problem with twentieth-century marmalade-making is that today's stovetops don't always oblige when it comes to getting large amounts of marmalade up to what old-fashioned cooks called a rolling boil, without which traditional marmalade stubbornly refuses to set. So when, in 1994, I tasted one of the best marmalades ever, I was thrilled to learn that the friend who had made it had cooked it long and slow – which solves the dilemma completely. Here is my version of Mary McDermot's original recipe, and it's the best I've ever tasted.

This recipe is extremely easy as long as you remember that it happens in two stages. So ideally begin the recipe one afternoon or evening and finish it the following morning.

For the first stage, lightly scrub the fruit and place it in a preserving pan. Add the water and bring it up to a gentle simmer. Now take a large piece of double aluminum foil, place it over the top and fold the edges firmly over the rim. What needs to happen is for the fruit to very gently poach without any of the liquid evaporating. This initial simmering will take 3 hours.

Remove the preserving pan from the heat and let everything get cool enough to handle. Place a colander over a bowl and, using a slotted spoon, lift the fruit out of the liquid and into this, reserving the poaching liquid. Now cut the oranges in half and scoop out all the inside flesh and seeds as well, straight into a medium saucepan.

Reserve the peel. Next do the same with the lemons but discard the peel. Now add 2½ cups of the poaching liquid to the fruit pulp, then place the saucepan over a medium heat and simmer for 10 minutes. Have ready a large nylon sieve lined with a 15 inch (38 cm) square cheesecloth, and place it over a bowl, then strain the contents of the saucepan through the sieve. Leave it all like this while it cools and drips through.

While you are waiting for it to cool, cut the halves of orange peel into quarters and then into chunky strips. The thickness is up to you, according to how you like your marmalade. Add these back into the reserved liquid in the preserving pan.

When the pulp is cool gather up the corners of the cheesecloth and twist it into a ball. Using your hands, squeeze all the pectin-rich juices into the preserving pan. Don't be fainthearted here – squeeze like

mad so that every last bit of stickiness is extracted and you're left only with the pithy membranes of the fruit, which you can now discard. When you have added the strained pectin, leave it overnight, loosely covered with a clean cloth.

For the second stage, the following day, preheat the oven to 325°F (160°C). Empty the sugar into a large roasting pan lined with foil. Place it in the oven and allow it to warm gently for 10 minutes. Place the preserving pan and its contents over a gentle heat and as soon as it starts to warm through, add the warmed sugar to the pan.

Now, using a large wooden spoon, stir the marmalade, keeping the heat gentle, until all the sugar has fully dissolved. What you must not do is let the marmalade boil until all the sugar is completely dissolved. Keep looking at the back of the wooden spoon as you stir, and when you are sure there are no more crystals left, turn up the heat and let the marmalade bubble away gently. It can take 3-4 hours for it to darken and develop its lovely rich flavor.

When the marmalade has been cooking for 2½ hours place some small flat plates in the refrigerator. After 3 hours, draw the pan from the heat and spoon a teaspoon of the marmalade onto a chilled plate to test for a set. Allow it to cool for a minute back in the refrigerator then push it with your little finger. If a crinkly skin forms, it has reached setting point. If not, continue cooking and do more testing at 15 minute intervals. When it has set, leave the marmalade to cool for 30 minutes before ladling through a funnel into warm sterilized jars. Seal the jars while they are hot, then label the next day when cold.

Four-Nut Chocolate Brownies

Makes 16 square brownies.

¼ cup each macadamias, brazils, pecans and hazelnuts

2 ounces (60 g) good-quality dark unsweetened chocolate (see note on page 256)

1 stick butter

2 large eggs, beaten

1 cup sugar

½ cup all-purpose flour

1 teaspoon baking powder

¼ teaspoon salt

If you've never made brownies before, you first need to get into the brownie mode, and to do this stop thinking "cakes." Brownies are slightly crisp on the outside but soft, damp and squidgey within. I'm always getting letters from people who think their brownies are not cooked, so once you've accepted the description above, try and forget all about cakes.

Heavily grease an 8 inch (20 cm) square cake pan and line it with parchment paper, allowing the paper to come 1 inch (2.5 cm) above the pan. Preheat the oven to 350°F (180°C).

Begin by chopping the nuts roughly, not too small. Place them on a baking sheet and toast them in the preheated oven for 8 minutes exactly. Please use a timer here; otherwise you'll be throwing burned nuts away all day!

While the nuts are cooking, put the chocolate and butter together in a large mixing bowl fitted over a saucepan of barely simmering water, making sure the bowl doesn't touch the water. Allow the chocolate to melt, then beat it until smooth. Remove it from the heat and simply stir in all the other ingredients until thoroughly blended.

Now spread the mixture evenly into the prepared cake pan and bake on the center rack of the oven for 35-40 minutes or until it's slightly springy in the center. Remove the pan from the oven and leave it to cool for 10 minutes. Cut into roughly 16 squares and then, using a metal spatula, transfer the squares onto a wire rack to finish cooling.

ICED LEMON CURD LAYER CAKE

You couldn't get a more lemony recipe than this: layers of lemon-flavored sponge, filled with homemade lemon curd and then a lemon icing for the finishing touch. It's wonderful.

Prepare 2 (7 inch) (18 cm) nonstick cake pans, 1½ inches (4 cm) deep, by greasing them, lining the bottoms with parchment paper and greasing the paper, too. Preheat the oven to 325°F (160°C).

Measure all the cake ingredients into a mixing bowl and beat – ideally with an electric mixer – until you have a smooth, creamy consistency. Divide the mixture evenly between the 2 prepared cake pans and bake them on the center rack of the preheated oven for about 35 minutes or until the centers feel springy when lightly touched with a little finger.

While the cakes are baking, make the Lemon Curd. Place the sugar and grated lemon zest in a bowl. Whisk the lemon juice together with the eggs, then pour this over the sugar. Cut the butter into little pieces, add to the bowl then place it over a pan of barely simmering water. Stir frequently until thickened – about 20 minutes. You don't have to stir constantly – just come back from time to time to give it a stir.

When the cakes are baked, remove them from the oven. After about 30 seconds, turn them out onto a wire rack. When they are absolutely cool – and not before – remove the parchment paper. Carefully cut each cake in half horizontally, using a serrated knife. Now spread the curd thickly on top of one half and sandwich the cakes together. Place on a serving plate.

To make the Icing, sift the confectioners' sugar into a bowl and gradually stir in the lemon juice until you have a soft, runny consistency. Allow the icing to stand for 5 minutes. Meanwhile, remove the zest from the lemon – it's best to use a zester to get long, curly strips. Spread the icing on top of the cake with a knife, almost to the edges, and don't worry if it runs a little down the sides of the cake. Scatter the lemon zest over the top and leave it for 30 minutes for the icing to firm up before serving.

FOR THE CAKE

1⅓ cups self-rising flour, sifted

1 teaspoon baking powder

1½ sticks butter, at room temperature

¾ cup superfine sugar

3 large eggs

Grated zest of 1 lemon

1 tablespoon lemon juice

FOR THE LEMON CURD

⅓ cup superfine sugar

Grated zest and juice of 1 large juicy lemon

2 large eggs

½ stick unsalted butter

FOR THE ICING

Zest of 1 large lemon

½ cup confectioners' sugar, sifted

2-3 teaspoons lemon juice

POLENTA *and* RICOTTA CAKE *with* DATES *and* PECANS

1 cup chopped dates

3 tablespoons Amaretto

½ cup pecans, roughly chopped

1⅓ cups polenta

1½ cups self-rising flour

2 teaspoons baking powder

1 tablespoon ground cinnamon

1 cup superfine sugar

1¼ cups ricotta cheese

1 stick melted butter

Scant 1 cup warm water

1 tablespoon brownulated sugar

This is a very unusual cake, quite different in flavor and texture from anything else. It's Italian in origin, and polenta gives it a sandy texture, while at the same time ricotta cheese and Amaretto liqueur gives a wonderful moistness. It also freezes very well, but as you won't have any left over you might as well make two – it's so easy!

Line an 8 inch (20 cm) loose-based cake pan with parchment paper. Preheat the oven to 325°F (160°C).

Place the dates in a small bowl, pour the liqueur on top and let soak for 15 minutes. Meanwhile, place the pecans on a baking tray and toast them in the preheated oven for 8 minutes – use a timer so they don't get overcooked.

In a large mixing bowl, sift the polenta, flour, baking powder and cinnamon. Keep the sieve held high to give the flour a good airing and add the grains from the sieve to the bowl. Add the superfine sugar, ricotta, melted butter and water and beat with an electric mixer until everything is thoroughly blended (about 1 minute). After that,

thoroughly fold in the nuts, the dates and the liqueur in which they were soaking. Spoon the mixture into the prepared cake pan and smooth the top with the back of a spoon. Scatter the brownulated sugar evenly on top, then pop the cake into the preheated oven on the middle rack, where it will take between 1¾-2 hours to cook. When it's cooked it will feel springy in the center when you make a very light depression with your little finger. If it's not cooked give it another 10 minutes and then do another test.

When the cake is ready remove it from the oven and let cool in the cake pan for 15 minutes. Then remove it from the pan and leave it to cool completely on a wire rack. Store in an airtight container.

QUICK APRICOT, APPLE *and* PECAN LOAF CAKE

If you've never made a cake in your life before, I promise you that you can make this one – whether you're male, female, age 6 or 106, it really is easy, but it taste so divine you would think it took oodles of skill. The only important thing to remember (as with all cakes) is to use the right size pan.

Lightly butter a 2 pound (900 g) bread loaf pan measuring 3½ x 6½ inches (8 x 16 cm). Preheat the oven to 350°F (180°C).

Spread the pecans out on a baking sheet and toast them lightly in the preheated oven for about 8 minutes, using a timer so that you don't forget them. Remove from the oven and let cool a bit before chopping them roughly.

In a large mixing bowl, sift the salt, baking soda, cinnamon and both flours, holding the sieve up high to give the flour a good airing and adding the bran from the sieve to the bowl as well. Add the rest of the ingredients except the fruit and pecans. Using an electric mixer, begin to beat on a slow speed; then increase the speed to mix everything thoroughly until smooth. Lightly fold in the apricots, apple and pecans. Add a drop more milk if necessary to make a mixture that drops easily off the spoon when you give it a sharp tap. Pile the mixture into the prepared pan, level off the top and sprinkle with the crushed sugar and cinnamon. Bake in the center of the oven for 1¼-1½ hours or until the cake feels springy in the center.

Remove from the oven and let cool for about 5 minutes before turning it out onto a wire rack. Let it cool completely before transferring to an airtight container, which may not be needed if there are people around, as this cake tends to vanish very quickly!

1½ cups pecans

A pinch of salt

1½ teaspoons baking soda

4 teaspoons ground cinnamon

1 cup whole-wheat flour

¾ cup all-purpose flour

1 stick butter, at room temperature

¾ cup brown sugar

2 large eggs, beaten

3 tablespoons milk

1 cup dried apricots, each chopped in half

1 cooking apple, cut into ½ inch (1 cm) chunks (about 1 cup)

FOR THE TOPPING

4 cubes brownulated sugar, roughly crushed

¼ teaspoon ground cinnamon

Rich Fruit Buttermilk Scones

Makes 12 Scones

1¾ cups self-rising flour

⅓ cup superfine sugar

¾ stick butter,
   at room temperature

½ cup mixed dried fruit

1 large egg, beaten

3-4 tablespoons buttermilk

A little extra flour for
   dusting tops

These tempting little scones are so quick and easy to make that you can have them on the table in less than half an hour after you first thought about making them. Don't worry if you don't have buttermilk; just use ordinary milk.

Remember that scones do not keep well so they're best eaten on the day they're made. Any leftover, however, will freeze perfectly well.

Lightly grease a baking sheet and a 2 inch (5 cm) pastry cutter. Preheat the oven to 425°F (220°C).

Begin by sifting the flour into a bowl, sprinkling in the sugar, then rubbing the butter in lightly until the mixture looks crumbly. Sprinkle in the dried fruit, pour in the beaten egg and add 3 tablespoons of the buttermilk. Start to mix the dough with a knife and finish off with your hands. The dough should be soft but not sticky, so add more milk, a teaspoon at a time, if the dough seems too dry.

Form the dough into a ball and turn it out onto a lightly floured work surface. Roll it out very lightly to a circle at least 1 inch (2.5 cm) thick. Cut the scones out by placing the pastry cutter on the dough and giving it a sharp tap. Don't twist the cutter, just push the dough out. Carry on until you are left only with trimmings, then roll these out and cut an extra scone. Place the scones on the prepared baking sheet and dust lightly with the extra flour.

Bake the scones in the top half of the preheated oven for 10-12 minutes or until they are well risen and golden brown. Remove them to a wire rack and serve fresh from the oven, split and spread with butter.

STICKY GINGERBREAD PUDDING *with* GINGER WINE *and* BRANDY SAUCE

Serves 8

For quite a long time now I've been trying to come up with an idea that matches the charm and popularity of the Sticky Toffee Puddings in my Christmas book. This is quite definitely it – it has the same degree of lightness and this time the fragrance and spiciness of preserved ginger, which takes the edge off the sweetness beautifully.

If you want to make these puddings in advance, they freeze beautifully, and after defrosting should be reheated as below.

Preheat the oven to 350°F (180°C). First of all place the pieces of preserved ginger in a food processor and turn the motor on for about 7-10 seconds. Be careful not to process for too long – the ginger should be chopped small, but not puréed! After that sift the flour and spices into a mixing bowl. Then add the eggs, butter and brown sugar. The way to deal with the molasses is to grease the spoon first and, using a rubber spatula or another spoon, push it into the bowl to join the rest of the ingredients. Now add the freshly grated ginger. Then, using an electric mixer, beat everything together gradually, adding the water until you have a smooth mixture. Finally fold in the apple and preserved ginger.

Now divide the mixture among 8 well buttered ¾ cup pudding cups, stand them on a baking sheet and bake in the center of the oven for 35 minutes or until they feel firm and springy to the touch. After that remove them from the oven and let them stand for about 5 minutes, then run a metal spatula around the edges of the cups and turn them out. Allow the puddings to cool completely and keep them wrapped in plastic wrap until you need them.

To make the Sauce, all you do is gently melt together the brown sugar and butter until all the sugar has completely dissolved, then whisk in the ginger wine and brandy, add the chopped ginger, and the Sauce is ready to serve.

To serve the puddings, preheat the broiler to its highest setting and arrange the puddings on a heatproof dish or tray. Spoon the Sauce over, making sure that no little bits of ginger are actually on the top of the puddings, then place the whole thing under the broiler so that the tops of the puddings are about 5 inches (13 cm) from the source of heat. Now allow them to heat through – this will take about 6-8 minutes, by which time the tops will be slightly crunchy and the sauce will be hot and bubbly. Serve with the chilled heavy cream.

4 ounces (100 g) preserved ginger in syrup (8 pieces)

1⅓ cups self-rising flour

⅓ teaspoon ground cinnamon

⅓ teaspoon ground cloves

¼ teaspoon ground ginger

2 large eggs

¾ stick butter, softened

⅔ cup dark brown sugar

1 tablespoon dark molasses

1 heaping teaspoon grated fresh ginger root

¾ cup warm water

1 medium Rome apple, peeled, cored and chopped small

Heavy cream, well chilled, for garnish

FOR THE GINGER WINE AND BRANDY SAUCE

1 cup dark brown sugar

1 stick unsalted butter

¼ cup ginger wine

2 tablespoons brandy

2 pieces preserved ginger, chopped small

D

E

F

*Thank you for choosing to explore
the fabulous world of GREAT FOOD.*

*N*ow that you've met the GREAT FOOD chefs and tried some of their magnificent dishes, perhaps you'd like to hear more of GREAT FOOD - the availability of more cookbooks, cooking products and more from the chefs. Please fill out the form below and send it to us.

We'll get you the information you 're looking for along with lots more up-to-date news from GREAT FOOD.

Name

Address

City   *State*   *Zip*

Telephone (   )   *E-mail address*

          (optional)   *(optional)*

Comments/Discoveries/Suggestions:

☐ *Add me to your mailing list.*   ☐ *Send me a catalog.*

DETACH AND MAIL TO: GREAT FOOD, C/O WEST 175 PUBLISHING,
P.O. BOX 84848, SEATTLE, WA 98124
OR PHOTOCOPY AND FAX TO 206-233-0753 OR E-MAIL US AT mail@greatfoodtv.com
1-800-288-7834